Portrait of
NOTTINGHAM

EMRYS BRYSON

Foreword by
ALAN SILLITOE

Photographs by
FRANK WOOLCOTT
and others

ROBERT HALE · LONDON

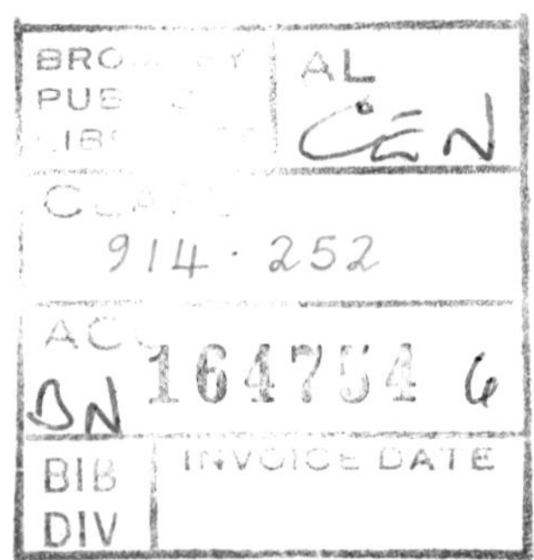

Printed in Great Britain by
St Edmundsbury Press, Bury St Edmunds, Suffolk
and bound by Hunter & Foulis

FOREWORD

Another book on Nottingham? Yes, but this is a different piece of work to what we've been used to up to now. Mr. Bryson has put Nottingham in print, and between covers, so that whoever carries this book about will have the soul of the city as an intimate companion.

The author was not born in Nottingham, but this is an advantage, if anything. It is said that if you like a city, then that city likes you, and the mutual affection will work to the advantage of both—something which is proved beyond all doubt by the appearance of this book.

The illustrations are delightful, and certainly nostalgic, but the text is excellent, being so compressed that it is like having several volumes in one. I feel that there isn't much about Nottingham Mr. Bryson doesn't know, and no books on it that he hasn't read.

For here is Nottingham as it is and was, a story with the lid off, so that we who were born in its boundaries know exactly what the people went through during its long history. It isn't a question of kings and queens, or facts and figures, but of flesh and blood people—including all the horror and squalor they had to put up with.

The people of Nottingham always were, and are, argumentative and opinionated, sometimes to their advantage, and on other occasions not, but we certainly know what Mr. Bryson means when he says: 'Through most of the eighteenth and nineteenth centuries, the characteristic sounds in Nottingham were the noise of jeering crowds, the whine of musket balls, and the smashing of glass.' And one might add that a typical sight was the rise of flames upon the midnight sky.

It is easy to recognise ourselves in this hugger-mugger of real people, milling around well-known stomping grounds. As a picture of Nottingham today it is invaluable, and will be more so in the future for those who will want to know what it was really like in the 1970s.

In fact Emrys Bryson is modest in calling his book a 'portrait', because to me it seems far more than that. Not that I would quibble with his choice of words—he knows very well how to use them—but maybe I would say that this is a portrait in depth, since it takes us, more than any other tome I know, under the skin of the place. And we can't ask for more than that.

There are many stories, some horrifying, others edifying. We are told about Squire Horne who, sentenced to death for infanticide, rides to the gibbet in his own coach. There is an account of the Lowdham apprentices, a tale whose counterpart could only be found in the Nazi concentration camps.

As it says in the chapter called 'The Valley of the Shadow', working conditions in Nottingham at the beginning of the Industrial Revolution were appalling, and the slums in which the people had to live were the worst in Europe. It makes you think that if they are the 'good old days' people talk about thank God they are over! But that is a small section of the book, and the achievements of the city are also dealt with.

Anyone coming to Nottingham with this volume will also have a factual guide, discreetly hidden perhaps, but practical nevertheless. Not only is it a book for those unfamiliar with the locality, but it is also something for local people to enjoy.

It is said that whoever reads the story of Nottingham will know the history of England, a pursuit which, if this is so, Mr. Bryson has made pleasurable and rewarding.

Alan Sillitoe

CONTENTS

ILLUSTRATIONS

The author is grateful to the following for their help
and kindness in the use of some of the illustrations:
Richard Iliffe and the Nottingham Historical Film
Unit (Plates 2, 3, 19, 20, 24, 25 and 29); Nottingham Castle Museum and Art Gallery (Plates 10 and
11); T. Bailey Forman Ltd. (Plate 21); Allan Hurst
(Plate 32); Paul A. Bloomer (Plates 12, 16, 22, 23,
30, 33 and 34); and H. Tempest (Plate 35).

For three genuine Nottinghamians—
my children Paul, Kate and Victoria

NOTTINGHAM

City and county borough in the county of
Nottinghamshire.

Lat.	—52.57 N.
Long.	—1.07 W.
Av. temp.	—Jan. 37.9°; July 61.9°
Prevailing winds	—mainly westerly
Climate	—equable
Av. annual rainfall	—24.68 inches
Population	—299,758
Area	—18,364 acres
Av. ht. above sea level	—215 ft.
Surrounding country	—hilly

River Trent —navigable as far as
Nottingham. Depth of deep water
channel at Trent Bridge: 8 ft. Width of
river at Trent Bridge: approx. 300 ft.

Distance from London —124 miles

Nearest airport —East Midlands Airport,
Castle Donington, 15 miles south-west of
Nottingham

Railway station —Carrington Street

Chief industries —textiles: lace, hosiery,
and associated industries of bleaching and
dyeing; light engineering and machining;
cycles; cigarettes and tobacco; coal
mining; pharmaceutical products;
brewing

Geology —several strata of vary-
ing hardness. The hard limestones and
sandstones, having withstood the wear
and tear of ages better than the softer
sands and marls, now rise above them,
forming the hills which often constitute
bold and distinct features in the landscape; while rain and rivers, combining
with frost and ice, have removed much
of the softer strata lying in between, and
have thus carved out broad, low-lying
vales

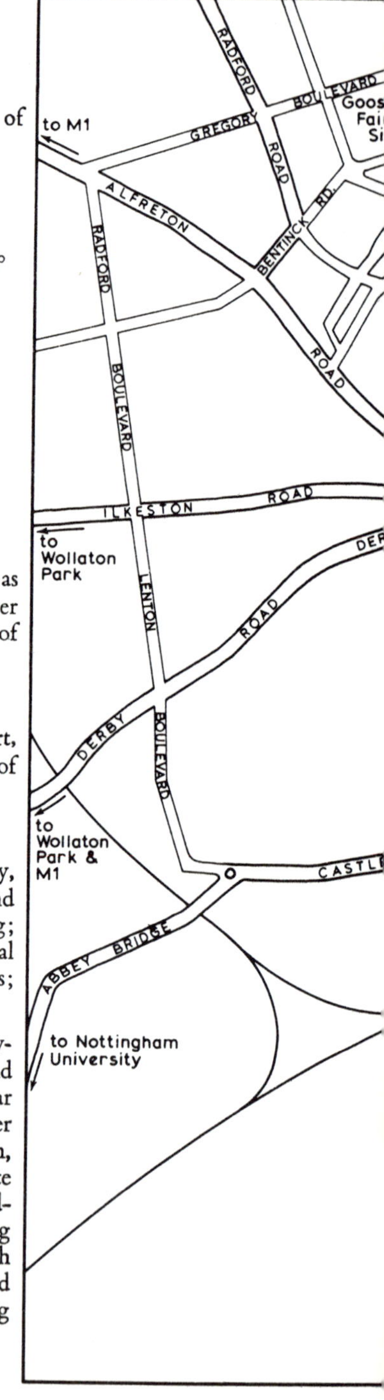

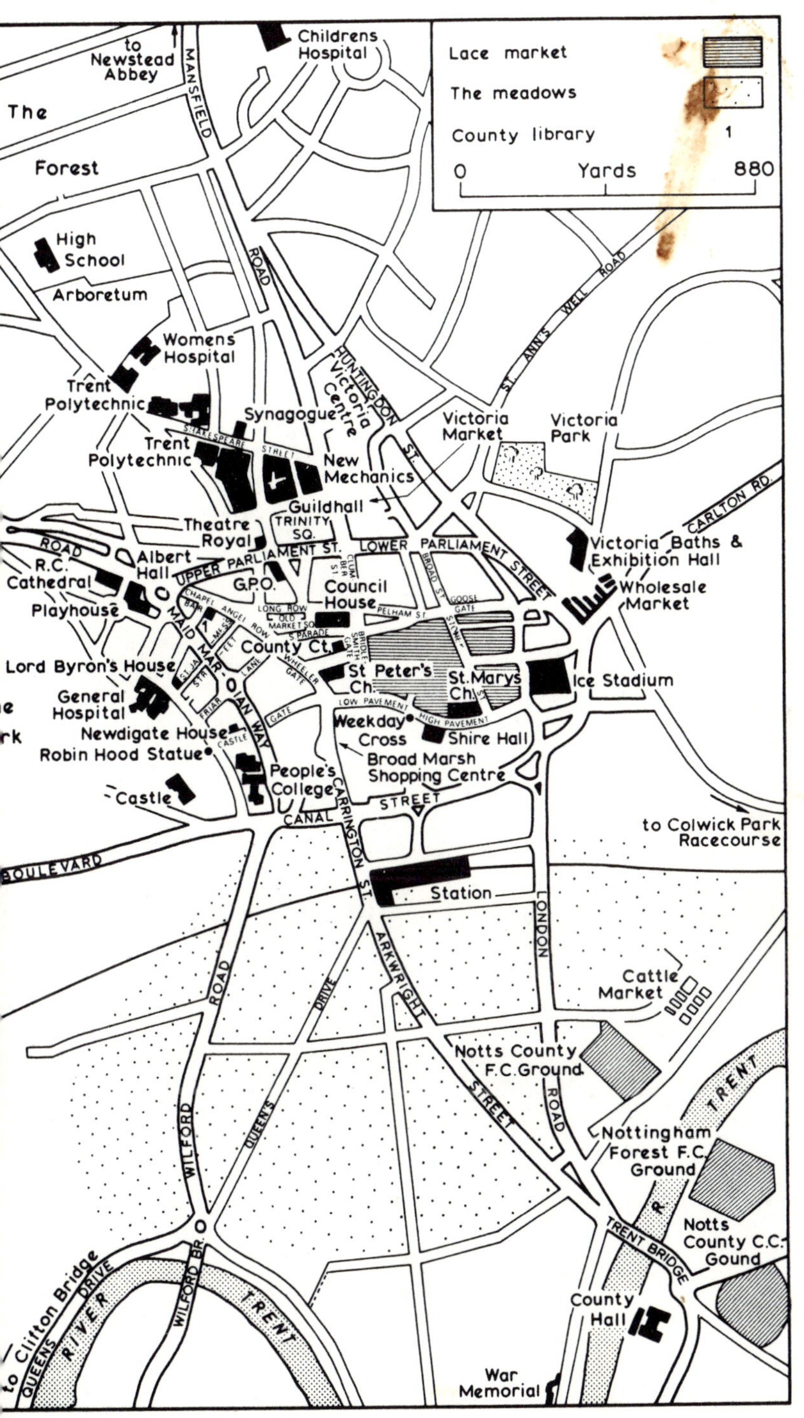

to Newstead Abbey
The Forest
Childrens Hospital
Lace market
The meadows
County library
0   Yards   880
1
High School
Arboretum
Womens Hospital
Trent Polytechnic
Synagogue
MANSFIELD ROAD
SHAKESPEARE STREET
HUNTINGDON
Victoria Centre
ST. ANN'S WELL ROAD
Victoria Market
Victoria Park
Trent Polytechnic
New Mechanics
Guildhall
TRINITY SQ.
Theatre Royal
CARLTON RD.
Victoria Baths & Exhibition Hall
ROAD
R.C. Cathedral
Albert Hall
UPPER PARLIAMENT ST.
LOWER PARLIAMENT STREET
LOWER PARLIAMENT ST.
G.P.O.
Council House
CLUMBER ST
BROAD ST
Wholesale Market
Playhouse
CHAPEL BAR
ANGEL ROW
LONG ROW
OLD MARKET SQ.
PELHAM ST.
GOOSE GATE
MAID MARIAN WAY
S PARADE
County Ct.
SMITH STONEY
BRIDLE SMITH GATE
Lord Byron's House
FRIAR ST
ELIA STREET
WHEELER GATE
St Peter's Ch.
LOW PAVEMENT
St. Marys Ch.
Ice Stadium
General Hospital
CASTLE
Newdigate House
GATE
Weekday Cross
HIGH PAVEMENT
Shire Hall
Robin Hood Statue
People's College
Broad Marsh Shopping Centre
Castle
CARRINGTON ST.
CANAL
CARRINGTON STREET
to Colwick Park Racecourse
BOULEVARD
Station
LONDON ROAD
WILFORD ROAD
QUEEN'S DRIVE
ARKWRIGHT DRIVE
Cattle Market
STREET
Notts County F.C. Ground
TRENT
to Clifton Bridge
QUEENS DRIVE
WILFORD BR.
RIVER TRENT
Nottingham Forest F.C. Ground
R TRENT BRIDGE
Notts County C.C. Gound
County Hall
War Memorial

PERSONAL PREFACE

To be perfectly honest, I didn't know just where Nottingham was until I went there in 1946 to get a job. Evidently, though, some of my friends did, quite intimately, on the strength of having been posted to one of the neighbouring R.A.F. stations during the war.

'You'll be all right there, mate,' they leered knowingly. 'On Long Row they reach out and pull you in by your braces.' Memories of enchanted nights when the blacked-out delight of Nottingham's Market Square had been a sandalwood-scented Shangri La to airmen from the flat boredom of Lincolnshire.

The day I went for my interview, Nottingham's carnal charisma and I missed each other. I learned afterwards that in getting to the offices of the *Evening Post* I had actually walked on Long Row, trodden the hallowed stretch which ran the length of the square and which had caused so much lip-licking. But all I noticed of Nottingham that day—apart from the Dickensian interior of the *Evening Post*, with its squeaky revolving door, and counter clerks who perched on stools and scratched at ledgers with cindery pens—was that the men had square faces and nearly all of them wore blue shirts.

Not much of a first memory, I admit, about the place of which I was about to become a citizen and ratepayer. But it didn't amount to much else. The managing editor and chief reporter who had interviewed me had had big square faces. And blue shirts.

I sat on a stone bench in the square and ate the sandwiches my mother had carefully packed for me in case Nottingham—fully sixty miles away; change at Lichfield and Burton—did not have such things, and noted that Nottinghamians seemed better fed than I was. The very pigeons which strutted at my feet were choosey about my crumbs.

I was used to the Black Country, where people were small, wiry, tended to be slightly deformed, and had paler, rattier faces. And now all around me were these large confident people, striding about their city as if they owned it. I didn't see a single pair of overalls. There seemed no traces of austerity. No heaps of tidied rubble. No bomb sites. The stonework of the square, the buildings, the bench I sat on, were not grimy black as they were back home, but light fawn and pearl grey. The buses were not garish blue but a relaxing green. The huge square was excited with the fat new leaves of April.

With nearly an hour to wait before the return train, I wandered —like a holidaymaker—out of the square, and found the Oriental Café along the curve of Wheeler Gate. I remember it had a magnificent, carved ceiling which seemed positively opulent for a café, and downstairs the dining-room was partitioned into roomy but snug wooden stalls. And there in my own padded stall I sat revelling in the fumes of roasted coffee beans, and buying cakes with some of the lunch expenses they'd given me at the interview. I hadn't told them that my mother had packed sandwiches.

It was past three o'clock but the dining-room was still full of men who didn't seem worried about getting back to work. They laughed and joked and seemed like holidaymakers too. I looked at the newspaper which my prospective employers had handed me, staring at the close-printed and incomprehensible advertise-ments for flat-lockers, bar-tackers and twin-needle binders, and nonchalantly hoped that my stiff white collar would not be noticed by these soft-collared sophisticates. The waitresses were kind (were *they*, perhaps, the eager girls over whom my col-leagues had enthused so warmly?), and they didn't bellow at you, as they did in the milk-bars I knew, to clear out as soon as your cup was empty. And when I paid the bill, my waitress said: 'Ta, duck!'

It was my introduction to what struck me almost as a definite little animal, some endearing creature called the Nottingham Ta Duck. On the way down Carrington Street I bought some cigarettes and the man behind the counter said 'Ta, duck!' At the Midland Station the girl in the sweet-kiosk sold me a bar of chocolate and said: 'Ta, duck!' As he let me through the barrier, the ticket-collector said: 'Ta, duck!' I pulled away from Notting-ham like some orphan child given his first glimpse of the sea;

wrenched from a soft and shining coast where the shirts were for ever blue and where the lesser-tufted Ta Duck played on the sand all day. If the *Evening Post* could find enough charity in its Dickensian heart to let me become its most junior reporter, then I vowed that my first wages would be spent on a blue shirt.

A lot of water has flowed under Trent Bridge since then. Within a month I was back through the revolving door of Forman Street, passing myself off as a Nottinghamian. 'Notts in May!' I declared wittily. The cherry trees and the almond blossom were out along the main roads, and unashamedly I stared astonished at the vast traffic roundabouts, at the sheer luxury of a town which could put vast circles of tulips and wallflowers not only in parks where they belonged but in the middle of a road, for the benefit of passing lorry-drivers.

I was to learn far more about Nottingham than my wistful pals back home could ever have dreamed. I saw their lusty ladies of Long Row (and a raddled lot they were, too) as they collected their fines or their gaol sentences, while I sat on the Press bench of the sooty Victorian Guildhall. In a very short space of time I absorbed my quota of nasty shocks concerning Robin Hood (I had six years to wait before Nottingham got round to putting up a statue of him), the legendary Nottingham Castle (which turned out to be a house and an ugly one, at that), and Sherwood Forest (which is miles away; the 'Forest' in the city turned out to be a few playing-fields, a tree-lined walk, some lavatories and a huge stretch of concrete).

I found out that The Meadows, Bluebell Hill, and Hyson Green were anything but sylvan. I never saw any lace in the Lace Market nor a goose at Goose Fair. Broad Street was narrow, and Narrow Marsh was not marshy. It was a blow when I headed for the various boulevards, expecting a Parisian whirl of gaiety with accordions and pavement cafés, and found merely a ring road.

My love affair with Nottingham began in that Maytime of 1946 and is still continuing. Sometimes it has been more of a love/hate relationship, when I felt that I could walk right away from it and never come back. It is one of the occupational hazards of journalism that a town frequently appears to be composed of backstairs politicians, smooth grafters, insolent officials, hypocrites on the make, and loafers on the scrounge. Of them, Nottingham has its share.

But it also has its abundant share of kindness and friendliness and lightness of heart; a fascination which has held me to it. Another newspaperman before my time—Graham Greene, who worked on the old *Journal* in the twenties—experienced the same strange pull. 'The memory of it,' he wrote in his autobiography, 'would stay with me over the next forty years like a photograph of a woman which one preserves in a drawer, one doesn't know why, even when the relationship has seemed a long time dead.'

Greene was converted in Nottingham to Catholicism. I was converted to Nottingham. I loved to prowl around its streets and odd little alleyways, in which the mediaeval atmosphere was still strong. I would sit at night in the soft mist along the river, watching the bars of gold thrown from the Embankment lamps across the glassy water, and try to imagine the splendour of Richard III's cavalry as it clattered its fateful way to Bosworth across the old Trent Bridge. Two archways of that bridge are preserved in the swirl and thunder of today's traffic, in a sunken garden fifty yards or more from the present water's edge.

Further upstream, past a delicate suspension bridge, which most people think is a graceful footway for pedestrians but which is primarily to carry water mains, I found the ugliest pair of trousers in England. They belong to the statue of Sir Robert Clifton, local coal-owning M.P. of the 1860s. He still stands there, banally holding a lump of coal.

It is this blend of beauty, bathos, and oddity which has kept Nottingham fresh for me. A jeweller's shop with a card saying 'Ears Pierced While You Wait'. A road junction called 'Ation Corner' because its buildings consist of a school (education), a church (salvation), a pub (damnation) and a pawnbroker's (ruination). Until it was swept up in road widening, there used to be a house on the end of Park Row which—shared by a post office and a hairdresser's—had, set in it, some windows from the old Houses of Parliament. Aptly enough, they were a few yards from Parliament Street, but true to form, Nottingham only gave that thoroughfare its name out of whim. It was known tersely as Back Side until some eighteenth-century property owner with a burning ambition to be an M.P. put up several boards proclaiming it 'Parliament Street'. He was held to be feeble-minded, but the name stuck.

I am quarter Welsh, quarter Black Country and more than half Nottingham. The arithmetic may be impossible but the sentiment is correct. I have lived here for over half my life, and the fact that I came from another town gives me the chance to see it with an outsider's eye, warts and all. They used to claim that there were two women for every man in Nottingham. I looked around for my two and finished by marrying not even one, but a girl from Lincoln. Our eldest child was born in a maternity hospital with a garden full of gooseberry bushes.

Nottingham has given me a certain amount of exasperation and a lot of fun. In my bachelor days I lived in a multitude of 'digs'—starting just over the river in West Bridgford ('Bread and Lard Island', as scoffers call its lace-curtained gentility), working my way through the council estates of Cinderhill and Bilborough and the mean streets of Hyson Green and Sneinton, to the more affluent districts like Wollaton where the white-scutted deer skip around an Elizabethan mansion.

In the course of time I have seen Nottingham change so that Graham Greene would not recognise it. Even the boy who un-wrapped his sandwiches in 1946 has a hard time recognising it. The Dickensian *Evening Post* and its morning *Guardian* took over their rivals the *News* and the *Journal* and became big and fat and computerised. The morning paper, the *Guardian-Journal*, vanished during an industrial dispute in 1973. The Oriental Café has long gone, along with its cosy cubicles—although its marvellous ceiling is in store somewhere. (I eventually learned that it was contem-porary with Milton's *Paradise Lost*.) I watched that café replaced by a streamlined, all-night Boots, littered every midnight with anxious drug-addicts waiting for their daily fix. Paradise lost indeed.

Technically speaking, Nottingham is a big place. A century ago it was small and packed, and we shall see how it was finally forced to gather in parts which are now taken for granted as the city conurbation. What used to be separate village communities like Radford and Hyson Green have been absorbed into Notting-ham proper. Others, like Arnold, Carlton and Beeston belong to the county, and have had their own district councils—but their history is sometimes so linked with that of Nottingham that they cannot be excluded in any portrait of the city.

Likewise, I shall occasionally stray deeper into Nottingham-

shire. But essentially this book is a picture of the city of Nottingham and the fine and frequently foolish people who live in it.

This city and those people have given me some strange
moments. I have known it solemnly agreed that Enid Blyton's
Noddy books should not be allowed on the shelves of the public
library. I have seen schoolchildren compiling records of passers-by
who could curl their tongues into a U-shape. I once heard a man
play a piano for a week, non-stop. I never did discover why
everybody in Nottingham seemed to be wearing blue shirts the
day I came for my interview. It still delights me to encounter the
Ta Duck, just as I like to imagine the National Union of Small
Shopkeepers emerging from their Nottingham headquarters
through a tiny doorway three feet high. And although I realise
perfectly well that it's a town and not a name, I still laugh to see
a Corporation bus labelled 'Arnold'.

It would be easy, in this personal preface, to become very sober-
sided and pontificate about the changes I have observed in my
time as a quasi-Nottinghamian. There will be plenty of that later
on. Instead, let's keep it light with a limerick written to mark the
meeting in Nottingham in 1937 of the British Association for the
Advancement of Science.

> The heads of the sages of varying ages
> Can be studied in sequence in Nottingham,
> All bulges and bumps
> Like men with the mumps.
> But think of the brains that they've got in 'em.

ONE

IMPERIAL EYE

This cosmopolitan, gay but wicked city.
Clerk to the Nottingham Justices

'NOTTINGHAM? The Robin Hood place. They have a Sheriff, don't they?'

Anything else?

'Well, they make bikes. And lace. And there's a football team—Notts. Forest. . . .'

Actually, no. There are *two* football teams. Nottingham Forest and Notts. County, but even the television commentators get them mixed up, so let that pass. What more do you know? Where *is* Nottingham?

'Up north somewhere, up the M1. Past Birmingham, anyway. Somewhere up there. . . .'

What's it like?

'All right, I suppose. Cleaner than most. The girls are pretty. . . .'

And that will be about all. Nottingham in an instant-knowledge kit. London: Nelson's column, the Queen, the Houses of Parliament, St. Paul's. New York: skyscrapers. Chicago: gangsters. Stratford: Shakespeare, Ann Hathaway's cottage. And so Nottingham: Robin Hood, lace, bicycles, pretty girls. All to be found vaguely up north, 124 miles along the M1 from London, or, as the British Railways posters triumphantly put it: '1 hour 47 minutes by InterCity. Beat that!'

Well, Nottingham can beat that. The eighth city in England is something more than a location 107 minutes from somewhere else. It does indeed make lace for the brides and the windows of the world. It still has a Sheriff, who lets awestruck visitors fondle his chain of office and does a public-relations job which any city could wish for. Certainly the girls are good-looking, and, thanks to Brian Clough, the football has perked up for Forest. And Raleigh Industries do continue to turn out the finest bicycles in the world.

But where would the lips and lungs of the world be without a Player's cigarette to smoke? Try to imagine the surgeries, the wards and the bathrooms bereft of the drugs, the pills, the potions, the soaps and the face powders (to say nothing of the one million cascara tablets a day) that come out of Boots' factory. Nottingham hosiery keeps the legs of women beautiful and the feet of men warm.

Would there have been a Salvation Army hostel, canteen, or band if William Booth had not been born in the curiously-named Nontintone Place in Nottingham? Could a decent cricket bat be made anywhere but at the home of Trent Bridge, on whose ground some of the greatest Test Matches have flickered? How long would children's libraries have had to wait if a Nottingham man had not turned the first page? Would Leicester's Thomas Cook have sent people off in all directions without Nottingham's example to follow?

Manchester can congratulate itself on having become the cotton capital of England, but it got it second-hand from here. You rarely see Nottingham credited with the invention of railways, but it had the first set of rails—a two-mile stretch at Wollaton colliery way back in the sixteenth century—waiting patiently for someone to invent a train.

If ever Nottingham decided to put up plaques and monuments to itself, the place would be as tagged as a museum. Partly out of modesty, partly out of indifference, Nottingham prefers to hide its light under a bushel, but it has no need to keep its trumpets muted. A historian need take no better step than into Nottingham to see the warp and weft of England. He can find a well-documented outline in the lovely new county library, and the evidence is still there in the streets, if he skips out of the way of the bulldozer.

Nottingham has been the centre of a rich regional life for a thousand years; the melting pot for Anglo-Saxons, Danes, Normans and now 22,000 immigrants from Poland, the Ukraine, Latvia, Ireland, Pakistan and the West Indies. Integration has become rather a habit.

Its castle was the seat of monarchs and parliaments. One of the earliest of its chroniclers, Dr. Robert Thoroton, in 1677 knew of 'no other place so far distant from London which hath so often given entertainment and residence to the Kings and Queens of this realm since the Norman Conquest'.

In the industrial revolution it was a prototype town, an inventive town, a suffering town. Nearly engulfed, it turned itself into a productive city with a peculiar and unique character. It was a hotbed of dissension and revolt. William Cobbett loved 'fair Nottingham' for its public spirit in 'carrying on the noble struggle'. Its fight for political, religious and industrial action gave England (and in Victorian times this meant the world) an example of protest.

And if that is a concept too vague for you, come down to a more material level and thank Nottingham for keeping your taxes down. Every day, in the vast Player's factory, a man writes out a cheque for nearly £1,500,000, the duty on the tobacco they get through. Nottingham thus pays for about a third of the entire National Health Service. Without that man at Player's the government would have to put another five pence on income tax.

Nottingham is officially in the East Midlands, a sort of no-man's-land in that absurd, intangible attitude which separates the north and south of this country by means of the River Trent. No one could lump it with London, but neither can you class it with Birmingham or Manchester. It is the Byron country, the D. H. Lawrence country, the *Saturday Night and Sunday Morning* country of Alan Sillitoe. In the acute summary by architect/traveller Ian Nairn: 'Neither Northern nor Midland, yet with a strange, black-souled vein of its own.'

Michael Drayton, the Elizabethan poet, called Nottingham 'the North's Imperial Eye'. And in Oliver Cromwell's time a sermon was preached (and printed two years later, for some reason) citing the desire of a man who had travelled the world to live and die in Nottinghamshire. 'In the southwest corner,' said this enthusiast, 'sits the fair town of Nottingham, delicately, like a Lady upon the Rocks. The best of all Situations, saith the Naturalist, her chair being flanked with the hills East, West and North, to keep off those churlish winds that might give her a cold in her Neck; her beautiful face only displayed to the warm

Southerly Sun where she beholds from on high the flowery Meadows, and the Trental streams, with no small delight; a Town situate so near the River that she may have the conveniences of Prospect, Fish and Navigation; and yet at such a distance that she is exempted from the crude, raw and anguished vapours thereof.'

Not everybody has raved about it. 'A frightful old town,' wrote Lady Hamilton's friend, Elizabeth Wynne, in 1811. 'The streets narrower than any I saw. Oppressive, smoky, riotous from the number of people employed in its manufactures. The inn detestable—but the beds good.' For Hilaire Belloc in 1925 it was 'like hell, getting beastlier and beastlier'. Nottingham 'stinks worse than Liverpool' says Sillitoe in *The Loneliness of the Long Distance Runner*, his nostrils wincing from memories of the sullen whiff of stale fish-and-chips that still hangs around the Ilkeston Road where he lived.

True, the 'Imperial Eye' has grit in it—what place doesn't where two or three hundred thousand are gathered together? 'A fine city for a lot of people—but if they live in the wrong parts, then the Lord help them' . . . 'A characterless place with no interest in its past and only a sleepy interest in its future' . . . 'Barmy planners with minds like Goths and Vandals. . . .'

There is a strong streak of complacency about Nottingham—that's what comes of having a stable economy which for several generations has not had to ride the switchback of boom and slump. It also has slums—that's what comes of allowing unbridled free enterprise to make free with its enterprises. It can be indifferent to visitors, secretive with its own citizens, downright suspect in its methods. A city which buys its Lord Mayor a £10,000 Rolls-Royce while there are over 7,000 defective houses clamouring for attention, and is capable of designing a housing estate like Clifton which looks good from the air, but so devoid of social life and entertainment for its 30,000 people that it has been called 'a graveyard with lights'. Typical of municipal reaction was the response when in 1967 the Adult Education Department of the University produced a report saying that in the area of St. Ann's—'a slum which crawls wearily on over more than 300 of Nottingham's dirtiest acres'—fifty per cent of the children were living in poverty. It was denounced as 'rubbish' and the leader of the City Council called its main compiler 'a bearded nit'.

But, to be fair, it also evoked an equally typical action, to be found when Nottingham is prodded enough. The Corporation embarked on massive redevelopment to clear up the dense legacy which eighty of Nottingham's greediest years had inflicted on St. Ann's. One of Nottingham's redeeming features is that it can and does pull its socks up with a will, eventually.

But it can be amazingly smug. The average Nottinghamian carries around him a ring of confidence, as if warding off the bad breath of other less favoured towns. His city is a compact, feminine town, particularly dainty when contrasted with tougher, masculine places like Sheffield or Newcastle-upon-Tyne. Brushing aside false claimants like Leicester, a Nottinghamian will refer to his city as the 'Queen of the Midlands' without embarrassment. It is surprising that the traffic signs on the outskirts do not actually carry the sub-title *Queen of the Midlands*. But then, Nottingham does not set out particularly to impress passers-by.

The city is in a happy pocket, physically and mentally. Fifteen minutes by road—once threaded through the tangle of traffic lights, with the little green men now prolifically enrolled in the fight to keep the city moving—and you are into the rich farmlands of Nottinghamshire with their plump fields of wheat and sugarbeet (the stuff that made Hilaire Belloc so disgruntled when he was obliged to churn out publicity blurbs in Nottingham). Another half-an-hour and you are among the oaks of Sherwood Forest. Strike out in any direction from the city centre and you may have your pick of a chain of castles and mansions in the Stately Home League—Belvoir Castle in the hunting grounds of Leicestershire, the Dukeries with Thoresby Hall, and the quick mountains of Derbyshire with Chatsworth and Haddon and Hardwick. Lions and miniature locomotives at Stapleford, near Oakham, or fairground and cable railway at Alton Towers on the Staffordshire border—they're all there within easy range. The city's own personal Stately Home, Byron's Newstead, sits in cloistered calm nine miles from the city centre, complete with abbey arch, ghost, poetical relics, Japanese gardens and the tomb of the dog Boatswain. And nearer still, the deer frisk round the Elizabethan magnificence of Wollaton Hall, well within the city boundary.

In that pocket, Nottingham has thrived since the fifth or sixth century. In fact there have been men living here since Palaeolithic times, and evidence of an early British settlement was turned up during the making of the suburb of Broxtowe three miles away. A Roman crematorium was found on the site of Nottingham Castle, but the Romans virtually bypassed Nottinghamshire, once it had served to conquer the Midlands.

Asser, biographer of Alfred the Great, wrote in A.D. 868 of Nottingham being called 'Tigguocobauc', or 'House of Caves'. For most of Nottingham lies on soft, yellowish Bunter sandstone, sedimentary rock laid down millions of years ago and going down to two hundred feet.

Generations of troglodytes have scooped themselves homes in it. Entering the town at the beginning of the seventeenth century, Bishop Corbett exclaimed: 'Why, the people live not in howses but are earthed in holes!' If a man was destitute, explained one writer in 1639, 'he has only to go to Nottingham with a mattock, a shovel, a crow or an iron, a chisel or a mallet, and with such instruments he may play the mole, the coney, and work himself a hole or burrow for his family where over their heads the grass and pasture grow, beasts do feed and cows are milked.' The caves in the area of the castle have been used as mushroom farms, cockpits, gambling dens, privies, drinking cellars and burial vaults. During World War II, some factories enlarged them as air raid shelters for their workers. Today the caves house social clubs, a rifle range, store-rooms and a cosmic-ray research centre. From time to time somebody gets even more exotic ideas for them—such as linking them together for a Tube railway or turning them into atomic shelters, to be reached quickly by people sliding down on mats as if on a helter-skelter.

Builders, of course, regard them as a nuisance and a hazard, and refuse to give a firm quotation for work in the centre of Nottingham. But the tours of underground Nottingham run for the 1972 Festival proved so popular that the city has woken up to its subterranean history as a tourist attraction. The thirteenth-century tannery (the only underground one in Britain) revealed in the multi-million pound Broad Marsh development, has been spared.

It was overlooking the Broad Marsh that Nottingham began. Led by a founding father called Snot, a sixth-century Anglo-Saxon tribe—probably from Schleswig Holstein—chose not the obvious height of the present castle rock but a more modest outcrop of sandstone half a mile to the north-east. Here they had a low but steep cliff looking across the marshes to the river, and they fortified the other three sides with a ditch and bank topped by a palisade. They carved themselves dry homes in the soft sandstone, and the place became known as Snottingaham—home of the followers of Snot. (It is now called Nottingham because when the Normans arrived they had difficulty pronouncing 'Sn'.)

That original settlement spread over some thirty-eight acres, in such a strategic position that when Danes came marauding up the Trent and occupied it they were able to thumb their noses at King Ethelred of Wessex and the nineteen-year-old Alfred, who came hurrying to try to get it back for their brother-in-law Burhred, King of Mercia, in whose territory it lay. Nottingham became one of the five boroughs of the Danelaw, and evolved into a trading town, which it has been ever since.

About A.D. 920, Alfred's son Edward the Elder retrieved the family honour by a counter-offensive. He recaptured Nottingham and consolidated its future as a military point by building the first bridge across the Trent; fortified at one end, and a vital point between north and south as it was on one of the only two roads between London and York.

Irish-based Vikings swept back and re-took it in A.D. 940, and by the time that William the Conqueror's men arrived (after Canute's steadying reign), Nottingham was more or less a fully integrated community, a Royal Borough with its own mint, a population of about a thousand, and one church listed in Domesday Book.

Where that church stood is now the perpendicular splendour of St. Mary's, the parish church of Nottingham since before the fifteenth century; where the nave took a hundred years to build; where the founder of the Quakers, George Fox, barged into the service in 1649 to harangue against Steeple Houses and was flung into a stinking cell for his pains: and where, two centuries later when the piers of the tower had weakened, a congregation pelted out in terror as an umbrella clattered to the floor.

The ornate dignity of St. Mary's now rears up, proud but confused, like an old aunt at a discotheque. For this area was the heart of Nottingham and much was bashed down. Nottingham has never bothered to mark the place where it started, and only recently began to conserve what, from pre-Conquest days until deep into Victoria's reign, was the core of the town. From here radiate the narrow streets proclaiming their Danish origins—Barker Gate, Fletcher Gate, Warser Gate. ('Gate' was from the Scandinavian for street and had nothing to do, as visitors often assume, with the presence of the castle.) Here were the elegant town houses of the Georgian gentry, in turn replaced by the warehouses of the Lace Market, and many butted into rubble. Weekday Cross, the original market place and for centuries the seat of local government in the Guildhall, has been swept aside with only a memorial plaque high on a wall to mourn its passing. Here was the narrow, winding Drury Hill, the main artery from the London Road until the sixteenth century. Inoffensive and quaint, it is now buried in the steel and concrete of the supermarkets and office blocks of the Broad Marsh scheme. St. Mary's stands worried and uncertain among the devastation, looking for reassurance to the Shire Hall across the road.

The Shire Hall is not mediaeval and not particularly beautiful, but it is a bit of the county within the city. When Henry VI gave Nottingham its most important charter in 1449 he decreed that this place, then the King's Hall, should be—along with the castle—extra territorial. A judge was conducting an Assize there in 1724 when the floor gave way and a beam nearly fell on him. The judge slapped a £2,000 fine on the county authorities, to be remitted if they built a new hall; but they took their appeal to the Privy Court. They won, although they spent half as much money in litigation as the new hall, thirty-five years later, eventually cost. And even then a slipshod eighteenth-century stonemason carved the words COUNTY GAOL as COUNTY GOAL. On the steps of the Shire Hall you can see where the gallows used to be socketed on hanging days. An odd little island in the middle of a city, the Shire Hall was the smallest parish in England, until local government tidying up in 1974—two voters, the caretaker and his wife, in a quarter acre. As the boundary passes through the centre of the court, the judge sits in the city while the prisoner stands in the county.

Looking more like an Anglican church than a nonconformist establishment, High Pavement Chapel is still there, a reminder that its congregation held virtually a monopoly of Nottingham's political life in the eighteenth and nineteenth centuries. And continuing down Low Pavement the town houses of the Georgian aristocracy and squirearchy raise their elegant frontages behind graceful wrought-iron railings. Some of them carry the brass plates of solicitors or accountants, others the more garish advertisements of insurance companies. Now that Low Pavement has been smartened up, it is a joy to wander down its slope before plunging into the frenzy of Albert Street and its throng of Woolworth's and Marks and Sparks.

Nottingham is a hilly town, and most of its streets gravitate towards the market place. The Old Market Square—half-contemptuously referred to as Slab Square since the cobbles, the setts and the market itself were finally ousted in 1928—is the centre of Nottingham. This five-and-a-half-acre concourse has been a pride and joy for a thousand years or more. 'The fairest in all England' was how Henry VIII's antiquary John Leland saw it, and it is pretty fair even today when sliced up into stone 'gardens' and used as a glorified Piccadilly Circus by traffic.

There used to be a wall right down the centre of this square, from east to west, which was supposed to keep the English and the French from fighting on market days—an unlikely theory since it was only breast high, with openings at intervals. More likely it was merely a trading facility, separating the livestock from the hardware and market produce. It mouldered on until 1713, a mild symbol of apartheid in a split-minded community. The English kept to their quarter around St. Mary's and the original Saxon market at Weekday Cross; the Normans built up their own culture in the shadow of the Conqueror's castle. It was a nice distinction that if there was bloodshed on the English side of the market wall the fine was 6/4d., but three times as much if French blood was spilled. The two communities ultimately overlapped and merged, but the terms 'English Borough' and 'French Borough' were used until the fifteenth century. Separate juries were called for the Quarter Sessions until the late seventeenth century, and two sheriffs and two coroners were elected as late as 1835—a custom commemorated today by the twin silver maces carried in procession before the Sheriff of Nottingham.

The only things kept apart nowadays in the Old Market Square are the underground lavatories at one end and the parking space at the other, an area rigidly designated for visitors to the Council

House despite a spectacular campaign led by a city solicitor who maintained that it was all illegal.

Henry II's charter, over eight hundred years ago, declared that 'the men of Nottinghamshire and Derbyshire are to come to the borough every Friday and Saturday with teams and pack horses'. And come they did. Until it became respectable and dispersed its stalls elsewhere and neatly under cover, Nottingham's market place was a vivid, noisy, bustling bazaar, ringing with the shouts of stallholders and the rattle of hooves over cobbles, clinking with pottery, clanking with the work of the town's famous little smiths, reeking of cabbage and burning coke, rumbling with wheels, fragrant with hot pies and chestnuts, gay with coloured awnings, clamorous with the bleating of sheep and the quacking of ducks mingled with the trillings of caged canaries, squelchy with mud and rowdy with the bellowings of cattle.

Nottingham's famous Goose Fair—that three-day orgy expelled half a century ago to an eighteen-acre site called the Forest a mile away (which hardly looks like a wood let alone a forest)—was naturally held in the square. Marshal Tallard, a prisoner of war from the Battle of Blenheim in 1704, was once taken to see Goose Fair. Up to then he had kept up a stream of encouraging letters to the King of France reporting that England was drained of men. Now he called for pen and ink and wrote: 'I would earnestly counsel your majesty to yield the war, as today I have seen as many men in one English market-place as would conquer the whole of France.'

From noisome swamp to hard slabs, the Old Market Square is soaked in history. Here a disguised Robin Hood is supposed to have taken part in that celebrated archery contest. Here Richard III reviewed his troops, before leading them to Bosworth and being hacked down. Here wrongdoers were whipped, and banns of marriage read. Here women and children have been sold as casually as a sow with piglets. Here, on November 23, 1688, the first open act of the Glorious Revolution took place when the Duke of Devonshire, Earl Howe and others declared their public acceptance of William, Prince of Orange. Here the Wesley brothers preached and were pelted with filth.

This square has blazed with the bonfires of rioters, echoed to the sullen tramp of hungry stocking-makers, flinched at the crackle of musketry and the swish of sabres. Election gangs have clashed like blind rhinos. Here a wild Irish barrister named Feargus O'Connor came, with other Chartist firebrands, for the 1842 election to stand against John Walter of *The Times*; he jumped from his cart, arms flailing like windmills, bored his way through the crowds, and sent his Tory opponents scuttling for the safety of a pub at the other end of the square.

This focal point of the city is a provincial Speakers' Corner for orators, religious revivalists and Salvation Army bands; a stage for pop groups, ballet and Punch and Judy. Its fountains are handy repositories for beer cans and the stubs of hot dogs. From time to time a lukewarm attempt is made to get rid of the pigeons, but they are plump and affectionate so people step tolerantly around them.

Dividing wall or no, fights still go on in the square—particularly at turning-out time on Friday and Saturday nights. The drivers of the black-and-cream taxis keep a sharp eye open for 'pirates'. Occasionally a squad of 'bovver boys' will go on the spree until yanked off by some very tall policemen. Nottingham used to own five sets of stocks and a pillory in the square; a few citizens sometimes wish they were still there.

They don't know quite what to do about the Old Market Square at the moment. Most of the big stores have been siphoned off to the Victoria and Broad Marsh Centres. On opposite flanks, these, the biggest market complexes in Britain (world's largest branch of Boots, etc.), have sprung up harsh and gigantic, and moved the shopping pivots of the city. Instead of being the natural hub, the market place could turn into a backwater. Nottingham is crossing its fingers and keeping a wary eye on ideas for 'pedestrianisation' or 'leisurisation', or even the prospect of a vast underground car park rumbling beneath 'the fairest in all England'.

Whatever happens will be shaped by the people who occupy the leather-padded seats of local government in the Council House, which rears its half-million-pound white bulk at the east end of the square. The Council House looks rather like St. Paul's; indeed, its Portland stone came from the same quarry. The keystone of the centre arch of the front loggia was a block intended for one of Wren's churches, and left lying near the Thames's edge since the City churches were built. If anything, Wren's churches are more accessible than Nottingham's Council House, which firmly resists all attempts by those who feel that the public should be able to wander around on an organised basis. Nottingham Corporation has a history so steeped in the cloak-and-dagger attitude that it has rubbed off on to the twentieth century. Council members complain that other council members make decisions without consulting them, and members of the public sound off that *they* are kept in the dark until the *fait accompli*. The situation may not be unique to Nottingham; it may not even be accurate. It just looks that way. The cynic may be forgiven for supposing that the special seaweed behind the tapestried walls of the debating chamber is there not so much to improve the acoustics as to prevent the rank and file from hearing what is happening.

But despite the acrimony surrounding its erection, there is no doubt that the Council House and its shopping arcade (modelled on that of Milan) is a handsome civic edifice. Its archways are flanked by a pair of Landseer-type lions (often scribbled with lipstick); the bronze lamps are from originals in a palace in Florence; and the two-hundred-foot-high dome is painted with non-fade murals showing great events in Nottingham's past—the Danes capturing the town, William the Conqueror ordering a castle to be built, Robin Hood about to speed a trusty clothyard on its way (the artist took archery lessons to get the stance correct), and Charles I raising his standard.

Little John is more vociferous. It's the nickname for the ten-and-a-half-ton bell in the nine-foot clock up in the dome. It is one of the loudest and certainly the deepest toned (E-flat) of any in the British Isles. On a good day you can hear it for seven miles, but mercifully it is silenced between 11 p.m. and 6.15 a.m.

Inside the Council House all is municipal opulence—sweeping staircase of Italian marble, phone kiosk in bronze, walnut and black marble, sprung parquet dancefloor as per London's Savoy Hotel. . . . Over the Greek columns on the frontage, under such high flown figures as Justice, Literature and so forth, a frieze carries reminders of the ancient trades of the city. Eight little children toting a great bell, eight little miners chipping and drawing tubs of coal, more youngsters working in alabaster and leather. Not one of them has a cigarette in his mouth, or a bike, to represent a less ancient trade.

Give or take a few gaps, the shops round the perimeter of the Old Market Square echo the idiom of piazza and colonnade from

Old Market Square and Council House

the Georgian past. And there is still an intriguing hotch-potch of styles to give the city centre a hybrid charm. Right next to the Council House, for instance, stands the deep-gabled 'Flying Horse Hotel', in excellent health despite its signboard of 1483—the year in which the Princes were murdered in the Tower. In its heyday the gaping sawpits outside it must have proved a terrible hazard for revellers.

Lift your eyes above the plate-glass shop windows and you discover an immense variety of architecture not yet erased by functional concrete. Black-and-white rubbing shoulders with Scotch baronial; clean-limbed Georgian mingling with the jokey, red-brick Victorian whimsies with which Watson Fothergill stamped Nottingham. Step across the tiny mouth of St. James's Street at the east end of the square and you come across an unplanned but not unpleasing conglomeration. Among the shops selling wallpaper, jewellery, shirts and off-the-peg suits is the ancient 'Bell Inn'. Once the refectory of a monastery, a billet for the Royal Regiment of Horse Guards at a time when Nottingham was usually under martial law, it still has the original flagstones along which travellers led their horses to the stables at the rear. A yard or two more along Angel Row, sandwiched between a record shop and one specialising in hipster trousers, you may open the graceful eighteenth-century door of Bromley House into a serene garden. Built in 1752 for Sir George Smith (of the family which started the country's first private bank at the other end of the square), Bromley House was put up so meticulously that its bricks were soaked for a fortnight before being laid. The elegant library of the gentry, it was used in 1819 as a strongpoint by troops who rushed in a wagonload of ammunition during rumours of revolution.

This Georgian oasis is in turn a neighbour of ultra-modernity in the form of the world's first automated Odeon. And across the road you can step briskly back into several different centuries at 'The Talbot'. It bears the date of 1380, when it sported the hunting dog badge of the Earls of Shrewsbury—who would need accommodation at Nottingham Castle's frequent parliaments and councils. Rebuilt in 1600, it later became a leading music hall for the Victorians, then had a Palm Court existence (complete with gentle trios) in the tea-room society of the 'twenties and 'thirties; as well as a leisurely and civilised dining-room underground, it

Approaching Nottingham by train in 1839
Goose Fair in the old Market Place, 1910

now incorporates a Yates' wine lodge in which Hogarthian figures drink docks of sherry from vast tuns at a long bar that could have come from the Wild West.

The three focal points of Nottingham have naturally been St. Mary's, the Old Market Square and the castle. Up at the top of Friar Lane (which, by the way, has nothing to do with Friar Tuck), the castle is still called a castle. But it hasn't been one since Oliver Cromwell (who didn't knock it about at all and was intensely annoyed when somebody else did) had it knocked from under him by the man he had put in charge of it. As a residence, it was built by the Duke of Newcastle three hundred years ago. It is a museum now, but when you tire of the bric-à-brac and have sneaked a touch at the cracked leather of the phaetons and the tarnished rivets of the sedan chair, wander into the sudden draught on the parapets. It is still the best place to stand to view Nottingham.

At the foot of the castle's sandstone cliff there used to curl a pleasant little river called the Leen. Before the Industrial Revolution, trout lurked and salmon flashed in the Leen; and in the mile between it and the broad loop of the Trent lay The Meadows, blazing in spring with carpets of crocuses. They are still called The Meadows, and many an unsuspecting radio announcer has waxed lyrical on reading out a record request from an address in Crocus Street, The Meadows. But those purple carpets were pounded flat when Nottingham expanded after the 1845 Act of Enclosure, and were replaced by the teeming slums and factories which followed the railways, like dirty seagulls round a ship. The Leen is now a sewer and a canal, diverted through the industrial streak of Castle Boulevard with its warehouses and car salesrooms and the marshalling yards of British Rail.

Hugging the western side of the castle lies the dusty foliage of The Park, once the royal hunting grounds and fishponds, and turned in the mid-nineteenth century into a private estate of 'superior' houses. It is still technically private. The cars of the common herd are not supposed to nip through it, and the gates are ritually closed one day a year to maintain its status. An address in The Park still sports an aura of prestige, even though many of the tall palaces of the Victorian lace kings have had to come to terms with the prams and cycles of the tenants of subdivided flats.

At the north tip of The Park estate, a few yards from the castle green where sprawlers ogle the girls and drop their choc-ice wrappers, King Charles I stood one windy August evening in 1642 and watched his long pennant of war being raised. One would assume the spot to have become a guarded highlight on Nottingham's tourist beat, a treasure pointed out proudly, something to bring the colour of history into the city's cheeks. But unless you happen to work in the General Hospital you can't get near it. A tablet near the mortuary jerks an imaginary thumb '80 yards to the rear', but the only thing raised by the ghost of King Charles is a tall boiler chimney.

Such victims are legion in the city's historical casualty lists. Apart from a gasp or two of mediaeval gable or Georgian façade, Nottingham has wasted the area round the castle, pulling down fine-looking almshouses and other legacies (generally the public finds out too late) in favour of concrete and glass shoeboxes of office blocks, of which twenty-five per cent are estimated to be empty anyway. And what is saved from the wreck is put to poor use. Up Castle Gate, at least one can see the calm grace of Marshal Tallard's house—Newdigate House—and the City Architect operates from a splendid row of Georgiana. There is now the small Costume Museum, which not many people find, but on the whole the city's heritage seems only to embarrass.

Looking deceptively placid, the river swings vigorously beneath Trent Bridge, with its triple satellite arenas for cricket and football. 'The smug and silver Trent', Hotspur calls it; but it isn't very silver these days except when the barges on their way to the Humber ports nose aside the clouds of detergent foam. As thousands of anglers realise only too well, the Trent has the dubious honour of being the worst polluted river in England. Its diseased fish, however, do not seem to bother the swans. They breast the currents firmly on the city side of the river—not because the County Hall on the opposite bank is inhospitable, but because on the city side the water is slightly warmer, thanks to the Wilford Power Station a mile upstream.

Just past that power station, relief to the bottleneck of Trent Bridge has been brought by the building (and doubling within fifteen years) of the Clifton Bridge, a £3,000,000 complex for the outer ring road, tempting such projects as Player's vast new Horizon factory with its cigarette-shaped chimneys, and encouraging the growth of new industries in the space entitled Midway

City. Between this new area and the northern housing estates of Aspley and Bilborough (those well-planned estates of council houses which surged along in the 1920s and after the Second World War) Britain's first medical school to be built this century has taken shape. Appropriately, it is placed adjacent to Nottingham University, the white tower of which looks over what must be one of the handsomest campuses in the country. Close-barbered hills of grass roll down to the boating lake with its public open-air lido and play spaces.

Jesse Boot gave a million pounds to make that university possible. He had little schooling himself, having to leave at thirteen to take full charge of a tiny herbalist's shop in Nottingham's Goose Gate. He built his fortune (and the fortune of thousands of Nottinghamians since) on shrewd cash chemistry—hitting on the device of selling cheaply by buying in bulk more cheaply. The idea of buying a ton of Epsom Salts and selling it for a penny a pound appalled the opposition, especially as they were marketing it for a penny an ounce. The bust of Sir Jesse, who died the first Baron Trent, might well look satisfied as, with the university behind it, it faces across a mile-long boulevard towards the gigantic Boots' factories. It has had a last and long laugh not only at those rivals who tried to discredit Boot but at D. H. Lawrence, who, picking up a free education, turned out a scornful little poem saying that:

> . . . future Nottingham lads would be
> cash chemically B.Sc.,
> that Nottingham lights would rise and say
> 'By Boots I am B.A.' . . .

In Lawrence's student time it was still a University College in the city's Shakespeare Street, a Gothic pile planned, somewhat remarkably for the 1880s, as an educational complex with public library and natural history museum. The old college, mostly full of lace machinery, is now part of the far wider layout of the Trent Polytechnic, its washed pinnacles cleaner than the streaky white tower behind it. In that skyscraper tower, surmounted by a radio mast that looks like some giant's Olympic Games torch, one wall is virtually composed of glass. Students float in layers, a window-cleaner's hoist perpetually crawling over the face of their transparent hive. The Polytechnic is spreading like an amoeba in the streets bearing names like Goldsmith, Dryden, Chaucer. Once select, the seedy area has become the students' quarter—at least one new seat of learning, abutting on the florid pomp of the Victorian College of Art, was designed with a prison-like exterior to offer as few windows as possible to vandals.

'A magnificent town,' wrote A. L. Rowse about Nottingham, 'full of improbable splendours.' That was nearly forty years ago, in 1945, and plenty of the splendours have gone. But the improbability can still be found. Like the house where the ten-year-old Byron penned his first poems in 1798. It's at the top of St. James's Street, near the castle, staring at the brutality of a multi-storey car park. It shares with Charles I the proximity of the General Hospital mortuary, but also has to cope with a lawyer or two on the premises, and the north midland Rechabites.

Pedestrian subways are not the usual place for plaques, but a couple of hundred yards from the Byron lodgings one beneath Maid Marian Way commemorates the fact that a sermon preached in the old Friar Lane Baptist Church in 1792 launched the Baptist Missionary Society. Indeed, it was a Nottingham man, Thomas Helwys, of Broxtowe Hall, who built the first Baptist church on English soil, at Spitalfields, in 1611.

There are still enough improbable oddments to make Nottingham interesting. A whale's shoulderblade over the door of 'The Royal Children' pub in Castle Gate; a souvenir left by some whaling skipper. The 'bug hole' caves in the castle rock, where plague victims used to be isolated. The lace warehouses built like country mansions. The 'Nag's Head', up Mansfield Road, where condemned men were offered a final drink just before the gallows. (In one case of supreme irony a criminal refused, pressed onwards to his fate and so missed a reprieve which arrived five minutes later.)

The corrugated fly tower of Nottingham Playhouse, neon-lit in a discreet quarter occupied mainly by doctors, dentists and barristers, looks brazenly at its neighbours of Methodist mission and Catholic cathedral. Likewise the new Post Office of 1972 meets eyeball to eyeball with the Theatre Royal, opened in all the cosiness of red plush and golden cherubs in 1865. Up at the top of the road to Derby, where the traffic does a whirligig dance as seven roads converge at Canning Circus, is the spot where they used to bury suicides. At opposite sides of this crossroads, where any roaming, restless spirit would have been squashed by a bus long ago, a funeral parlour and a tombstone maker ply their trades. An uneasy feeling for the old people in the almshouses in Canning Circus; their backdoors open into the General Cemetery.

Most of the improbabilities to be seen around Nottingham happened by chance and expediency. Wheeler Gate, leading off the Old Market Square, owes its serpentine curve to its origin as a path beside a rivulet. Ancient, overlapping tangles of streets have led to one side of a road being called say, The Poultry, while the other is Cheapside. And another road becoming Beastmarket Hill, Angel Row and Chapel Bar in the space of a few yards.

But the most striking juxtaposition was planned. When the super- and hyper-markets of the Victoria Centre began sucking in trade in 1972, the red brick clocktower of the Victoria Station—run off the rails after existing for exactly seventy years—was left as a deliberate memento. It stands among the glowering off-white canyons as a souvenir of another era. So far as ugliness is concerned, there is little to choose between the two.

A strange mixture, Nottingham. It likes to think of itself as a queen but sometimes acts like a drunken navvy. A feminine town, but one which repaints its 10,000 lamp posts from green to black to prove its masculine virility. It is ringed with coal mines and power stations, and grows the most beautiful roses in the world. Where delicate lace comes out of tough-looking factories. Where the shire horses of Shipstone's brewery clop with their drays of barrels round desperate gyratory traffic systems. Where people boast about the city's clean face but drop greasy chip wrappings and bus tickets and plastic cups as though at a chimps' tea-party.

A paradox of a place. Which for centuries welcomed kings but became a Parliamentary bastion. A town of trade and peace which spawned the violence of the Luddites. A happy city with a booming crime sheet. Where half the budget is spent on education, yet where the young put half the phone boxes out of action, systematically smash every light in some districts, and use aerosols to write their graffiti.

A stubborn community, with all the trappings of a city—complete with prison and drug addiction centre—yet obstinately parochial. Which destroys its own charm and grumbles when visitors seem disappointed. Which prides itself on its heritage but knocks it down. Which can practically ignore legacies like Robin Hood and the sort of history most other towns would give their eye-teeth for.

A split-minded town. It fusses over the magnificence of the flowers in its traffic roundabouts, yet puts up blocks of flats like Alcatraz. Whenever the papers print pictures of homeless doggies or bewildered budgies there is a rush of offers of shelter. But the annual RSPCA returns prove that Nottingham has the worst record for miles around. Howls of protest went up when, for a production of *The Seagull*, Jonathan Miller asked for a newly-dead seagull. In the end he got the props. department to make a dummy one. 'If I'd asked for a dead baby, hardly anyone would have bothered,' he said. Even in the short time he spent in Nottingham Dr. Miller had diagnosed a condition of schizophrenia.

Nottingham can appear strangely bloody-minded. Putting questionnaires to its aged and infirm inquiring what help it can give, yet sending them stumbling down the steps of subways instead of making the cars go round. It worries about the high illegitimacy rate but quibbles about the cost of family planning. It votes money to give gold medals to retiring Lord Mayors and Sheriffs while overworked midwives must pay themselves for a telephone extension to their bedrooms. It decrees that films like *Ulysses* and Ken Russell's *The Devils* will corrupt the citizenry (and therefore must be banished across the city boundary), yet it doesn't notice how clients seeking the prostitutes near the Forest are also accosting the local schoolgirls.

Nottingham, on the other hand, can be immensely warm-hearted, full of gaiety, brimming with fun. It argues about every-thing and rarely apologises. A Nottinghamian will hardly ever admit openly that he can be wrong—but, after a decent interval to save face, he will put the matter right and make it appear that it was his own idea. He may not be strong in tact or diplomacy, but he is sincere.

Some day a sociologist should explore the dual personality of Nottingham, the twin tributaries that flow through its character. At the moment the case-material is still available, the story of a settlement which flourished a thousand years ago, merged with a different culture, kept its double identity but hammered out a single one. He could speculate on its neutral relationship to north and south; theorise on the economic factors which have kept it afloat; examine the blend of determination, craftiness, obstinacy, gentleness and cussedness by which it has been shaped.

Nottingham is alive and well. Occasionally sodden, sometimes mulish, very proud, frequently exasperating, self-satisfied . . . and extremely lovable.

Nottingham is a book you can't put down, a woman you can't forget.

A frightful old town? Getting beastlier? A black-veined queen? A magnificent town full of improbable splendours?

We shall see.

TWO

DOUBTING CASTLE

> If the Americans will pay £1½ million for London Bridge,
> then they would certainly pay ten million for Notting-
> ham Castle. This would solve the Corporation's financial
> problems for a few years and rid the city of a blot on the
> landscape.
>
> Reader's letter, Nottingham *Evening Post*

THANKS to the city's most notable resident, whose plastic statuette
is the staple line in the knick-knack shops, Nottingham Castle is
numbered with the great and fabled. Aided and abetted by Errol
Flynn, Walt Disney and various other bands of merry men,
Robin Hood has given the world a legend to rank with Camelot.

The people of Nottingham are aware that they are expected to
produce a cross between Prince Charming's castle and the Tower
of London. And they get very apologetic when camera-slung
Texan romantics or coachloads of schoolboys from Harlow New
Town head brightly for the battlements and bowslits of their
dreams. Nottingham Castle today is an inferiority complex.

Nowadays the only arrows turned on it are one or two timid
street signs pointing to where it perches on a 133-foot-high sandstone bluff, understandably trying to hide behind the trees which
foam around the rock.

Reaching it from the General Hospital side, you merely walk
into a park on roughly the same level. But turn off Castle
Boulevard by the labour exchange and approach it that way, up
the steep hill of Castle Road, and at least the castle does try to look
impressive. Acting as a sort of advance agent for it, the ancient
pub 'The Trip to Jerusalem' valiantly attempts to set the scene.
Nestling into the castle rock itself, the 'Trip' has a floor so porous
that spilled beer will dry before the barman can get a cloth to
mop it up. Heavy with the smell of earth and proclaiming itself

the oldest inn in England (labelled 1189), it is supposed to have been a good pull-up ('tryppe' was old English for 'halt') for Crusaders when they left for the Holy Land.

A tiny aperture in the cellars is said to be the mouth of a speaking-tube chiselled through the living rock, for before it became a public house this was the brewhouse to the castle. Like the fortress it served, it lay outside the town boundary until 1877. Brewhouse Yard, with its cluster of ramshackle houses, inns, brothels and caves, evolved into an untouchable haven for cut-purses, vagabonds and other 'ill-conditioned persons'. Even the Victorian rogue Charles Peace is alleged to have found sanctuary in its warren.

Agog with this whiff of the twelfth century, the seeker after Nottingham Castle will be further conditioned by the 'Salutation' inn, with its thirteenth-century oak beams and rumours of high-wayman Dick Turpin; and the mediaeval timbers of the former Severn's Restaurant, rescued from the jaws of the bulldozers, on the other side of town, and reassembled here.

Robin Hood himself, no less, is there to spur him on, sturdily drawing his bow (if somebody hasn't snapped it off) outside the castle walls. A pudgy, peculiar statue this, with fat legs and a squat frame, not a bit like Errol Flynn. His henchman Friar Tuck reads intently, Little John concentrates on repairing his bow, Will Stukeley sings, and Alan-a-Dale strums his harp for Will Scarlet. They all deliberately seem to avoid the visitor's eye, as though anxious not to be the one to disillusion him.

A yard or two more and the tourist stands on the very threshold of Nottingham Castle, eager with his memories. Crossing a pattern of cobbles (*circa* 1968, Design Centre Award) he clicks through the turnstile of a restored but feasibly ancient gatehouse, where portcullis once clanged and drawbridge creaked beneath the weight of mailed knights. Even at this stage he is ready to settle for at least the debris of glory, the ruins of towers and turrets; prepared to imagine the boiling oil, the clink of shields, a hint of kings, the flash of heralds, a floating of muslinned wimples, the clash of lance against breastplate.

But not only has the castle gone. The glory has gone. Leaving not even a ghost. Above the neat municipal lawns, where summer-time crowds munch their sandwiches round a tiny bandstand (silent since a Corporation economy drive) is the understudy for a dream. Nottingham Castle. Not a castle, but a seventeenth-century mansion. And not even Nottingham's until thirty years ago when the Corporation had to buy it for £16,000 from the Oxford University Trust. That was £2,000 more than the original building price for William Cavendish, Royalist supporter and the first Duke of Newcastle, who began it in 1674 when he was in his eighties. And £5,000 less than the infuriated fourth Duke received in compensation when incensed reform rioters set it ablaze in 1831.

After its gutted shell had stood roofless for over forty years, it was transmuted in 1878 into the country's first municipal museum and art gallery; a curious Victorian manse, made from one of England's earliest Palladian palaces.

Even cleaned up to its original, unsettling fawn colour, it remains a constant, traumatic jolt, especially when floodlit. Most people take it to be a prison. And in its heart Nottingham would prefer a fragment of crumbled keep or decayed dungeon, the stumps of a romantic castle, to a building which hands out such a swipe to the legendary past. But in his zeal to build his new house, the eighty-two-year-old Duke had several feet of the castle rock cut away, and so almost entirely obliterated the ground plan of the ancient fortress to the chagrin of historians of three centuries.

Small wonder, then, that down there by the bandstand the statue of Captain Albert Ball, twenty-one-year-old air-ace V.C. of the First World War, seems to be buckling on his bronze flying coat in a gesture of defiance. The dead Nottingham hero might well be warming up his Nieuport Scout in a gallant but mis-guided gesture to protect the balustraded box behind him.

Crossing a wooden footway over what was once the dry moat, you may queue for a cup of civic tea in a vast high hall containing the massive ducal ovens. It takes some hard imagining, as you sit at your plastic table, to wonder if Henry II and his draughtsmen pored over their plans on this very spot. Or, as plastic oranges swirl languidly in their tank above the ham-rolls, whether Richard the Lionheart sat there between two archbishops in 1184 and indicted his brother John for treason. This baroque mansion—with its uniformed attendants shifting on uncomfortable tubular and canvas chairs beneath the heavy gilt frames of indifferent paintings and guarding the uniforms from faded wars—lays a deadly hand on history. Even the small specimen of thirteenth-century town wall, which, thirty feet high and seven feet thick, crept around Nottingham for seventy years, lies in the grounds like a neat stone packing-case.

A century ago the earnest Victorians cleared out the ivy and birds' nests from the charred hulk of the Duke of Newcastle's ruin. Characteristically they added ingenious hot air and ventilation systems (walls and floors made fireproof this time) and connected the first telephone in town—prudently to the constabulary. To make their cultural institution suitably splendid, they knocked into two storeys a building designed for three. The resulting windy spaces were enshrined, for the opening by the Prince of Wales, in an eighteen-verse ode by Philip James Bailey, whose epic 'Festus' was allegedly a favourite with Queen Victoria and whose bust is now set—with those of Byron and lesser local literati—in the entrance portico.

'Lift up thy head, Art Fortress,' urged Bailey, 'mid strongholds of our land, an Intellectual Beacon burning bright.' The Art Fortress, filled initially with exhibits from the South Kensington Museum, borrowed and returned over 60,000 pictures and objects in its first twenty years. (It was a charitable traffic that occasionally encountered bottlenecks—as when some ladies in Altrincham, prepared to loan a huge oil painting, put it in their hall and were hardly able to leave the house, let alone their dining-room, because the museum forget to collect it.)

Slowly the hybrid castle accumulated its own permanent collections, a jerky beg-and-borrow process dependent on the whim and purse of whatever political party happened to be in control of Nottingham. The struggle by dedicated but penny-pinched keepers, curators and directors is painfully obvious today. As recently as 1960 the entire staff of the castle museum was four—the director, his deputy, a clerk and a shorthand typist. The Corporation did not even recognise archaeology until the 1960s, when it eventually cleared a little space for the two rooms in which now lie Nottingham's strongest links with its remote forefathers—a couple of thirty-foot Bronze Age dugout canoes, dredged from 2,500 years of Trent mud, and dried out under fifteen tons of wet gravel (gradually, to prevent disintegration after so long a burial) and found a resting place in the congested castle. It was only in 1972 that Nottingham bothered to appoint a resident archaeologist, who is understandably appalled at the years of neglect he will have to clear up.

Largely through gift and bequest rather than a policy of purchase—for the city fathers have never been lavish with the arts—the museum now bulges with material crying out for adequate space for storage or, more important, display. The visitor is faced with an amazing mixture of coins, machine guns, Wedgwood (one of the finest collections in existence), bone-shaker bicycles, mediaeval Nottingham glazed ware, alabaster, wrought iron, glass walking-sticks, coaches, assegais, blunderbusses, medals (including the Victoria Cross of that young airman outside), statues, lace, English silver, French glass and Japanese armour.

Like so much in English history, Nottingham Castle was fathered by William the Conqueror. Within two years of the Battle of Hastings, William splashed across the ford of the Trent in person and, pausing on his punitive route to deal with the rebellious north, quickly sized up the greater military advantages of the rock with its sheer drop on three sides, as distinct from the cluster of the Anglo-Danish settlement.

From his orders to 'bridle the English' grew a speedily-built castle of the 'motte and bailey' type, a simple affair of a tower, on the summit, surrounded by a strong palisade and an outer ditch.

Nevertheless, Nottingham's castle (governed by William Peverel who was also granted Sherwood Forest and 162 manors) was planned not only as a strategic buckle in the bridle, but as a royal residence. It was to grow, and solidify the role, for the next five hundred years; the most important castle in the Midlands and one that was to accommodate eighteen crowned heads, their attendant Parliaments, and a mixture of won and lost causes.

Like iron filings drawn round a magnet, a Norman community settled in the shadow of the Conqueror's castle, co-existing reasonably enough with the Anglo-Danish population. There was never much question of marked hostility towards the newcomers. Nottingham was already a trading town; a royal residence would bring more prosperity. Never particularly war-like, Nottingham settled down as a Norman manor with the king as Lord of the Manor. But the presence of the castle brought its miseries. In 1140 during the troubled reign of Stephen one of the more troublesome barons, Robert Earl of Gloucester, tried to break in, failed, and vented his wrath on the town instead. Women and children were butchered in the streets or burned in the churches to which they had rushed in horror.

Thirteen years later the town was incinerated again, as a defence measure. One spirited merchant lured some marauders into his house promising them loot, slammed the door on them, and burnt jointly house and raiders.

But this time the man who had besieged the town—then Duke of Anjou—showed his contrition in a practical way. Almost as soon as he gained the throne as Henry II, he rode into Nottingham (in February, 1155). By way of compensation he gave it a shot in the arm by halving the taxes to allow rebuilding, and giving the right to levy tolls on rivers and roads and to hold markets on Fridays and Saturdays; he also conferred on it the monopoly of dyeing cloth within a radius of ten miles.

Brisk and businesslike, Henry was the one who transformed the wood-and-earth castle into the vast stone complex we carry in our imagination, with cleancut battlements like stone teeth gnashing the skyline, rattling chains at the portcullis, and minstrelcy and the smells of boar's head and roast sucking-pig.

It was a prize which eventually Henry's son John coveted so strongly that while the new king, his brother Richard Coeur de Lion, was away at the Crusades he laid claim—thus acquiring one of the eight castles in the kingdom equipped with a bath. Lionheart returned in 1194 and, the dust of Jerusalem still on his chainmail, made a beeline for his castle in Nottingham. John was in France at the time. Richard headed the army himself, crashed through the outer defences (there is record of a payment of six guineas for bringing shields, arrows, javelins and Greek Fire from London), and three days later made the Governor wilt into opening the gates without resistance.

Then, during a four-day session of Parliament in the main hall, Richard called upon his brother to answer for his treachery within forty days. The following year the brothers were reconciled at the intercession of their mother, and John was soon back in his favourite castle, behaving himself so well that on his deathbed the Lionheart named him as his successor.

The latest royal resident spent a great deal of time at Nottingham during the seventeen years of his reign. The hunting was good in Sherwood (the 'shire wood', twenty miles long and eight from east to west, stretching to the outskirts of the town) and this powerful castle was a handy mobilisation centre for forays against the rebels in Wales.

John was an increasing paranoiac—once, he took it into his head that a member of his Exchequer was swindling him and 'did him to death by a strange torment; he closed him in leade and so, by depryvinge him of al ayre, bereft him of his life withal'.

It was this same unbrookable fury that led him to carry out the bloodiest act in the history of the castle. Storming into Nottingham in 1212, furious at rumours from Wales, John refused to eat a meal until he had seen with his own eyes the twenty-eight Welsh hostages—sons of the most illustrious families in the Principality—hanged from the castle walls. The boys, mostly aged twelve and fourteen, were seized as they played games and carried to the ramparts, yelling and struggling in bewilderment and terror.

Throughout the Middle Ages, Nottingham's castle—'so well defended by nature and by art that it was almost impregnable'— was a constant base for the monarchs of England. As a home, a refuge, a prison, a Parliament (for Parliament was wherever the king happened to be) or as a secure platform from which to curb or crush opponents.

The artistic Henry III and his queen commuted there regularly from 1244, sending ahead minute instructions for decorations; fixing new candlesticks in the bedrooms, putting in new windows, a new altar for the chapel and new wainscotting in the queen's apartments.

The castle changed hands several times during Henry III's tussles with Simon de Montfort, a period which seemed on the point of echoing the old days of violence, and set Nottingham building its town wall; an expensive and abortive project that continued spasmodically for the next seventy years.

Relations between town and castle were cordial enough under Edward I, even if his queen, Eleanor of Castile, did complain that the smoke of the fires drove her away in 1257.

It was to the safety of Nottingham that Edward II sent Queen Isabella when the Scots tried to kidnap her in 1318. And twelve years later it was there that, having condoned the bestial murder of her husband at Berkeley Castle, she was wrenched from her affair with the man who had arranged it—Roger Mortimer, ex Marcher Lord and now the power behind the throne.

With the ingredients of a rattling good tale of treachery and intrigue ready to hand, Nottingham Castle today makes quite a feature of the business—even though the signboard outside the secret passage called Mortimer's Hole does get it wrong. The eighteen-year-old Edward III did not, as it states, enter the stronghold through it on that night of October 19, 1330. He was already there, a virtual prisoner of his mother's lover and his bodyguard of wild Welsh mercenaries. When Edward's party of conspirators had crept up through the tunnel (history is a bit vague about how they got through what would have been the most heavily guarded sections of the whole fortress) he joined them in the courtyard and took them straight to Mortimer's room, next to his royal mistress. A brisk set-to, a couple of stewards run through, and the Hamletian affair was over. Its villain, Mortimer, was dragged on a hurdle to Tyburn to be hanged, drawn and quartered. But unlike the queen in *Hamlet*, Isabella survived for another twenty-eight years, on reasonable terms with her son and enjoying the freedom of her several manors.

And Edward himself had half a century's reign, hunting at his royal lodge at Bestwood (which, centuries later, another monarch, Charles II, gave to Nell Gwynne for services rendered), and waging war on the Scots, and sending back prisoners like their regent the Earl of Murray. The Scottish king David himself is supposed to have languished for eleven years in one of Nottingham's dungeons, scratching the scene of the Passion on the rock wall (with his fingernails, some say, rather wildly). But despite two excavations for the purpose in 1720 and 1864 King David's cell remains unearthed. He did no worse than the regal quarters of the Tower of London, where he spent some time.

What is more accurate is that Edward III used Nottingham Castle as a gaol for the Speaker of the House of Commons who had spoken out against the king's mistress. Flung in for life, he was liberated two years later when the king died.

More important to the prosperity of England in general, and of Nottingham in particular, was Edward's momentous Parliament in 1337 which invited the cloth workers of Holland to come over. It was a move that not only laid the foundations of England as a manufacturing country; it was, along with Henry II's

St. Mary's, the city's parish church
The Shire Hall

Willoughby House

modest granting of the dyeing monopoly one hundred and eighty years before, a vital step in establishing Nottingham as the centre of a textile industry.

The splendour of Nottingham Castle unrolled like a rich tapestry. Richard II brought the Lord Chief Justice and four other judges scurrying up in 1387 to condemn those who opposed him over the issue of Parliamentary writs. And five years later, after a row with the City of London which refused him a loan, he took umbrage and removed the whole Court of Chancery to Nottingham. Another five years and he was holding another council to dispose of his main opponents; his uncle the Duke of Gloucester (soon murdered on his instructions), the Earl of Arundel (beheaded), the Earl of Warwick and the Archbishop of Canterbury (exiled).

Henry IV imprisoned Owen Glendower within Nottingham's powerful walls. The future James I of Scotland was also moved here for several years. And Henry V, who in 1421 showed off his bride Katharine of France on a proud tour after her coronation, used it a year later as a lodging for two dozen of her countrymen, as captives.

Since gaining some rights under Henry II's charter, Nottingham had been inching towards autonomy. When, three centuries later, Henry VI arrived, it acquired the most important charter of all. In 1449 Henry made the borough a county in itself. Nottingham could choose its own rulers, a Mayor and six aldermen picked from a strangely chosen list of fifty leading men called The Clothing. It could administer its own justice. Its two bailiffs were to be known as sheriffs, and even royal officials could be prevented from entering the town. In effect the borough became a tiny self-governing republic. True, the charter meant little to the rank and file for the Corporation was a select and self-perpetuating clique; a state of affairs which was to take it well into Victorian times. But the 1449 charter meant that control by the castle on the cliff-top, already technically outside the town, was prised loose from it.

Yet although feudalism and the Middle Ages were sliding towards their death, Nottingham Castle was still too important not to play its part. It was one of the few major fortresses that the Yorkish sovereigns Edward IV and Richard III bothered to maintain. Edward, who in 1469 used it as a base against the northern

rebels of Lancaster, had himself proclaimed king in Nottingham
in 1471, and set in motion a massive building programme including a splendid octagonal tower at the north-west corner of the
inner bailey. His crookbacked brother eventually added a vast
range of state apartments adjoining it, their seven mullioned bay-
windows glinting richly in the sun. In his princely 'Castle of
Care' as he called it, the last of the Plantagenets would take
himself off to his sumptuous turret, writing to his subjects in
Ireland to tell them of his accession, rounding off the peace with
Scotland, and arranging the marriage between his niece and the
Scots king's eldest son.

But the sun of York was setting, and it was Nottingham which
caught the last rays. Aware that Henry Tudor might land in
Wales, Richard had his Master of the Rolls bring the Great Seal,
in its white leather bag, from London and posted relays of horsemen at intervals of twenty miles along the roads leading to
Nottingham. He was hunting at Bestwood when the news came;
five days later the red rose of Lancaster was reported blooming
as near as Lichfield forty miles away.

On Friday, 19th August 1485, his standard of war was hoisted
at the flagstaff on his tower, next to the white rose emblem.
Richard, wearing his richly gilded steel armour topped by his
golden crown, mounted his favourite white Surrey covered with
gorgeous cloths—the gay, golden lions of England and the lilies
of France—and reviewed his troops in the Market Place. Then,
preceded by his cavalry, his bombards (gunpowder was coming
in), and his infantry ranged five abreast, he led the glittering
column out from his castle for the last time. The townspeople
watched it go, clinking and jingling across the town bridge and
over the arches of the old Hethebeth Bridge across the Trent, and
winding over the hills at Wilford until lost to sight by those
staring from the ramparts of the castle.

Three days later, Richard III's bloody and grimy corpse was
picked up from the battlefield at Bosworth, near Leicester, and
flung over a horse. The crown, they say, was found dangling on
a hawthorn bush.

The new wearer of that crown, Henry VII, proved to be 'the
personification of politeness and affability' when he closed in on
Nottingham to test local loyalty. But after Henry had disposed of
Lambert Simnel's army at East Stoke near Newark, where 7,000

men were butchered in a gulley that became aptly known as the Red Gutter, it was the beginning of the end for Nottingham Castle. Today's disappointed American tourists, whose country was being discovered in Henry's reign, can blame him to a great extent. For as part of his policy to dispose of castles by demolition or neglect, he did no more to maintain Nottingham either as a palace or a military station.

The florid Henry VIII visited the castle in 1511 and testily dashed off an order for 1,000 ells of canvas to line the tapestries. A touch of luxury which, nineteen years later, the sad, dying Cardinal Wolsey could scarcely have appreciated on his single night's sojourn before being urged on by 'the iron Constable' of the Tower of London. In 1537 the Earl of Rutland stocked up men and provisions to seal off the north, rising against Henry's new religious regime; but they were not needed, except for a short, revolting business at the great Clunaic priory at Lenton two miles away when the prior and one of the monks were hanged over their own gateway.

By the time that the king's antiquary John Leland visited the castle in 1540, the west side and the great hall lay in ruins, even though the east and south 'were well towered, there being a stately bridge, with beasts and giants, three chapels, three wells and the most beautifullest and gallant building, Richard III's tower'.

The great days were over. Despite 'extensive reparacions' mooted for the castle, and a buzz of rumours for a magnificent meeting in 1562 between Queen Elizabeth and Mary Queen of Scots, the old place was unfit for human habitation. When James I's Queen Anne and her son Prince Henry passed through Nottingham in 1603, it was to Wollaton Hall, the recently completed fantasy home of the Willoughby family, that they turned. Likewise, for his half dozen visits from 1612 onward, James I stayed at Thurland Hall, the forty-seven-roomed mansion built in the heart of the town by the immensely rich wool stapler Thomas Thurland, and bought by William Holles who, son of a self-made merchant Lord Mayor of London, was equally well-heeled.

Charles I also relished the comfort of such stately homes, but recognised the psychological value of the castle as a backdrop in his theatre of war. Ruin or not, the ancient fortress was the spot on which to raise his standard. On August 12, 1642, Charles issued the call urging that 'all subjects who can bear arms northwards of the Trent and southward twenty miles' should rally round. At 6 p.m., ten days later, surrounded by a small body of militia and 800 horsemen, he had the proclamation read out. The herald had hardly begun when some scruple arose in Charles's mind. He motioned the herald to stop, took the document on his knee, scribbled a few corrections and handed it back.

From then on it was like an extravagantly ill-conceived play. As the blustery wind dried the ink on the parchment, the herald stumbled over the amended script. Prince Rupert and other extras on the scene played their roles with zeal, shouted 'God Save the King', and tossed their plumed hats into the blustery breeze. With a flourish of trumpets the standard itself was brought forward on a pole like a long, red maypole. It was a large silk pennant, painted by a local craftsman, involving the cross of Saint George, two lions on crowns, a hand pointing to the royal arms and the hopeful motto: 'Give Caesar His Due.'

It was held by Sir Edmund Verney who declared stoutly that they who would take it from his hand must first wrest his soul from his body. Everybody seemed vague about the actual ritual, and where the top-heavy flagpole could be planted. They scratched unsuccessfully in the rock with daggers, and for a few hours a couple of dozen of the supporting cast struggled to hold it up after the principals had left the stage. Following Richard III's precedent, 159 years previously, they took it back into the castle and fixed it to Richard's tower. Where that night, like an omen, the wind blew it down.

The Great Recruiting Show scripted and stage-managed by Charles ran for three weeks, received thin houses (a mere 300) and moved elsewhere. Nottingham Castle, still sufficiently intact to form a considerable stronghold, spent the Civil War, paradoxically, not as a last bastion for a king but as a Roundhead island in a hostile sea of Royalists. In fact, of the seven aldermen of the town council only the Mayor was firmly for Parliament, but a defence committee was formed in which, as the issues clarified, Nottingham came down on the side it felt had the best chance. The command of the Nottingham garrison was given to Colonel John Hutchinson. In the strange turbulence before the war actually began, Hutchinson had foiled a cool attempt by

Cavaliers from Newark to filch the town's gunpowder supply. Refusing the Earl of Newcastle's bribe of £10,000 to defect to the Royalist cause, Hutchinson removed the armoury to the castle, caused quite a stir by building cannon platforms there rather than trying to defend the town itself, and offered to let the townsfolk stow themselves or their goods in the fortress if they repaired the place. He made his determination clear by arresting an alderman and fourteen other men as troublemakers and sending them off to prison in Derby. And the regulations under his military government included stiff fines and imprisonment for drinking, swearing, and 'idlely standinge or walkinge in the streete in sermon-tyme'.

If the Royalists wanted to take this poor castle, he asserted with vigour, they would have to wade through blood. To a certain extent they did. One September night in 1643 a surprise party of Cavaliers from Newark crept in (Alderman Francis Toplady was said actually to have let them in) and held the town for five days, capturing many of the garrison's soldiers while they were sleeping at home, and raking the castle ramparts with musket fire from the tower of St. Nicholas' church. (Hutchinson later had the church pulled down.) A relief force from Leicester and Derby saved the situation, but at intervals during the next few years the men of the castle garrison had to rush down to indulge in bitter hand-to-hand fighting. One daring bunch of Cavalier commandos disguised themselves as shoppers on their way to market, to pounce on the outpost at Trent Bridge with iron bars and pistols up their sleeves. And when the Nottingham garrison beat off a 1,000-strong force which penetrated the streets right up to the castle, the retreating Royalists left a great track of blood, which froze as it fell on the January snow.

When it all ended, so did Nottingham Castle. In 1651, nine years to the day since Charles I had hoisted his flag of war, and two years after his beheading at Whitehall, Oliver Cromwell rode through Nottingham on his way to defeat Charles's son at Worcester. The demolition of the castle was ordered the following year, oddly enough not by Cromwell but by John Hutchinson. He had seen that 'the poison of ambition had ulcerated Cromwell's heart' and hastily got Parliament to sanction the destruction in case his ambitious master used the castle to his own advantage. He may have been right. When the Lord Protector found out about it, he expressed himself as 'heartily vexed'.

And so ended the castle on the rock, relatively free of whimpers but loud with the bang of the demolition men's gunpowder. Anything of value 'likely to be embezzled' was shipped to the Tower of London. And the masonry, trodden by the feet of kings, was sold in job lots as paving stones for the feet of ordinary men.

The mansion which was to take the castle's place looked over an utterly different Nottingham where the great families were to build an elegant pyramid, toppled in turn by the industrial revolution. The colourful courts of the Henrys and the Richards and the Johns were to be grimed by the smoke of factory chimneys in the lush meadows below. The jingle of harness as kings went a-hawking was to be replaced by the deafening snarl of twentieth-century lorries on a road named after Maid Marian and described as 'the ugliest road in Europe and an insult to Maid Marian'.

Even in its heyday, the mansion which replaced the old fortress had dwindled to a glorified boarding-house. After the fire of 1831, when it was attacked and burnt by rioters angered by the quashing of the Reform Bill, the Duke of Newcastle left its carcass as 'a memento of the folly of, and a standing disgrace to, the inhabitants of Nottingham', although from time to time they were let into the grounds for festivals, balloon ascents, flower shows or, as in 1842, a party to 'commemorate the triumph of Conservative principles'.

The area which was once the outer bailey of the mediaeval castle was rented out as allotments, and the ruin on the crown of the hill was soon complemented by clusters of smaller ruins, as gardeners' summer-houses and tool-sheds mushroomed. Starting with six embarrassed recruits on the first parade, in 1859, the Robin Hood Rifle Corps built itself into a crack unit within the grounds, getting rid of the double flight of steps to the front entrance because it obstructed manœuvres.

What is now known as Nottingham Castle is a minor reminder of major history; a trademark for Player's cigarettes, a place to hold Scout and Cub parades, a backcloth for an open-air performance of *The Yeomen of the Guard*. All that remains of Richard III's grandiose tower stands in a garden in The Park, where the householder's children use the stones as a play-castle. The most impressive banner even seen over the ancient rock was a gigantic flag in a visual-arts experiment, simply bearing the word FOG.

In 1976, an archaeological dig—done on a shoe string, naturally—excitingly revealed the Black Tower, buried beneath the courtyard which was filled in to become the present Castle Green. Together with a section of the outer wall, the find gave hope that there may be a lot more of the medieval castle than was supposed.

With almost every vestige of the real castle gone and the Georgian quarter at its base practically wiped out, yet with streams of visitors anxious to see at least something, Nottingham Corporation lately decided to hang on to what it had. Through 1972 it spent £15,000 to stop erosion of the castle rock. Otherwise the castle—cleaned-up Palladian dignity, Victorian bric-à-brac and all—would eventually tip off the edge.

An event which would have given the ghost of the 'heartily vexed' Oliver Cromwell no little satisfaction.

THREE

WILL THE REAL MR. HOOD
PLEASE STAND UP?

Robin Hood, Robin Hood, ridin' through the glen . . .
—TV series signature tune

THE name of the President of the First National Bank in North Carolina, U.S.A., is Robin Hood. He married a girl with the surname of Frye whose friends, before she became Mrs. Hood, used to call her Frye Tuck. Their son John was inevitably known as Little John.

Another American Robin Hood is in the sand and gravel business in Denham Springs. One day he phoned a local restaurant, trying to locate one of his drivers who bore the name of Jesse James. When he told them that Robin Hood was calling, they hung up.

Minor tragedies like that are being enacted all over the States and the rest of the English-speaking world, as the organisers of the Nottingham Festival found out when in 1970 they canvassed for five Robin Hoods to come over as VIP guests. They received more than a hundred letters, ranging from heartcries by those who had suffered lifelong accusations of insolence in school or army, to a wistful four-year-old girl whose parents christened her Robin Hood 'because they wanted her to be outgoing and popular'.

A photograph of the chosen five, grouped round the Robin Hood statue, was the first record of their trip. Whenever a photographer is stuck for a quick subject in Nottingham, Robin comes to the rescue. Half a ton of him, in half-inch-thick bronze, stands in the shadow of the castle walls, twanging an invisible arrow from an invisible bowstring. Invisible because the mediaeval outlaw has lost his fight against twentieth-century vandals. Robin used to be able to shoot a measured mile; now he can't shoot an inch. Since the seven-foot effigy was manœuvred on to its two-and-a-half-ton base in 1952—the gift not of the city but of a local businessman—the Corporation have wearied of replacing stolen arrows at £55 a time. Then one night half the bow was snapped off. So they surrounded Robin with a mini-forest of prickly bushes, gently turning down suggestions of a moat of coloured dye, a built-in siren, or an electrically-charged bow and arrow 'which would shock but not actually kill'.

By 1970, and a few arrows later, they gave up the struggle against souvenir hunters, and sculptor James Woodford himself agreed. 'Leave the arrow to the imagination,' he said.

It was a typical Nottingham solution. One can hardly visualise the Swiss at Altdorf allowing William Tell to stand on his plinth minus his crossbow. Nottingham was prepared to let visitors be baffled at Robin Hood's stringless stance. The entire Hood affair exists only in the mind, and Nottingham doesn't exert itself to make it real.

It is real enough to other people. Throughout the world, people who have never smoked a Nottingham-made cigarette, hung a Nottingham lace curtain at the window, or swallowed a Nottingham-made pill, all know about Robin Hood, whether they call him 'Hróa Hött' in Iceland or 'Robin Good' in Russia (where they buy their Olympic bows from a Nottinghamshire firm). They might give him a strong anti-imperialist propaganda value, and be more concerned about his struggle against the Reactionary Capitalists than his love life, but along the line Nottingham gets a plug.

It is ironic that the one thing for which Nottingham is universally famous is not there at all. The Shakespeare industry at Stratford, has, after all, the plays to show. Nottingham, with only a legend on its doorstep, isn't too bright with abstract ideas unless someone else has shown the way. So, although it mentions him in holiday brochures, Nottingham gives Robin no museum, no reminder on its traffic signs at the city boundary, no official backing, not even a Robin Hood section in its castle. True, there are no guaranteed relics to display, but there are enough pictures, books, films, theories and assorted international mementoes to turn Robin Hood into a major Nottingham industry.

Imagine the trade to be picked up if tourists were able to come to a Robin Hood Centre, in the very town with which he is associated, and there saturate themselves with his exploits. They could listen to talks and ideas, handle contemporary clothes, see a replica of a town of his period, examine mediaeval manuscripts, compare the stories of other countries, hear the ballads about him, read the first-known accounts and the subsequent volumes that line bookshelves, and wallow in the films that have been screened around him. No one could be expected to come up with the genuine bow or accredited quiver—but if as near as possible to (or even on the site of) Nottingham Castle, Nottingham Corporation took its outlaw to heart, it would not only make up for the disappointment of the castle but would prove a copper-bottomed moneyspinner. But there are signs that the city is beginning to wake up to the outlaw's pull.

After all, Nottingham has actually pardoned Robin Hood. On October 9, 1966, seven centuries after the last 'WANTED' poster was tacked on to the trees of Sherwood Forest, the Sheriff of Nottingham, wearing his robes and accompanied by his mace-bearer, drove to the Major Oak at Edwinstowe, Robin's famous hiding place, and officially exonerated him and his archers in a proclamation which cancelled any suggestion of villainy. It added that he 'shall be welcome in the city at all times'.

As things are at the moment, the welcome is a bit scrappy. Robin is there on a mural in the Council House dome (a footballer and a doctor's wife respectively modelled Little John and Maid Marian), and one or two hotels possess a 'Robin Hood' cocktail bar. You can walk down a Robin Hood Street, a Robin Hood Chase and a Robin Hood Terrace. One of the electoral districts is Robin Hood Ward. A self-righting lifeboat launched on the Trent in 1867 was named after him. He drew a bow on the masthead of the *Guardian-Journal* every morning, and travels lithely on the back door of Barton's buses (but not on Corporation vehicles). There is a Robin Hood coach company, and a 'Robin Hood' pub. He is further immortalised by a driving school, a poster printer, a light ale, a television service, a garage and a chip shop. All of which evokes a picture of the merrie men hiring a charabanc, filling up at a petrol pump served by Friar Tuck, getting in a few crates of beer and taking fifty cod-and-four-penn'orths back to Sherwood Forest for Maid Marian to warm up.

If anything, the Sheriff gets better publicity. Holders of this office respond with magnificent aplomb, getting the glory from the Golden Arrow archery tournament every September, and riding round in the official Rolls. The Sheriff is a natural for merry quips about his erstwhile character, and has turned the historical 'baddie' into a splendid chap. One Canadian youth was so impressed after meeting him in the Council House that he wrote in his school essay that the Sheriff of Nottingham even had golden sugar in his coffee. The city has grown so fond of him, in fact, that it has fought to save him from being scrapped with the reorganisation of local government.

But it seems to be the people outside Nottingham who take more interest in Robin Hood (the M1 dining-room at Trowell, complete with waitresses in jaunty feathered caps handing over the olde-Englishe menu, is called 'The *Sheriff's* Restaurant'). The country is littered with rock pillars and megaliths connected with him. Robin Hood's Stone, a mass of rock in Lunedale, supposedly kicked from the top of Shacklesborough; an earthwork in Wiltshire, Robin's Bower; a megalith near Halifax, Robin Hood's Ringstone. From Robin Hood's Butts in Shropshire he was alleged to have shot an arrow at the weathercock of Ludlow Church. There is Robin Hood's Tower at Richmond Castle. A hamlet is named after him in Derbyshire.

Nottinghamshire itself does try more than Nottingham. Even without the promised theme park, 40,000 visit Sherwood Forest on a summer Sunday and the county authorities have done something about the degeneration of the area through erosion and use. Big plans are in hand, so they say, to realise Sherwood's potential as a major zone of countryside leisure. For some years it has been possible to sponsor a new tree in the forest. America—where eight million people belong to associations connected with Robin Hood—has paid avidly its £10 per oak, getting in return a gold and scarlet document on handmade paper.

The 1,500 acres leased to the Ministry of Defence were freed by 1978, and there is a nice visitors' centre, but the approach from Edwinstowe to the Major Oak is a sort of blasted heath as leafless trees stand stark and grotesque from blight and lack of water. The Oak itself, 1,400-year-old headquarters of the men in Lincoln green, is a sad old thing now, propped with iron shackles and patched with lead sheets. But it still stands gnarled and proud, the slit in its belly polished by the bodies of tourists who squeeze inside and imagine they have given the Sheriff the slip. Tree surgeons are called in periodically and minister to it, lopping off rheumatic limbs, flushing out dead wood and fungus, spraying with protective paint. And every year acorns plop down fresh and hopeful from its upper branches. The equally famous oak, Robin's Larder, was blown down in a gale in 1966—its corpse is now dissected by disabled workmen at Portland Training College and fashioned into plaques, barometer-stands and similar souvenirs. Some of them are sold in Nottingham in company with the Robin Hood statuettes made in Hong Kong.

The Sherwood in the city of Nottingham, of course, is merely a suburb along the Mansfield Road; and the Forest a recreation ground. But the greenwood of Sherwood Forest used to edge there, right up to the common fields bordering the old town. The Royal hunting forest was originally an ellipse between Nottingham and Edwinstowe.

The fact that it connected with the woodlands of Yorkshire has lured Yorkshiremen into the trap of claiming Robin Hood as their own. Particularly as they can produce evidence of at least two *Robert* Hoods. One, mentioned in the pipe roll of 1230, was a fugitive from justice in the West Riding. The other, born in Wakefield about 1290, joined the rebel Earl of Lancaster, fought for him at the Battle of Boroughbridge and was later outlawed.

Nottingham men will concede that Robin (the true Nottinghamshire product, that is) is *buried* in Yorkshire. The eighty-seven-year-old hero was treacherously bled to death, according to the legend, on Christmas Eve 1247 at Kirklees Cistercian nunnery, four miles north-east of Huddersfield, by the prioress, a kinswoman anxious to protect the family name. Clearly the action of a sly Yorkshirewoman. Little John, who came hurrying along in response to Robin's 'weak blasts three', was all for burning down the nunnery in revenge; but, gentleman to the last, his master would not permit it. Instead, he shot one final arrow with his ebbing strength and commanded that he be interred where it fell.

Television series by partisan and biased Yorkshire-TV notwithstanding, Nottingham rests calm in the knowledge that it owns the right man. You could snap him in half and find 'Notts.'

lettered right through. There is talk that Robin was born in Loxley, Staffordshire, that his real name was Fitzooth, and that he was the rightful Earl of Huntingdon. But then, there is so *much* talk about his identity. Why, even Rumania claims him.

Robin, says Nottingham with as much authority as anybody else, was probably born about 1160 'in Locksley town, in merry Nottinghamshire'. But his point of origin is not important. The strong thing is that he centred on Nottingham.

Yards of books still grow, seeking the 'truth' about Robin Hood (alias Robin Hode, Robertus Hood, Robyn Hode and Hobbehod), niggling away at the traditional encounters with Richard the Lionheart and King John. Most of the disclaimers hinge on quibbles about his longbow (not introduced until twenty-five years after his traditional death, and not in common usage until the Battle of Halidon Hill in 1333). Or about his choice of friends (Friar Tuck couldn't have existed anywhere in England until 1221 and there were no friars locally until 1272). Or the carping point that there was no actual Sheriff of Nottingham until 1449 (Robin's arch-enemy would have been the Sheriff of Nottinghamshire and Derbyshire). And that if Robin had indeed been related to the Earl of Huntingdon, then he would also have been Crown Prince of Scotland which title was vested with the Earl's heir, and surely *that* would have been recorded somewhere.

Robin got his first press notice about 1380, in William Langland's *Piers Plowman*, linking him with Randolph, Earl of Chester —whose lifetime spanned the reigns of Richard I, John and Henry III. Robin was a well-established character by 1377, and some of the earliest ballads were brought together about the end of the fifteenth century in *A Lytell Geste of Robyn Hode* printed by Wynken de Worde. But earlier, about 1420, Wyntoun in his *Scottish Chronicle* makes note under the year 1283 of the outlaw and 'King Edward'.

It is easy to understand how the ballads grew up. The penalties for breaking the forest laws were savage. Blinding and mutilation for poaching deer were not abolished until 1217, and imprisonment and banishment lasted for a long time afterwards. Since the public then regarded poachers as criminals no more than the eighteenth century so regarded smugglers, a dashing figure, or a composite of several, would naturally leap to mind and tongue. If Robin Hood did not exist it would have been necessary to invent him.

Handed down orally, embellished by every telling, the original stories about the outlaw are now impossible to unwrap with any accuracy. Not that Jim Lees will ever give up the fight for his hero. Mr. Lees—a sixty-five-year-old Nottinghamian ex-shirt-maker, part time square-dance caller and legal clerk—is Robin Hood's supreme champion. His ruling passion is to establish without doubt that Robin was alive and well and came from Nottingham.

He dismisses with contumely the impertinent Yorkshire tykes trying to climb on the bandwagon. The Barnsdale in which they place Robin, he maintains, was corrupted from the Bernydale of the earliest printed ballads. And Bernydale was Bryunsdale (or Brymsdale) where the merrie men had their main camp. Near Bestwood Park; in the parish of Basford; which is a suburb of Nottingham. Firmly in Sherwood Forest and nowhere near Yorkshire.

After twelve years of eye-straining research, Mr. Lees has discovered 'indisputable' proof of Robin's noble Saxon birth, his justifiable claims to the Earldom of Huntingdon and the Lordship of Loxley, and his strong religious ties. Ever keen on schemes to take visitors on a grand tour of the traditional haunts (one of them was slap where Nottingham's Council House now stands), and to organise a (so far unsuccessful) Robin Hood Festival worthy of the city, Mr. Lees springs terrier-like to the defence should anyone make a spurious claim or utter a harsh word about Robin.

He had plenty of opportunity when a writer, in the *Justice of the Peace and Local Government Review*, dared scoff at the 'stealing from the rich to give to the poor' idea. The miscreant described Robin as 'the greatest bandit of them all' who had deserted his lawful wife for fun and games with Maid Marian ('no better than she should be, and certainly no maid'), and who would, if he were alive today, 'be eligible for a good, long spell of preventive detention'. With warm dignity, Mr. Lees (backed by the Sheriff of Nottingham, no less) scotched such calumny by stressing Robin's sterling goodness. He restored Maid Marian's honour by pointing out that she was already his wife Matilda (from Wake-field—how that name does seem to crop up) who changed her name on becoming a co-outlaw. Far from being a sort of Bonnie and Clyde of the longbow they were a devoted couple who never actually robbed anybody.

Alas for his gallantry! Mr. Lee's subsequent probing uncovered no trace of Maid Marian, and he was forced to scrap her as a myth. Robin—fifty-two years old, not eighty-seven—went to his grave (in 1278) a bachelor, he found. And with the courage of the true scholar, Mr. Lees gulped and had to explode another legend —that Little John was in fact a small man.

According to a survey (by the indefatigable Mr. Lees) most people believe that Robin Hood really existed. Out in the Sherwood Forest country at Papplewick, one man has spent three months and £1,500 restoring the ancient cave reputed to have been Robin Hood's stable, and the hundreds of visitors—including the Argentinian football team—who make the pilgrimage to the hallowed spot prove the magnetic interest he holds.

Some day, somewhere, someone will come on irrefutable proof. After all, Little John was always supposed to have been buried at Hathersage in Derbyshire, and sure enough when the grave was opened in 1728, were not bones of enormous size found inside? (With apologies to Jim Lees.)

For all its neglect of him, Nottingham is proud of Robin Hood —even though that statue, cleanshaven and skull-capped, makes it feel uncomfortable. Robin is still the classic 'goodie', the universal symbol of the fight for justice on behalf of the underdog. Not for nothing did the Luddites meet in Sherwood Forest.

With this quiet confidence, Nottingham doesn't mind that Frank Sinatra turned him into a gangster in the film *Robin and the Seven Hoods*. It is so used to the Fairbanks/Todd/Greene athlete of cinema or TV that it laughed delightedly when in the Frankie Howerd film *Up the Chastity Belt* he was shown as a raving queer, with a band of gay rather than merrie men.

Robin Hood is used to hard knocks, having been anything from a euphemism for the Devil to a leggy principal boy in pantomime. He must have had a twinge when local film-makers announced in 1972 that interest in him was so lacking that they intended to find backers in Spain, Yugoslavia or even Japan. And a slight prickle that the latest Walt Disney cartoon depicts him as a sly fox. It must hit home that the East Midlands Archery Society, wanting to banish the Robin Hood image for ever, has urged its members not to take part in events involving dressing up—to the extent of refusing to wear the feathered hats sent by the Oregon team which competes by transatlantic telephone. It must worry him that, out of 18,000 archers in Britain, his home county has only one per cent, the lowest number of open clubs in the land. And that Nottingham is the only education authority in the country which does not allow archery to be practised in its schools.

But, as he grips a bow which at last has an unbreakable arrow—made out of steel used in tanks—and peers through the female underwear which students occasionally drape over him, Robin can keep his family pride. He still has 'em worried. For when in 1971 the girl who was Maid Marian at the Nottingham Festival flew to America, security men confiscated her bow and arrow. In case she hi-jacked the plane.

Nottingham Castle

FOUR

A TOWN IN A GARDEN

Nottingham has more gentlemen's houses in it than any
town of its bigness in Great Britain.

—Cox, 1730

IN 1972, Wollaton Hall, an Elizabethan mansion three miles from
the centre of Nottingham, came twelfth in the British Tourist
Board's popularity list. The Tower of London was understandably
first. Nottingham Castle, with half a million visitors, took sixth
place. Wollaton Hall drew a sturdy 345,000.

One of the most important Renaissance houses in England,
worth the equivalent of a million or two, Wollaton Hall was
picked up in 1924 by Nottingham Corporation, who did a neat
deal with the eleventh Lord Middleton for £200,000. It was a
spectacular bargain. The city promptly sold less than a third of its
774 acres to tasteful builders and so got the place free.

Wisely it has resisted the temptation to turn Wollaton Park
into a funfair. It laid out a picturesque and exclusive golf course,
and permits pricey fishing on the Chekhovian, reeded lake with
its solitary boat. Cars are not allowed to stream along the avenues
of magnificent lime trees. A small café is tucked away between
lake and stables (where the police horses are quartered). There is
one phone box, one refreshment caravan tolerated as an eyesore,
a hut or two near a couple of football pitches, and a discreet
adventure-playground for children. Occasionally the Corporation unbends and lets the park be borrowed briefly for a caravan
rally, a Scout jamboree, some mock-mediaeval jousting, a hot-air
balloon festival or even the inanities of television's 'It's A Knock-
out'. But once the beer tents have folded and stolen away, and the
last firework tube has been removed (one firework display was
ordered to the far side of the lake, lest it disturb the nesting of a
grebe), Wollaton Park sinks back into a civilised sanctuary. The

Clocktower of the former Victoria Station
Wheeler Gate

spotted deer pick delicately through the golf trollies, and peace is restored for dog-walkers, goldfish-admirers, kite-flyers, flower-sniffers and lonely long-distance runners whose plimsolls patter over the fallen twigs.

The Hall itself emerges from the morning mist like some castle on the Rhine, a fairy-tale vision of Gothic traceries and pepper-pot turrets, seemingly moored to its green hill by stone gondola rings carved round its walls. Walk through its lofty entrance, and the painted saints swirling on the ceiling look down on stuffed gorillas, pickled jellyfish, shaded cases of Brazilian butterflies and silent foxes frozen in mid snarl. For Wollaton Hall is now a natural history museum.

The house was finished in 1588—Armada year—the eight-year extravagance of Sir Francis Willoughby. He was a coal tycoon who probably cared little for the philosophers and poets whose busts he installed in niches around his rococo creation. With no male heir or brother to keep alive the family name, he built his princely and ostentatious palace as matrimonial bait for his eldest daughter. Evidently it worked. She married her cousin, one of the Kent Willoughbys.

At least, that's the story. It has the outlandish aura that hovers round not only the house itself (which looks as if cut out of cardboard for a film set) but round the entire Willoughby family. There is even a tale that one of them, taking a stroll in the grounds, was incensed to see a stranger looking calmly over the wall. Angrily he ordered an extra course of bricks to be laid on the whole seven-mile length—and then learned that the man had been a giant from Goose Fair.

The dynasty began with a wealthy Nottingham wool merchant in the thirteenth century. He carried the prosaic name of Ralph Bugge, but by the third generation the surname (it meant 'hobgoblin') was dropped in favour of the more aristocratic Willoughby, from Willoughby-on-the-Wolds where the founding father had bought up parcels of land. Stretches of Wollaton had also been acquired by marrying the heiress of the lord of its manor. But there was something in the Willoughby make-up which made its menfolk push on beyond the mere gathering of riches. Sir Richard Willoughby, for instance, refused to stagnate as a country squire and became Lord Chief Justice of England. Travelling on circuit to Grantham in 1331 he was kidnapped by a band of outlaws not entirely in the Robin Hood tradition. Calling themselves Gent's Savages, they kept Sir Richard in a wood until ransomed for £60.

Sir Hugh Willoughby was another who declined to loll back and take things easy. In 1553 he took command of three ships trying to pierce a north-west passage to China between Russia and the Pole. His 120-ton *Esperanza* was discovered by Russian fishermen the following year, its crew of thirty-five frozen or starved to death. Sir Hugh, his journal and his will in front of him, was found stiff in his captain's chair.

Sir Francis—the flamboyant originator of Wollaton Hall— looked nearer home for his fortune. Working from 6 a.m. until 6 p.m., his shallow pits at Wollaton yielded 20,000 tons of coal a year. Smoky stuff, by all accounts. As the old rhyme went:

> I cannot without lye or shame
> Commende the Town of Nottinghame.
> The People and the Fewel stinke.
> The place is sordid as a sinke.

Stinking or not, Nottingham Corporation was keen to follow his success with black gold, and in 1630 sank pits on its common land under the Coppice Wood, but lost money heavily.

The fabric for Sir Francis's grandiose hall cost him nothing. His pack horses would set off loaded with Wollaton coal and bring back Ancaster stone from the Lincolnshire quarries in exchange. Even so he spent more than £80,000. Not that the cost bothered him. It was an investment; just as when he had set up an ironworks, experimented with glass manufacturing, tried out new pumping equipment for his mines, dabbled in schemes to send his coal to London via Hull, and even grown woad for dyeing.

He lived handsomely, with a demanding wife, twelve daughters and a host of servants to support. A check-list of 1598 showed nearly fifty people in residence, ranging from the eight footmen to a slaughterman. And he kept going the forty-three-roomed old hall in Wollaton village as an annexe for guests.

When he was not worrying about business problems, nagging wife or contingent of headstrong girls, Sir Francis compiled a rulebook of instructions to his staff. It was, for example, the usher's duty to notify his master if guests 'of the better sort' arrived, so that they could be entertained accordingly. Or, if they were of the meaner variety, 'to know the cause of their coming'. He must make sure that 'no stranger be suffered to pass without offering him to drink', to 'have good regard of every person', and to 'reform all disorders, saying with a loud voice "Speak softly, my masters!"' Any food left over was to be put out for distribution to the poor. And the butler was to see that no beer or bread was filched, for his was 'an office both of good credit and great trust'. Even with such a sharp eye on wastage, Sir Francis's household expenses for fourteen months amounted to £1,394 18s. 8½d.

The Willoughbys were typical of the rich landowning families —the Cliftons, the Strelleys, the Manvers, the Stanhopes, the Byrons—who constituted the Nottinghamshire squirearchy and began building their elegant town houses in Nottingham.

Ever since becoming one of the five Midland Danelaw boroughs, the town had been thrusting with commerce. The Danes, as Sir Arthur Bryant puts it, had taken to trade as the next best thing to piracy. Something of their clear-headed traits stayed with their descendants. From the twelfth century the street names of old Nottingham advertised their wares—Barker Gate acrid with tanner's hides . . . Fisher Gate redolent of fishmongers . . . Fletcher Gate's flesh hewers or butchers . . . Lister Gate where the listers (dyers) spread their cloths . . . Pilcher Gate, home of the pilchmakers and makers of other fur garments . . . By the time it achieved county status in 1449, Nottingham was a well-ordered town of 3,000 people, with an embryonic council of aldermen, councillors and burgesses. King John's charter of 1189 had given it the right to a merchant guild, that kept a beady eye on anything and anybody who threatened the 'closed shop'. A non-resident had to leave quickly or pay £10 to become a burgess. In 1578 Thomas Nix had his ironmongery business closed down because he had not served an apprenticeship in Nottingham.

From early times the town was split up into seven wards. Seven aldermen, who took it in turns to become Mayor, controlled them—fixing prices, keeping a watch on things like rearing pigs in yards, making muckhills in the streets, and gambling with dice. They dealt on the spot with 'affrays of blood' (a punch on the nose carried a sixpenny fine in 1396), weeded out idle persons, and made sure that foreigners or 'skulkers' from other parishes were hustled smartly back again. They were particularly hot on trading offences, such as using false weights or 'forestalling' (buying up goods to sell again at a higher price). Even the Mayor himself was hauled up in 1512 for selling herrings at five a penny instead of seven. Market activity at the Weekday Cross near the black-and-white timbered Guildhall was so brisk that there was a special court of summary jurisdiction to keep pace with offences—the Piepowder Court which got its name from 'pieds poudreux', dusty feet, synonym for a pedlar.

One way and another, the Big Seven of Nottingham had it made. They regulated trade, assessed taxes, controlled town finances and charities, and decided who should serve in the army. They issued every kind of licence, pounced on the work-shy and excluded from the town anybody they wished—with the cast iron excuse of 'not wanting the plague to sparkle abroad'. And as magistrates they had the backing of a host of punishments. Women with bastard children were whipped, not for their immorality but because their offspring had become a charge on the parish. Bakers who gave short weight were paraded with a loaf slung round their necks. Scolds were soused on the ducking stool on Cuckstool Row (now the Poultry, by the side of the Council House) and continued to be until 1731 when one victim was drowned. The pillory and the stocks were usually occupied, and so were the filthy and airless dungeons under the Guildhall. 'Lewd persons' were carted round town in disgrace as the target for rotten vegetables. For stealing a bit of hay or a dress, old men or young girls alike were stripped to the waist and lashed until their backs were bloody. And, for the ultimate enforcement, there were the gallows standing bleakly at the summit of the Mansfield Road. In 1557 the borough accounts show payment for eleven days' work, felling and squaring three trees for a new scaffold. Eighteen years later, the bills included 'Five shillings for faggots and other kindling to help burn a traitor'.

But in all its viciousness—half drowning a shrewish woman, or carting a man backwards on his way to the noose—Nottingham was no different from other towns. Indeed it was better than most. Between the twelfth and fifteenth centuries it founded at least five hospitals or almshouses. Its wealthy merchants endowed schools and churches. Its coal, its wool, its alabaster (fifty-eight heads of John the Baptist were shipped to London in one consignment) made it prosperous, and caused some fine, solid houses to be built (glass and timber amid the wattle and thatch). And it had an alert, if oligarchic, body of leaders whose policy was to keep an eye on the main chance. Nottingham looked strictly after itself. Despite the momentous happenings emanating from its castle on the cliff, there is no recorded excitement over the Crusades, Magna Carta, the expulsion of the Jews, or the Barons' Wars. Nottingham kept a wary finger on the pulse of self preservation. No sooner did it get word, for example, that Richard III had definitely been defeated at Bosworth than a deputation rode post-haste to pledge Nottingham's devotion to his successor.

It paid its royal levies, and as each king reviewed its charters it nibbled another concession or an additional privilege. The same characteristic, of riding the storm and coming out of it slightly better off, is just as apparent today. Nottingham, of necessity, has had a lot of practice at it.

It was politic to keep in with 'the royals', even if it meant mortgaging £150 worth of town property to entertain and present 'three fair gilt bowles' to James I for a single night's stopover in 1612. Thrift exerted itself two years later; no gift was forthcoming. However, the owner of Thurland Hall was always eager to provide a pillow for a crowned head (he was dubbed Baron Holles and later the Earl of Clare for two down-payments of £15,000). In 1619, therefore, the king was back. He knighted a small queue of those who could afford the fee, commenting to one who had no other qualification: 'Hold up thy head, mon! I have more need to be ashamed than thee.'

Nottingham also regarded the patronage of Charles I as a good investment, sprucing up the plaster and paintwork of every house in town for the visit in 1634.

But the town became disenchanted. Charles was putting on too much of a squeeze, what with £200 a year Ship Money and forced loans. In July 1642 the monarch managed to get away with a £50 purse from the Mayor (who had the privilege of kissing the royal hand), but when Charles returned a month later to prepare for the raising of his standard the atmosphere was distinctly cool. Many of the locals sided openly with Parliament. Even the house in which Charles stayed was split; the second son of the

Earl of Clare—Denzil Holles, Charles's boyhood playmate, was one of the Five Members whom the king had tried to snatch from the House of Commons. After the disappointing flag-waving on Standard Hill, Charles was to see Nottingham only once more— in February 1647, trailing back in defeat *en route* for London and the headsman's axe.

Most of the colour left Nottingham under the Puritans. The town's arms and the twelve royal crowns were stripped from the mace; a card game became an underground pastime; missing a church service incurred a fine. Even the mother of the redoubt- able Colonel Hutchinson, the commander of the castle, found herself in trouble in 1653 for allowing music in her house.

But enough was enough. Despite its record during the Civil War, Nottingham chafed at Cromwell's idea of government. There were open clashes with the Roundhead troops. Hutchin- son's wife Lucy glumly recorded that after General Monck passed through in January 1660, on his march from Scotland to London to invite the Stuarts back, the town 'had begun to go mad, and to declare themselves so, in their desires of the king'. A man was gaoled in Nottingham for 'imagining the death of the king' even while the Commonwealth was still in operation.

With the Restoration there was some clearing up to be done. Nottingham's mutilated mace was sold and another, with a crown on, bought for £60. Colonel Hacker, from the Notting- hamshire village of East Bridgeford, jailer and commander-in- chief at Charles's execution, was hanged at Tyburn. Royalists rode back into Nottingham to reclaim their town houses. The Corporation weeded out its dissenters who, embedded during the Puritan regime, now refused to swear allegiance to the king. Six out of seven aldermen had to go.

In London, the body of Henry Ireton was exhumed from Westminster Abbey and hanged. Ireton was from Attenborough, seven miles from Nottingham. He had served on the town's Defence Committee, commanded Cromwell's left wing at Naseby, and had been made Lord Deputy of Ireland. He had also signed Charles's death warrant.

And so had Colonel Hutchinson. Mainly because of his final distrust of Cromwell—and no doubt through being a cousin of the loyal Byrons—Hutchinson was allowed to retire to Ow- thorpe. But in 1663 he was accused of conspiring against the new regime, and after a gruelling year of imprisonment he died—leaving a widow to rail caustically at a Nottingham which was 'cunning, specious and false-hearted'.

Exactly ten years later, William Cavendish, first Duke of Newcastle, cleared away the rubble of the old castle and began to build.

Cavendish came from a sturdy line. His grandmother, the shrewd Bess of Hardwick, daughter of a plain squire, married four times bettering herself each time; starting with the captain of Queen Elizabeth's Guard she ended with the Earl of Shrewsbury, by which time she had amassed the largest fortune of any woman in the country.

Her grandson took part in fifteen battles or sieges for the king, spending nearly £1,000,000 in the process. He was the finest horseman in Europe, a lover of the arts (he collaborated on plays with Dryden), and was already eighty-two when he commenced his Palladian mansion. He died three years before it was finished in 1679.

The new castle of the Newcastles brought back some of the glories of the past. Princess Anne of Denmark came to stay in 1685 and is said to have worked the tapestry in the dining-room. Nottingham Corporation remembering its last experience with royalty declined to maintain a guard of honour on the grounds of being broke (which it was; it only managed to buy two new sheriff's maces by making each holder of the office pay 10/–). The future Queen Anne returned three years later when, escorted by the Bishop of London who temporarily laid aside his Bible and packed sword and pistols, she was met by a jubilant army of Whig supporters. The Earl of Devonshire—who with Lord Delamere and Earl Howe had mounted the steps of the Malt Cross in the market square to declare soundly for William of Orange—had taken over the castle while his Tory kinsman Newcastle was away.

The junketing of the Glorious Revolution went on for a week before Anne and her whooping horsemen moved on to Oxford, leaving a rueful Corporation to mourn the loss of three pewter dishes and twelve plates, loaned for the Princess's use and never returned.

With its cedar wainscotting, half a dozen state rooms, fine picture gallery and tapestries so rich with silver and gold that three of them cost £1,500, the baroque home on the clifftop commanded a prospect of ripe meadows, thick woods, rolling cornfields and, according to that observant traveller Celia Fiennes, 'the neatest town I have ever seen, built of stone and with delicate, large and long streets much like London and the houses lofty and well built'. Admittedly, a plank footway had had to be laid in 1641 because of the mud, but by 1675 the topographer Thomas Baskerville could enthuse that 'here is Paradise restored', with 'fair built houses, fine women, many coaches rattling about and the shops full of merchantible riches'.

And it had the sort of social swim which welcomed a cultured French captive such as Marshal Tallard, taken prisoner by Marlborough at Blenheim. For eight years until 1712 he lived in a P.O.W.'s paradise—laying out the garden of Newdigate House until it was the admiration of the town, and introducing Nottingham to French rolls and celery.

The town began to blossom. It acquired (for £31 in 1708) a fire engine, a waterworks (as early as 1696, pumping up from the Leen to a cistern on Standard Hill), and a postmaster (from 1621; although the post office itself had to wait until 1737). Now that the restrictions on religious freedom were off, the nonconformist chapels mushroomed, notably those of the Congregationalists in Castle Gate and the Presbyterians in High Pavement. At least sixty-six mayors during the eighteenth and nineteenth centuries were from High Pavement, and the chapel's members were to hold a monopoly of the office of town clerk for 126 unbroken years. As late as 1833 when there were 12,000 nonconformist chapel attenders in Nottingham compared with 5,000 Anglicans, it was claimed that four-fifths of the Corporation's officers came from the same congregation.

In 1710 Nottingham got its first newspaper, the *Post*, run by bookseller John Collyer. Two years later the radically-minded and outspoken William Ayscough had his *Weekly Courant*—and within five years was fined for printing 'false and scandalous reflections on the Government'. Nottingham had seven weekly newspapers by the 1850s and four dailies going strong until 1953.

Banking, too, owes much to Nottingham. In 1658, six years before the establishment of the Bank of England and ninety-two before there was a bank anywhere else in the provinces, a draper named Thomas Smith used a deep rock cellar beneath his shop in the corner of the market place as a safe-deposit. When merchants wanted to keep their gold secure, who better than this mercer of integrity? Farmers also fell into the habit of leaving their market takings in his care rather than risk the footpads lurking between Nottingham and home. Smith kept a brace of blunderbusses within handy reach (they now hang on the wall of the National Westminster Bank at the corner of Exchange Walk), abandoned his drapery business and set up as a full-time banker. Smith's Bank went on to survive all the panics such as the aftermath of the Napoleonic Wars which toppled no fewer than thirty-nine banks in the ten years following Waterloo. It understood its customers and their resources well, and tempered its business acumen with charitable touches. Once, a merchant who owed the Smiths money pleaded that he had a large family. The debt was washed out on condition that he had no more children . . .

Respected alike in business and civic life (the Smiths had five seats in one House of Commons), the banking house was the first in the provinces to open a branch in London.

Nottingham in the 1730s held a comfortable 10,000 people, with 2,041 houses, 400 saddle horses, 130 coach, chaise and team horses, eleven private coaches, several sedan chairs and a couple of packs of hounds.

The Gothic west front of St. Mary's was rebuilt in the Classic style, as was fashionable. If it was also fashionable to drink and smoke in vestries, the parish church would seem to have been an exception. In 1724 the vicar intercepted a messenger returning with ale, pipes and tobacco for the Bishop of Lincoln who had retired to the vestry after a confirmation service. Turning the man out of the nave, the indignant incumbent declared that no bishop or archbishop was going to make a tippling house of St. Mary's.

After eight years of discussion, the market square—its muddy morass paved with boulders from the old Fosse Road—was graced with an Exchange, designed by the mayor, costing £2,400. It was a handsome civic building of red brick, 123 feet wide, with a twelve-foot-wide colonnaded piazza which is echoed in today's Council House. Three niches were allocated for statues of George I and the Prince and Princess of Wales, but somehow funds never ran to filling them. But there was just enough cash left for the topmost figure of Justice, which henceforth was swathed in blue silk on the king's birthday as a mark of Corporation respect. Later, in 1814, in the architecturally dark ages of George III, the Exchange was modernised. The piazza was enclosed, despite heavy grumbling from those who could no longer shelter from the rain, and turned into shops. The red brick was covered with stucco and presented a bald, shop-windowed front, rather like a warehouse.

Now that the crumbly old wall no longer bisected the market place, much to the relief of the local traders, and the profusion of swinging signs and posts was cleared away in favour of neater gibbet signs, the middle of Nottingham began to hum with trade. The country folk clung stubbornly to the original Saxon market at Weekday Cross, to sell their fruit and vegetables, but the central market square itself was a teeming bazaar in front of the Exchange. To recompense themselves for having provided the farmers with the luxury of a paved surface, the Corporation imposed a toll on all grain brought into the town for sale. The incensed farmers promptly retaliated by offering their grain by sample, bringing in just enough to give the customer a glimpse of his purchase and thus evading the tax. After a bit of thought, the Corporation hit back by setting up toll houses (there is still a Toll House Hill). When the delivery carts came into the borough with the order, collectors would trail them with the zeal of secret agents, and extract the toll before the goods were handed over.

In an effort at reconciliation the Corporation, by now feeling richer, rebuilt the Malt Cross, the most important gathering place in the square, which had been dismantled when the old wall went. Given six pillars, a tiled cupola, six sundials and a weather vane, it was offered to the farmers as a shelter in which to conduct their business in bad weather. The ploy did not help much. Farmers and toll men remained bitter enemies until the market was declared free of toll in 1799. The Malt Cross, having become 'a public nuisance, a harbour for filth and rubbish, a resort for the idle and a gaming place for apprentices', was auctioned in 1804 and finished up as somebody's summer house.

Mid-eighteenth-century Nottingham was a town in a garden, complete with a permanent Maypole. There was a row of fine elms in the market place, many poplars along what is now

Parliament Street and elms along Stoney Street. Places with names like Walnut Tree Lane, Cherry Street, Gillyflower Hill and Rosemary Lane abounded with what they described. Where nowadays you cannot find a blade of grass among the office blocks around the castle area, spacious gardens bloomed. Horses and sheep grazed on what a century later would be the Lace Market. The approach along the London Road, across the gentle, flat crocus meadows was one of the most beautiful miles in the kingdom. Charles Deering, a German doctor who, before he died in abject poverty in 1749, made a loving study of Nottingham, asked in delight: 'Were a naturalist in quest of an exquisite spot to build a town or city upon, could he meet with one that would better answer his wishes?'

Reaching this exquisite spot, however, could be execrable. Footpads and thieves were so thick in the bushes along the roads that a man setting off on a long journey would make his will as a matter of course. It was no great deterrent that the penalty for highway robbery was automatically death. Sentencing a couple of footpads to hang for robbing a traveller of twenty-three shillings, a judge in Nottingham commented that he 'would cause the laws to be executed with such severity as shall enable any gentleman to hang his watch by the roadside with the full confidence of finding it there on his return another day'. Bookseller William Hutton, for one, had his doubts about such a long-term policy. On his trips to London—three days going, three days there, three days coming back—he would keep some loose silver in his pocket as a sop to robbers and sew the rest in his shirt collar.

Rutted in summer, quagmires in winter, the roads around Nottingham were as despicable as those in the rest of the country. Three miles an hour was good going. Convoys of thirty or forty mules carried merchandise, the front mule with a clanging bell slung round its neck, and the train guarded by a packmaster 'riding shotgun' with pistols in his saddlebag. Heavy, springless vehicles carried passengers, the half-price fares being literally slung behind in a basket. The gentry made their journeys in ponderous but more comfortable carriages, laden on top with an array of trunks but fortified on the route with larders of food and bottles of whisky, black cherry brandy, sack or beer.

Such difficulties of travel gave even more inducement for the establishment of town houses. The castle mansion had led the way, and spacious, dignified residences soon sprang up for the nobility and the prosperous bourgeoisie. The Green Court of the castle was gay with the aristocracy of Nottingham—the ladies in stiff, pointed bodices, hooped petticoats and high-heeled shoes; their menfolk in coats of claret and sky blue with silver facings, embroidered waistcoats, cocked hats and powdered perukes.

'Many gentlemen of great fortune reside here,' was the report of any visitor to Nottingham. And indeed they did. Alderman William Trigge, for instance, who became Mayor for the fifth time in 1754, was able to give his daughter a dowry of £30,000 on her wedding day, besides leaving her another £50,000. Alderman Trigge and his wife would sit on high-backed chairs on the porch of their house in the High Street, in the shade of the elms, and hold court every afternoon—he in a suit of plum coloured velvet with diamond knee-buckles and large silver shoe-buckles, she in a *mantilla* of rich brocade, hooped petticoat, and toupéed head-dress, and almost bowed down with jewels.

The gentry had their Assembly Rooms on Low Pavement, decorous with dancing, card tables and a music gallery. Not to be outdone, the wealthy tradesmen opened rooms of their own in Thurland Hall, when the Earls of Clare had departed. For the *hoi polloi* there were a matter of sixty inns and public houses, about one for every 200 inhabitants, and an assortment of clubs like the one in Long Row which opened at four in the morning, and had a standing rule that anyone who had not emptied a quart pot of strong ale before the clock struck six should provide a gallon for his pals.

All three levels of Nottingham society met on the many bowling greens, at cock fights, at the race-course on the Forest where thirteen windmills breasted the ridge to catch the breeze, or at the theatre which opened in 1760 near St. Mary's. The townsfolk could enjoy the walks to St. Ann's Well, where the shepherds' races or mazes were considered to promote the 'due circulation of the juices and secretions of the body'. They went on fruit-gathering and nutting expeditions.

And there was excitement of other kinds, in the rough, tough manner of the eighteenth century. Crime and its punishment provided endless morbid fascination. For stealing a mare or a handkerchief, wrongdoers would be sentenced to transportation and branding. In all courts an iron instrument was affixed in front of the prisoner's dock; there the unhappy victim would have his hand branded with a red hot iron immediately after the judge's pronouncement. Public death was never far away in Nottingham's calendar of awestruck amusement. Gibbets rattled their grisly burdens on every common. Crowds jostled for vantage points as the latest tumbril jolted up the Mansfield Road towards the gallows. Highwaymen, simple-minded nursemaids, pickpockets, boy thieves—they all afforded a spectacle for the populace. That is, unless gaol fever claimed them first in their dank underground cells. Even debtors were not very much better off, although they enjoyed the benefit of being above ground. No food was officially provided for them, a point which led one town gaoler to release all his prisoners after he had been told that if any of them died on his hands he would be tried for murder.

Eighteenth-century society seemed to exult in stage-managing its executions with even greater macabre effect. When Squire William Horne was hanged on his seventy-fourth birthday, for infanticide, he was allowed to be driven in his own coach by his own coachman (after complaining that he would miss his traditional dinner of plum pudding). His body was dissected and put on view in a garden. And on the morning of *their* execution, two robbers were taken to St. Mary's, where they heard the Condemned Sermon and were then allowed to lie down in their graves to see if they fitted. They walked to the gallows in their shrouds.

Elections, too, were times of great exuberance. The candidates would be chaired in the streets and given a musically novel greeting by the town butchers banging steel against cleaver. The opposition would be borne in effigy on a litter of vegetables and rotten fruit and then 'hanged'.

Naturally, there was considerable striving to make loyalties known. One burgess walked all the way from Norfolk to register his vote, wearing a light blue velvet suit with buttons made of Queen Anne shillings. Another staunch Whig kept a blue-lined coffin in his house, and used it as a cupboard until it would be required. In 1727, Vincent Eyre got so elated at the news that the Tory candidate had won that he declared he wouldn't mind dropping dead. And did. His gravestone was lavishly inscribed by his fellow Tories:

In freedom's cause, he stretched his jaws,
Exhausted all his spirit.
Then fell down dead. It must be said
He was a man of merit.

Elections were also times of feasting, bribery and corruption. In 1714 the agent of Thomas Pelham, the great Whig Duke of Newcastle (who later became Prime Minister) wrote that £7000 would fix this borough as he had already given 500 electors a shilling apiece for a drink. Votes were hawked around openly for about 10/- and the current prices chalked up on shutters of houses. Much freehold property in Nottingham was owned by county magnates who were strongly Tory and controlled the voting of their tenants. And the Corporation made every effort to control the voting of its tenants. In 1763 the members solemnly pledged themselves to use all their influence in the Whig interest. Tenants who voted on the wrong ticket incurred serious displeasure, and on occasion the Corporation piled on the pressure, as when the rector of St. Nicholas's church voted Tory; he lost his Corporation subsidy for three years.

Three-quarters through the century, Nottingham stood poised between the two worlds of trade and manufacture. The omens seemed good. The Trent was a vast highway along which to send its coal, lead, timber, corn, wool, pottery, beer and cheeses, receiving in return bar iron, block tin, wine, oil, hemp, flax, drugs and groceries. Turnpike roads were coming in from the north and south. Ayscough's *Courant* carried the advertisement that the 'flying machines with steel springs' would set off from the 'Swan With Two Necks' Inn in London every Monday and Thursday morning at five o'clock, and, after an overnight halt at Northampton, drive through the yard gate of the 'Blackamoor's Head' in Nottingham the following evening—'if God permit'.

The brickyards at Mapperley turned out bricks at 10/- per thousand. The 'little smith of Nottingham, who does work no man can do',[1] hammered away. The town had a good reputation for bellfounding, tanning (the fumes of the trade were supposed to have afforded immunity during the last bubonic plague in England in 1667), glassmaking, brewing—and hosiery.

[1] Origin unknown, but probably mediæval.

The stocking frame had been invented in 1589 in the Nottinghamshire village of Calverton by, of all people, a curate, the Reverend William Lee. Some say he worked on his machine out of desperation because his girl friend was perpetually clicking away with her knitting needles during their courtship. More likely it was to while away the tedium of life in a country parsonage, and even to earn a little extra money. At any rate, Lee laboured hard over his wooden model and produced a machine capable of flat knitting with eight needles to the inch. It was coarse work, but it was a revolutionary advance over the painstaking, traditional method of making stockings on pins by hand.

Elated, the country clergyman tried to enlist the patronage of Queen Elizabeth, but she was not impressed and declared that she would not grant a patent to something that would deprive so many of her subjects of their employment. Lee went back and eventually evolved a finer-gauge frame with twenty needles to the inch, taught his relatives to use it, and so made Calverton the only place in the world where stockings were knitted mechanically. But opposition to the labour-saving machine increased, and James I proved as stubborn as Elizabeth had been. Like so many British inventors who succeeded him, Lee took his brainchild abroad—to a more encouraging France. He died in Paris in 1610, worn out by his labours and the disappointments of twenty years. The frame which Lee invented was fundamentally the same as all hosiery and lace machines in use today.

After Lee's death, his brother James came back to England with eight machines and all but two of the workmen, and set up in Nottinghamshire where, with a miller who had been apprenticed to William, they built improved frames at half the former cost. Progress was so slow that by 1641 there were only 100 frames in the country, and it was in London that the industry first developed. Framework knitters there concentrated on the limited but lucrative market for fancy goods like silk hose and waistcoats. On the other hand, Nottingham had an advantage in the production of worsted hosiery, since the sheep of Sherwood Forest were of a peculiar breed, 'small in size but covered with a fleece having the wool of the longest filaments and of a fineness equal to any in Europe'.

With lower wages, rents and prices prevailing in the provinces, and the desire to break free of London's Framework Knitters'

The Market Square in 1740; Malt Cross at one end and the Exchange at the other. (From a drawing by Thomas Sandby) Artist's impression of the castle in the sixteenth century

Company, the trade shifted to the Midlands. Between 1732–50, some 800 frames were transferred from London to Nottingham, giving it 1,200 of the 3,000 in the county. By 1780 there were 20,000 frames in Nottinghamshire, Derbyshire and Leicestershire —'domestic outworkers' scratching a living in their own cottages on frames owned by capitalist master hosiers.

The inventive curate of Calverton could never have imagined what he would set in motion. In 1730 the first pair of cotton stockings to be made in England was produced by a stockinger named Draper in Bellar Gate, Nottingham, using Indian yarn so fine that four threads had to be used for the leg and five for the heel. The success of the experiment started a new branch of the hosiery trade. The extreme whiteness of cotton stockings was actually preferred to the colour of silk, even though in 1745 the best Nottingham workman produced a silk pair weighing only one and three-quarter ounces. No great expansion of the cotton hosiery trade was possible, however, without adequate supplies. By 1739 a Londoner, Lewis Paul, was experimenting in Nottingham with a machine to spin four cotton threads at once. It worked, and so did other attempts in Nottingham between 1740—67, but the yarn was inferior to that handspun in the west of England. The search created a climate of invention to which in 1768, James Hargreaves, the Blackburn carpenter, gratefully brought his 'spinning jenny', which was attracting the attention of machine smashers in his home town. Another refugee came hard on his heels, Richard Arkwright, the Preston barber who had likewise thought it best to leave Lancashire. Nottingham capital enabled them to set up the first cotton mills in the world— Hargreaves in a passage off Wollaton Street (where the Central Co-op now stands) and Arkwright patenting his roller-spinner and establishing himself in Hockley. Arkwright's mill was powered by six strong horses harnessed to a twenty-seven-foot wheel. Horse power was succeeded twenty years later by a Boulton and Watt steam engine—but if Nottingham itself could not claim the first steam-driven mill in England, at least the county could. In the village of Papplewick, Robinson's mill was steam-powered in 1785. Before that it had installed a vast water wheel at great expense. Unfortunately it happened to be sited three miles downstream from Newstead Abbey where the fifth (and Wicked) Lord Byron used to have fun and games with a series of artificial lakes. He would dam up the river until all that reached the millpond was a flabby trickle, while the eccentric lord cavorted about in a twenty-gun battleship, popping away at his servants defending a mock fort.

Despite Lord Byron there were eight cotton mills in Nottingham and more than twenty more in the rest of the county by the end of the eighteenth century. Nottingham narrowly missed becoming the cotton centre of England. Arkwright went to Derbyshire with Jebediah Strutt, the farmer who in 1758 had adapted the stocking frame to produce a ribbed fabric. And, what with ideal humidity for the fine spinning of Crompton's 'mule', Lancashire finally cornered the industry.

But all this lay round a hidden bend for Nottingham, the town in a mid-eighteenth-century garden. It still had its naïvety, an aura of pastoral innocence. As when, at the funeral of an alderman in 1765, eighteen pallbearers and others were given scarves of China silk made on a stocking frame as a novel form of advertisement. Or when in 1773 more than 300 of Richard Arkwright's employees were led in procession from the cotton mill, headed by the foreman in white cotton from top to toe, to go gathering nuts in the Coppice.

As yet unknown, a squad of obscure mechanics were cudgelling their brains on mechanical innovations for Lee's Elizabethan invention. Much was to depend on their ingenuity and tenacity. For a blight was moving fast upon the garden.

FIVE

VALLEY OF THE SHADOW

200 Good Hands to work in the Lace Factory. From six
years old and upwards.

—Advertisement in Nottingham, 1810

IN THE first half of the nineteenth century, Nottingham—one of
the most pleasant towns in Britain and even Europe—began to
sink rapidly into slime. From a garden city it turned into a
slum second only to Bombay throughout the whole Empire. If
it had been sucked under, it would be remembered as a classic
memorial to greed, apathy, muddle, chicanery, violence and sheer
misery. And the irony was that it should happen to a town in a
physically lovely setting; like a pus-filled sore on a young girl's
cheek.

In 1750 Nottingham had 11,000 people. By 1800 it had 29,000.
All squeezed into the same space, one and three quarter miles in
perimeter, the same as for hundreds of years. Apart from small
gaps at Sneinton and Radford, hopelessly too small to relieve
much pressure, the town was clamped within a green but steely
ring of inviolable property rights. On the west—the Duke of
Newcastle's park and Lord Middleton's Wollaton Park. On the
east—Colwick parish owned by the Musters family. And to the
north and south—the common fields and meadows, the biggest
stumbling block of all.

Controlled by the Corporation, these 1,000 acres could have
prevented Nottingham from throttling itself. But they were
owned by some 3,000 freemen, an ownership enmeshed by a
tangle of mediaeval privilege such as the right to graze cattle
during several months of the year. Few of this 'cowocracy' even
bothered to exercise that right—never more than 185. But compulsory 'enclosure' of their life-giving lands would mean losing
their small privileges. To prise them loose would take a petition

to Parliament by the Corporation. The freemen elected the Corporation; and they hung on to their property like limpets.

Enclosure was the dirtiest of words in Nottingham, not only among the wealthiest freemen but among the poorest, who queued up in the hope of winning one of the 250 'burgess parts' of arable land which became available on a sort of lottery basis. Fierce battles brewed up over the question of enclosure. The election of 1787, fought solely on the issue, brought a record poll. Not only was the supporting candidate crushingly defeated; he was burned in effigy and his voters hauled round town in dung carts. In typical Nottingham style, vested interest was elevated into a high moral principle. Even those who had not the remotest dream of being allocated a 'burgess part' on which to raise a few pigs and calves, were scared of the bogeyman of enclosure. The common lands, they pointed out, were the 'lungs' of the teeming town.

Lungs they might be; but the heart was bursting. In the switch to industry, farm workers poured into the town. Labour was needed—cheap labour, women's labour, children's labour, skilled or unskilled. By 1796 the Nottingham canal linked the Cromford canal with the Trent, turning the borough into an inland port served by wharves made by felling the trees in the Coppice. The orchards and the old pastures went, along with the elms in the market square. The square reverted to a muddy slough; the streets leading off it filled in with back-to-back houses springing up like clusters of dirty mushrooms.

There was no control of building or drainage. Such things, the Corporation felt, were none of its business. Parish authorities resisted attempts to organise scavengers or cleaners and left the dirt to accumulate. Any schemes for improvement were snuffed out on the grounds of cost; such as the efforts in 1786 by a committee of the town's most enlightened men who saw their ideas of street widening collapse over a matter of £800. Such expenditure, they were told with heat, could only be made possible by the sale of some of the common land. And the streets of Nottingham would not be paved with the burgesses' gold.

The main thoroughfare, Bridlesmith Gate, could take only one carriage at a time. In fact it remained hopelessly narrow ever after—the tightest spot for coaches on the entire run from London to Leeds, and not made a one-way street until 1924. (It is now at last paved over as a pedestrian way.)

The chief artery to the north—Cow Lane—was a hideous bottleneck until 1811 when the Duke of Newcastle finally let it be widened by sixteen feet and renamed Clumber Street, after his ancestral home. The western gateway of Chapel Bar, built in 1643 with turret-like defences against likely royal invaders, was removed a century later, producing panic when, within twelve months, Bonnie Prince Charlie's army got as near as Derby. Nottingham's merchants scurried off to bury their cash in various wells and cellars; a memory which may have had something to do with the fact that Chapel Bar remained only twenty-six feet wide until the 1830s. In recent years it has been blocked off to allow for the sweep of Maid Marian Way and now echoes the gateway idiom with a £10,000,000 arch of offices.

There were no wide sweeps, however, in the early nineteenth century. Hardly a day passed, for example, without some unfortunate being crushed in Sheep Lane (Market Street now), either trapped between wall and wagon wheels or pounded to death as some terrified bullock from the cattle sales in the square stampeded through the chaos. But the Corporation blandly continued to veto road-widening plans for this 'populous and commercial place'. Then, in 1795, when it actually did agree to the idea of enlarging the entrances to the town by establishing a toll at Trent Bridge, the notion was scotched by the gentry of the county who, safely out of the low-lying areas periodically flooded by the river, did not see why they should subsidise the poor who lived there.

Nottingham had a neat General Hospital, opened in 1782 when the dry moat of the castle had been filled in. But it had had a work-house long before then; by 1795 dark, verminous, ill-ventilated and appallingly overcrowded.

Three-quarters of the population were illiterate. Day schools—such as the Bluecoat School formed in 1711 to teach sixty pupils the three R's and a knowledge of the Church—were painfully few. Sunday schools were non-existent until 1784; then laid the emphasis of their teaching on the virtues of hard work. And children knew plenty about that.

Up in the garrets of the knitters' cottages—long-windowed to catch every minute of daylight—even a baby of three or four had to make himself useful. Boys and girls of six and seven were carried to coal pits in darkness, and, after fourteen hours filling or hauling tubs, with chains chafing their little bodies, were carried home asleep, still in darkness.

At the Mapperley brickyards, shoeless seven-year-olds carried the new-made bricks from the kilns. The tiny, wiry chimney sweeps of Nottingham achieved a notorious fame, hardening their flesh in vinegar and being encouraged to hurry by their masters lighting a fire in the hearth. If occasionally one of these climbing boys suffocated as he squirmed in the sooty tunnels, it was classed as an occupational hazard.

Considerably more hazardous were the fortunes of pauper children brought jolting up from the swarming London work-houses to the cotton mills of Nottinghamshire. Lured, from the age of five, by promises of fine suits and meals of roast beef and plum pudding, they would agree to become apprentices until they were twenty-one, a goal many of them never reached. Arrived at places like Lowdham or Papplewick, they soon found the roast beef turned to black bread, the plum pudding suspiciously blue porridge, the fine suits the rags they stood up in.

Sick and fainting, supervised by an overseer with a horsewhip, they eked out their miserable existence in the roaring factories. Knuckles scraped to the bone, joints nipped by cogs, the children frequently collapsed with fatigue into the machines. Robert Blincoe, a workhouse waif who survived to write a book which made *Oliver Twist* read like a pleasantry, described seeing a girl of eight whose dress caught in a shaft. She was dragged into the machinery and spun round like a rag doll, her bones cracking and her blood spraying as if from a wrung-out mop.

Every fortnight the intricate machinery had to be taken apart and cleaned, which meant an extra sixteen-hour stint on a Satur-day. The children were taken piously to church next day; and once a year they were loaded into carts and treated to Nottingham Goose Fair with sixpence to squander.

They worked up to sixteen hours a day. They were subject to the whim of any brutal supervisor. They fought the institu-tion's pigs for delicacies from their troughs. They were given a standard cure for bed-wetting—being dragged across the icy mill-stream. And when they died, often gratefully, and in vast numbers through starvation, disease or suicide, they were dumped in wheelbarrows and shovelled into unmourned mass graves.

Generally in separate churchyards, to avoid scandal. In Linby churchyard near the Papplewick mill, 169 lie in one unmarked grave. The parish register tones it down by recording a mere forty-two.

While such children were the dramatic victims of early industrialisation, the people of Nottingham had to endure a long, slow stretching out on the rack. The main trade was hosiery knitting, and behind his long windows, the stockinger was gradually mastering the art of producing every known mesh by mechanical means. Guarding their secrets as best they could, an army of artisans—several of whom drove themselves beyond the brink of insanity—laboured to adapt Lee's stocking frame to create lace.

Since 1740 the phrase 'as poor as a stockinger' had been proverbial. It was a home industry; a life of grinding, stupefying toil, in which a knitter sweated for 7/– a week if he was lucky, and one in which his wife and every child had to sweat with him. A stockinger could be identified at a glance from his paleness and a certain degree of emaciation. His diet was mostly bread and cheese, gruel and tea. To cut down interruptions of the clacking frame, it was common practice to lull babies with a concoction called Godfrey's Cordial. One Nottingham chemist knew of four children in a single family who died through being drugged, or 'pacified' in this way.

A stocking-maker had plenty of burdens, apart from the sheer grind of labour. Worried sick by the fluctuations of his trade through the vagaries of fashion, he was screwed down by middle-men, the go-betweens for the hosiers who actually owned the frames, and who charged as much as twenty per cent of his earnings in rent. He had to pay that rent even when he was out of work, which was often. He lost half a day's earnings when he had to take in the finished product. He would often find himself paid in groceries or shoes or candles by hosiers who owned other businesses. And because of the scattered nature of the industry, a stockinger found it hard to build up any strong opposition, to stand up to the master hosiers.

The Framework Knitters' Company, futilely preening itself in London as a livery company, had been moribund since the 1750s. With no controls to check them, manufacturers paid what wages they liked and used what labour they chose. Inevitably wages were pressed as low as possible, and apprentices taken on from that limitless source, the work-house. It was a system tanta-mount to slavery. Parish officers were only too keen to get rid of young paupers; and even if the apprentices tried running away they were soon brought back as no one else dared keep or employ them.

In 1778, when wages were so low that a good man in Notting-ham could make no more than 4/6 a week on coarse worsted, the framework knitters petitioned Parliament to regulate wages. The hosiers, better connected and better organised, counter-petitioned and had the bill thrown out. When a second attempt a year later was rejected, Nottingham's stocking men erupted in fury at last. They burned down the house of Samuel Need, the master hosier who had led the opposition to their appeal, marched on Arkwright's mill which he had financed, broke every window, and tried to fire it. The property of every hosier known to have voted against the bill was attacked. Over three hundred frames were flung into the streets. The officers of the Oxford Blues, attending a ball in the pavilion of the race-course, hurried back, still in their dress uniforms, to marshal their cavalry. The Riot Act was hastily read, and 300 special constables sworn in before order was restored, three days later.

The hosiery employers took the hint. They promised vaguely to improve conditions; even made a small concession in prices. Coupled with a slight revival in trade, the gesture served to damp down the volcano for the time being.

In less than twenty years it heaved again. Trade slumped, hit by Napoleon's ban on imports of hosiery. And in 1795 stocking manufacturers introduced the practice of using 'cut-ups'. Instead of stockings being knitted to shape, the yarn was knitted into lengths of even width, which were then cut out and seamed together. It made for a spurious and inferior job which increased output and lowered wages.

The framework knitters—poor and powerless since their em-bryonic trade union had been stamped upon after the 1779 riots—shuddered into convulsive action. The Combination Act of 1799 had tightened the screw by making trade unions illegal, but even at the eleventh hour the Nottingham Framework Knitters Association tried to remedy conditions by legitimate negotiations —in so far as an illegal organisation can function legitimately.

But weary, sickened and angry at the endless poverty, at the contempt for their grievances and distress, there were others who favoured more direct methods. They gave the world a new word.

Luddism.

The first outbreak of frame breaking by Luddites was on March 11, 1811. After a stormy meeting of framework knitters in Nottingham's market square, a group of men assembled in Arnold, on the outskirts of the town, and smashed sixty-three frames. In three more weeks the number was up to 200. By February of 1812 the tally was 624 frames destroyed.

The Luddites were no hooligans smashing machinery for its own sake. Nottingham, after all, had welcomed the cotton pioneers and evolved painstaking developments. Except for the few cases in which mistakes were made by hotheads, only frames employed on spurious work or belonging to hosiers who paid low wages were attacked. The Luddites were not anti-machinery but anti the conditions of their trade, and they showed a selectivity and loyalty worthy of Robin Hood's outlaws.

Fittingly, they usually met in Sherwood Forest, often sworn to secrecy with oaths of death. Taking their name from a Leicestershire youth named Ned Ludlam who, in a fit of pique, took the needles from his frame and smashed them with a hammer, they operated in groups six to sixty strong according to the job in hand. Obeying an acknowledged leader called General Ludd, they would meet at a pre-arranged spot, post guards while the main body shouldered their way into a work-place and shattered the offending frames, then, after a quick roll-call, would melt away home. None of them was ever betrayed, despite the tempting bait of £500 rewards at a time when huge numbers of people were on starvation level.

Nottingham was wild with theories. That it was a Napoleonic plot. That it was inspired by feuding rivals in the trade itself. That the mysterious General or King Ludd was none other than Gravener Henson, the articulate, self-educated ex-stockinger who carefully picked his way through the thickets of the law and was connected with most of the trade combinations between 1808–40. There was talk of well-dressed working men meeting suspiciously in alehouses and running up bills which, they said, 'Ned Ludd would settle.' About £400 a week was supposed to be paid out among French agents in the town.

The authorities responded with energy characteristic when the

Establishment was threatened. The master hosiers formed a secret committee, with the town clerk George Coldham as its secretary, not only to fight the new menace but to disrupt the attempts of the knitters to regulate their trade. The Corporation quickly allotted £2,000—which did not need to be accounted for. The Lord Lieutenant, the ubiquitous Duke of Newcastle, personally instructed police officers on the need to listen at windows and keyholes to winkle out conspirators. Spies were paid to mingle in the taverns, to piece together a jigsaw of careless clues. A 10 p.m. curfew was imposed.

In February 1812, when between £6,000 and £10,000 damage had been caused, Parliament debated a bill to make frame-breaking punishable by hanging. In the Lords, the twenty-four-year-old Lord Byron, remembering the poverty he had seen in his boyhood streets, spoke passionately against it in a maiden speech that rang with vehemence.

'I have traversed the seat of war in the Peninsula,' he declared. 'I have been in some of the most oppressed provinces of Turkey. But never under the most despotic of governments did I behold such squalid wretchedness as I have seen since my return to the very heart of a Christian country.'

He had seen this once honest and industrious body of men meagre with famine, sullen with despair, careless of a life which their Lordships were about to value at something less than the price of a stocking-frame.

'Suppose this bill passed,' cried Byron in ardour. 'Suppose one of these men was dragged into court to be tried for this new offence by this new law. Still there are two things wanting to convict him and condemn him—twelve butchers for a jury and a Jeffreys for a judge.'

The bill was passed. Just before this, two young Nottingham men were transported for fourteen years for breaking seven frames. A boy of sixteen received seven years transportation.

Officers from Bow Street were seconded to Nottingham. Every available citizen was ordered to patrol the streets. Thousands of Redcoats were drafted into Nottinghamshire and set up camp on the Forest. Soldiers marched in church parades with fixed bayonets. They were billeted in every inn. Eventually, more troops and cavalry were tied up hunting Luddites than Wellington took with him to the Peninsular War.

But still the breaking went on, often by groups of about a hundred, within yards of where the soldiers were searching. Hosiers throughout Nottingham received handwritten or crudely printed warnings that they were on the Luddite list unless they mended their ways. The Mayor was threatened. An attempt was made to assassinate a prominent hosier, by a couple of men who shot at him from behind the tombstones in St. Mary's churchyard. A judge and jury were openly threatened with murder at the August Assizes in 1816; at the trial of two alleged frame-breakers, a well-disciplined group took over the court, refused to let a light be brought in except for the bench and counsel table, and meaningfully stationed a shadowy gang of armed men all around. Diplomatically or otherwise, the jury found the prisoners not guilty—and Nottingham very nearly lost its rights of Assize to Newark.

While this sort of thing was going on, Gravener Henson and his delegates were still pegging away through legitimate channels. At a time when combinations were outlawed, the remarkable Henson was virtually a full-time trade-union leader, perhaps the first. Rounding up support in London for a petition to Parliament, he dashed off sharp letters back to Nottingham for samples of work to show to anybody who would listen:

> 'Why the devil don't you send the silk stockings—are you asleep? Lord, how negligent you are! Damn the trade; they seem determined on their own destruction. They are the most backward, dilatory, unwilling-to-do-good race of men on earth. Send them, blast them to hell, send them or burn them! If they do not arrive instantly they will be of no use. If any man in the trade refuses to do his duty in the making of articles for the recovery of his trade, knock his teeth down his throat!'

It is hard to see how with such a fireball of a leader the framework knitters could fail. Their demands were not excessive. They asked that employers be made to tell their men the rates they were getting and stick to them; that they be stopped from making what was considered inferior goods; and that truck payment (in kind rather than cash) should cease.

But fail they did. Unfamiliar with London ways and Parliamentary procedure, they would wait for hours for a minister who failed to show up, or else be insulted, and smoothly delayed over technical points.

When they trailed miserably back, the men formed a co-operative to market their own products. That failed too, strongly opposed by the master hosiers. The books and papers of the Committee of Framework Knitters were seized, enabling George Coldham to make out an alphabetical list of people suspected of being Luddites. In 1814, when frame-breaking seemed to have died down somewhat, Coldham advocated disbanding the militia so that demobilised knitters should flood the labour market. When he was killed the following year—not, as might be expected, from a Luddite bullet but because the horse of his gig took fright and bolted—the Corporation recorded its deepest lamentation, ordered mourning for three months and affixed a memorial tablet in St. Mary's.

The hot impetus of Luddism cooled. There were sporadic bursts of frame-breaking but towards the end it was tending to lose sight of the original concept and to become an excuse for pilfering and general lawlessness. The final seal on its end came in 1817 when a dupe called William Towle of Arnold and six others were hanged for an attack on the Heathcoat and Boden mill at Loughborough and the attempted murder of a workman. Three more were transported. Gravener Henson himself, who travelled to London to seek clemency, found himself arrested on suspicion of high treason, but was released.

The army of General Ludd might break frames but not the system. Between 1811–17 they smashed a matter of 1,000 stocking frames and eighty lace machines. They achieved little or nothing, beyond a valiantly desperate niche in history. As a contribution to the betterment of their trade, their efforts were practically nil.

The Luddites carried the same doomed hopelessness as that of Jeremiah Brandreth, the twenty-six-year-old 'Nottingham Captain' who in 1817 tried to lead a national insurrection. Every move of the proposed rising was charted by spies, notably one called Oliver who infiltrated meetings at 'The Three Salmons' in Nottingham and egged on the conspirators with promises that Nottingham would be given up, that forces would come out of Yorkshire like a cloud, that there would be a provisional government set up in London and that there would be pleasure trips galore on the Trent. Brandreth started at Pentrich in Derbyshire, gathering recruits among distressed knitters. Five hundred strong, they swept exuberantly on through Eastwood and towards a

Nottingham which they confidently expected to be in revolutionary hands. Instead they found a solid force of soldiers. It rained steadily. Hungry, dispirited, and sodden, many of the would-be insurrectionists slunk away home, slinging their home-made pikes and pitchforks into the hedges even before the Hussars attacked. Only forty got through to Nottingham. Thirty-five were immediately arrested for high treason. In November, Brandreth and two of his followers were taken to Derby and hanged. Brandreth was the last man in England to be hanged, beheaded and quartered; his dismembered body was put on show in different parts of the country as an example to others. As his corpse was stretched out for beheading, a cog caught under the chin and turned its face to the hushed crowd, so that the black piercing eyes glared in final, terrible anger.

In Nottingham, exhausted by the struggle to get a few coppers more, the hosiery workers tried to organise a general strike in 1819. They brought in their frames, dragging them in borrowed carts, pulling them with ropes to the warehouses and leaving them at the hosiers' doors. Soon, 14,000 stocking workers had ceased work. Eventually sixty-seven out of the ninety hosiers in Nottingham were induced to sign a statement raising the price of making stockings from 8/- to 12/- a dozen; but in nine weeks the workers' funds had run out and they were forced to return, whether the increase was promised or not. Eight months later the prices were as low as ever.

Another strike in 1821—when scarcely two dozen pairs of stockings were made in two months, in the three counties of Nottinghamshire, Derbyshire and Leicestershire—had no more impression. Demand had become stagnant. Skilled men swept the streets and begged from door to door. In Nottingham, 5,000 men paraded daily, headed by women carrying placards: 'Pity Our Distress . . . We Ask For Bread . . . Help Our Children . . .'

The best the government could do was to rush six companies of troops, and wagonloads of ammunition, to turn the elegant Bromley House into a checkpoint against any possible revolution.

Suddenly, in 1823, came a brief and amazing spell of prosperity. The patent expired on Heathcoat's bobbin-net machine, which had adapted the hosiery frame to produce lace. Local mechanics threw themselves into a frenzy to copy it. More flocked from Birmingham and Sheffield to join the boom, and their output was snapped up in an orgy of speculation. The new aristocrats of the working classes were the twist-hands, arriving for work on horseback and finishing the day with a pint of champagne rather than a mug of beer.

But it soon went flat. The twist-net bubble burst. What had brought a return of five pounds dropped as low as a shilling.

In July 1824, at the height of the boom, the body of Lord Byron—dead two months from fever in the Missolonghi marshes —lay in state in the 'Blackamoor's Head', Pelham Street, having been refused burial in Westminster Abbey. Immense crowds, who remembered their champion of twelve years before, escorted the coffin to the family vault a few miles away at Hucknall. Eighteen months later their plight was grimmer than in 1812. Poverty and starvation took up their double-handed grip again. Four hundred families emigrated to the Cape Colony. By 1830, half of Nottingham's 50,000 people were in receipt of poor relief.

The burning of Nottingham Castle on October 10, 1831, was a twin symptom of both that misery and the welling surge towards a political change. Reform was 'the talk of the day and the dream by night'. At the election in May when both Reform candidates were elected, 12,000 people in Nottingham had signed a petition in support of Prime Minister Lord Grey's bill. Only 400 had opposed it.

On Saturday, October 8, the House of Lords squashed the Reform Bill. The man who had urged them to do so was the owner of Nottingham Castle, Henry Fiennes Pelham Clinton, fourth Duke of Newcastle. He was Duke by the fourth creation; the second Duke's sons had all died in his lifetime, so the Cavendishes were succeeded by John Holles, fourth Earl of Clare, killed hunting in 1711. The male line was to fail twice more.

The latest holder of the title was a throwback to feudal times. At Newark election, he had evicted forty of his tenants for voting against his nominee, blandly declaring that he 'had the right to do what he liked with his own'. Even Wellington confessed that 'there never was such a fool'. The Duke himself was rather proud of saying that he had only to show his face to cause a riot.

He had indeed not shown his face at the castle for years. Of late the building had been occupied by various wealthy lodgers, notably a Miss Kirby who specialised in breakfast parties on the terrace to watch a stag being uncarted for hunting in The Park, and in oyster suppers when all the barrels were draped with white satin and each guest's chair had an embroidered bag for the shells.

At the time of the Reform riots, the last lodger had moved out. The castle held nothing worth looting—an old bedstead or two, some 'starved tapestries'. But it was an obvious target when a stunned Nottingham learned the fate of the Reform Bill. On Sunday morning, October 9, hundreds were waiting as the mail coach from London rattled into the yard of 'The White Lion'. A few windows were smashed around the town as a kind of preliminary, and next day, systematic attacks were directed at the property of people thought to be anti-Reformers. A silk mill at Beeston was burned down, one of the Forest windmills destroyed, several shops looted.

The mob marched on Colwick Hall, home of the Musters family. Its owner, a well-known opponent of Reform, was away, and his wife (Byron's first love, Mary Chaworth) and daughter crouched terrified in the shrubbery as the crowd—some of whom had got drunk on looted wine—rampaged among fine furniture and paintings. A fire was lit but someone, thinking he was helping, tossed a mattress on to it and smothered it.

To divert the military, a feint was staged against the House of Correction in town, while the main body from Colwick Hall split up and reassembled to deal with the castle. Converging at about 7 p.m. they forced their way past the lodge, poured in through a broken window, smashed the doors, and set about making a vast bonfire of this hated, if deserted, symbol. They hacked holes in the upper floors and rammed in broken bannisters. The tapestries were sold as souvenirs for 3/– a yard. The busts over the windows were smashed, the equestrian statue of the first Duke pounded with a crowbar; (one leg of the horse was carried off as a trophy, while a foot of its ducal rider eventually turned up in a London antique shop).

By 9.30 p.m. the blaze was at its height, the air heavy with the scent of burning cedarwood from the wainscotting, and golden runnels of molten lead cascading from the roof. Vast crowds watched the spectacle, the light of the flames flickering on the tops of their wet umbrellas, and the silhouettes of men 'hurrying to and fro like restless spirits of some infernal incantation'. In the morning the castle was a charred hulk. Among the ruins were found the scorched bodies of two children.

Four men were eventually arrested for the burning of the castle, but were discharged. Three were hanged for the destruction of the Beeston silk mill—despite a petition for mercy, signed by 17,000 within twenty-four hours. Nobody has ever managed to answer various questions about the fate of the castle. Lord Melbourne, the Secretary of State, ordered a £500 reward but never received satisfactory evidence. The action of the Nottingham magistrates was odd—in not defending the castle even though they were supposed to have warning and a list of the places to be attacked. Was it merely because the castle was extra-territorial and not their province? Or did they—as Whigs—want the castle destroyed to revenge themselves on the Tory Duke of Newcastle? It is unlikely that we shall ever know. It may be significant that when the infuriated Duke begged for a seat on the commission to find the miscreants, the town replied by requesting his removal as Lord Lieutenant of the county. And to rub salt into the wound, Nottingham was held to be innocent of the burning, for Henry VI's charter expressly excluded the castle from the town's boundaries. So when the Duke of Newcastle obtained £21,000 compensation, it came not from Nottingham but from towns which lay in the 'Hundred of Broxtowe'—Basford, Bulwell, Arnold, and as far away as Mansfield.

Five months after the conflagration, a second Reform Bill was tried on Parliament. In case it was rejected again, many manufacturers in Nottingham refused to give out materials to their employees. A representative of the *Sun* newspaper sped from London in an open chaise, changing horses four times in nine hours, to bring the news that it had been passed. In the 'triumph' which Nottingham put on to celebrate the event, some 20,000 people paraded. There were fireworks, a tableau of 5,400 boys bearing flags that rippled like a carpet of tulips, and, appropriately, huge bonfires.

Although the Reform Bill eased the tension, Nottingham was still as taut as a watchspring, with the authorities keeping their trigger fingers flexed. Even the railings around the new Collin's Almshouses, built in Greyfrair Gate between 1831 and 1834, were designed in such a way that they could not be yanked out and used as spears by rioters. The town was packed with troops, fortunately under the command of General Sir Charles Napier who sympathised with the Chartist ideals and kept a cool head when

Wollaton Park
The oldest inn in England, 'The Trip to Jerusalem'

YE OLDE TRIP CO
JERUSALEM
1189AD
THE OLDEST
INN IN ENGLAND

mass demonstrations were held. Napier liked Nottingham. 'The poor people are good and, were they fairly treated, they would be perfectly quiet.' As a soldier he made it clear that 'if the mob break the peace, I will break their heads', but he also was quick to condemn magistrates for imposing stupid bans which the people ignored. Mainly through his tact and diplomacy, no blood was spilled when the Chartists organised a three-day protest in 1840.

Curiously, Napier lodged in a house in Wheeler Gate where, two centuries before, his great-great-great-grandfather Charles I had once stayed. 'He died in his right place,' Napier wrote in his diary, '—on the scaffold. And well he deserved it.' The suffering poor of Nottingham, however, were another matter. 'They are resolved to die rather than go into the Union houses,' he wrote.

They did not have much choice. When 30,000 hosiery and lace workers were out of work in 1838 there was no hope of taking them into the work-houses. In any case the municipal view was that to help the poor was to encourage idleness. It did not prevent the Corporation from helping itself. It made petty cash payments for soup kitchens, but it spent thousands of pounds on defending its right to elect aldermen and administer archaic estates, and on such perks as feasting at evening parties, while doing business which could have been got through in a fifth of the time. There were numerous dinners and balls involving plentiful expenses— all of which were rigorously upheld, no matter what hard times the town as a whole was going through. Membership of the Corporation was nicely carved up between a few select families. Three-quarters of the whole corporate body, it was found when the Municipal Corporations Commissioners delved in 1833, came from four families attending the three leading chapels. The Swanns and the Allens had eleven places in a body of thirty councillors and a dozen officials, spending £400 or more a year on entertainments, besides the £315 to enable the mayor to 'keep table and make friends'.

A seat on the council with such creature comforts as these, and various contracts for supplying the prisons and work-houses, was worth having. And worth buying. Would-be councillors each invested between £300 and £1,000 at election time, in judicious bribes among the 3,000 freemen who could vote, and who made known the going prices by chalking them up on inn doors. Once on the council, the ruling clique made sure of staying there, either

Bronze statue of Robin Hood

by holding no elections or by distributing appointments in such a way as to ensure their return to office.

They had a good reason to hang on: the slums they owned.

There were 8,000 back-to-back houses in Nottingham. Trapped in the twin vice of private property and the untouchable common-lands, the town had grown like a fungus from the inside. By the 1830s and 1840s the garden city had become one mighty prison of bricks and mortar—with fifty swarming filled-in streets in which there was no room for a garden the size of a dining table.

Back-to-backs were common in every industrial town. Nottingham's were unique, being arranged in narrow courts closed at both ends and entered by yard-wide tunnels eight feet high and twenty to thirty feet long. The houses in these 'rookeries' consisted of two or sometimes three rooms on successive storeys, each eleven feet square, with a tiny space for food and coal under the stairs. Some had cellar dwellings in the sandstone beneath. None of the houses (indeed no house built before about 1890) had a damp course. The drain was a channel down the middle of the court. At one end was a group of privies—one for the use of up to thirty people, and many of them under the bedrooms. When enough sewage had accumulated in the alleys it was sold to 'muck-majors' who dumped it in the streets until they had a bargeful to sell to farmers.

'Some parts of Nottingham,' reported a shocked Commission in 1844, 'are so very bad as hardly to be surpassed in misery by anything to be found within the entire range of our manufacturing cities.'

The Commissioners found that 'the condition of working inhabitants as respects their habits of life, occupation, dwelling, diet, clothing, bedding and fuel' offered a spectacle of the most lamentable description.

Many of the houses in these warrens were also workshops, thumping with the noise of frameworking or lace dressing. Lace in particular needed a high temperature and a humid atmosphere. Heated by stoves, hot water or steam, the thin, porous walls were alive with vermin.

By comparison, conditions in the factories 'were Elysian'. Children were kept up until 11 p.m. or midnight; boys of five winding yarn, little girls standing on stools, to be able to see the candles on the tables, as they stitched away at seams. Mothers would pin them on their knees, giving them a slap on the head if they fell asleep before their stint was finished. It was common to find fifteen or twenty children working in a low garret twelve feet square, for fifteen hours a day. When girls reached womanhood they were 'as uneducated for wives and mothers as if they had been brought up in the Sandwich Islands. The most clean and orderly of them invariably desponds, relaxes her exertions under the influence of filth, damp and stench, and probably sinks into a dirty, noisy, discontented and perhaps gin-drinking drab.'

Small resistance was built up on a diet of bread, potatoes, milk and herrings, with sometimes no meat for months. Nottingham was one of the most overcrowded and unhealthy towns in the country. The mean age at death was just over twenty-two—seven years lower than elsewhere. In some areas it was fourteen or fifteen, worse than any town in the British Empire. In one district in St. Ann's, it touched eleven. Nowadays about seventy per cent of people who die in Nottingham are over sixty-five.

The town as a whole had a population density greater than London—twenty square yards living space per person. In one teeming rookery, 4,283 people were found in 883 houses in an area of less than nine acres; an average of just over ten square yards each. With such an ideal breeding ground, it was incredible that when Asiatic cholera struck in 1832 there were only 330 deaths. Perhaps the greatest single factor in preventing a ghastly toll was the work of one man, a brilliant young water engineer named Thomas Hawkesley of the Trent Waterworks, who showed that it was possible to supply 8,000 houses, containing 35,000 people, with piped fresh water for a penny per week per house. He could have installed proper drains at 6/– a house, too.

But the slum landlords, running up their jerry-built hovels cheaply, reaping rents totalling £40,000 a year, didn't want to know. Why should they eat into their profits by such luxuries? Why support any hare-brained notion which might empty some of their 2/– a week coffins?

'There is no want of public nuisances in Nottingham,' reported the Commissioners of 1844. 'The entire quarters occupied by the labouring classes forms but one great nuisance!'

SIX

VICTORIAN PATCHWORK

The English are town birds . . . but they don't know how
to build a city, how to think of one or how to live in one.
—D. H. Lawrence

AT TWENTY minutes past eleven on the morning of December 4,
1843 a salute of guns boomed out, from the rock of burnt-out
Nottingham Castle, to announce that a very special train was in
sight along the four-year-old tracks of the Midland Counties
Railway.

The band of the Inniskilling Dragoons struck up a jaunty air.
The 64th Foot presented arms. And young Queen Victoria, her
hair loosely braided under a white straw bonnet with blue
ribbons, accompanied by her handsome Prince Albert, walked
along the crimson-carpeted platform. In a flower-bedecked
landau, the royal pair clip-clopped towards Nottingham beneath
nine triumphal arches, including one on which was perched the
wherry *Nautilus*, and its entire crew in full naval costume.

Nottingham might be living in squalor; juvenile prostitution
might be rife; in the rookeries, two out of three babies might
never reach their fourth birthday; children, if they were not
exhausted from work, might have to play among the dungheaps
in the foetid courts. But the town was nothing if not loyal. So the
cheers rang loudly as the glamorous couple, like visitors from
another planet, were borne to civic feasting along their route
from Chatsworth to Belvoir Castle.

They only stayed a few hours. But what was really significant
was not their visit, but the actual road under the wheels of their
rosette-studded carriage. For that road, specially completed for
the occasion, ran across the common lands of the Meadows. At
last, and in the nick of time, Nottingham was being allowed
elbow-room.

100

The Municipal Reform Act of 1835 had ended government of towns by charter, and abruptly, even curtly—with a few caustic comments to boot—had despatched the 'select body' of seven aldermen and a few councillors which had run Nottingham for four hundred years. As soon as the new council got into its stride, with a good Town Clerk and a good Mayor to guide it, pressure was renewed to give breathing space to the gasping town. First a modest enclosure of fifty-two acres, in 1839, broke through the hard core of opposition, although it still left another 1,068 acres subject to the grazing rights of the 'cowocracy'. And then, in 1845, a general enclosure. It took another twenty years before three commissioners untangled all the claims and arguments, but freeing the common lands was like knocking away the chocks beneath a ship waiting to be launched.

With a gasp of relief, Nottingham creaked down the slipway and gathered momentum. Its slums—as is the nature of the beasts —were to stink in its nostrils for many decades to come. But at least there was a chance to tip out some of their teeming thousands. In fact, Nottingham's slum dwellers only found themselves in newer, slightly more spacious slums. In the Victorian free-for-all, speculative builders ran up some hideous places in which not a single acre of open ground was left for public use. The old crocus-fields of the Meadows became criss-crossed with railways; factories blossomed; and in the flood-lands some builders adroitly built below water level.

Naturally, the passing of the ancient Meadows did not go unmourned. A local poetess (Anne Gilbert, who also wrote *Twinkle, Twinkle Little Star*) came up with a flower's eye view of the disaster. After penning a harrowing picture of the crocuses succumbing to a brick-red trance of industry, she had them giving one gentle shriek and uttering:

Spirit of giant trade! We go! On wings of night we fly,
Some far-sequestered spot to seek where loom may never ply.
Come line and rule—come board and brick; all dismal things in one.
Dread Spirit of Enclosure, come—thy wretched will be done!

What with the rush to build, and the delay in sorting out complicated claims, Nottingham lost its chance to plan itself as a complete whole, with graceful squares and promenades. But this has proved in some ways an unwitting blessing. The enclosure commissioners of necessity kept to the pattern of the old field paths, with the result that even the harsh building lines of modern Nottingham are softened by natural curves and undulations.

As if to make up for its past record, an unusually enlightened Corporation insisted, in the 1850s, that 130 acres be set aside for ever for recreation; one of the earliest statutory provisions in the country. This space—the Forest, the twelve-acre Arboretum laid out in 1852, and the tree-lined walks of Elm Avenue, Corporation Oaks and Queen's Walk—then represented one-seventh of the old town. It has since kept Nottingham reasonably green and open compared with other towns which were turned into brick jungles in the same period.

At the same time, strict rules were laid down for development in the area—again a rare step in the right direction—and, despite the grumblings of speculative builders, some well spaced streets of houses showed the way to avoid the horrors of the back-to-backs.

But, on the whole, Nottingham hardly reformed overnight. The availability of land outside the old boundaries made some improvement in the standards of working-class life, but for the most part, in the words of Professor Asa Briggs: 'Contemporaries were satisfied by the rhetoric of urban pride rather than by its substance.' Forty thousand people continued to swelter, for another half century, in their rookeries, although a sharper eye was kept on their health and sanitation. But Pugin's ugly Catholic Cathedral was built at the bottom of Derby Road in 1844; there were public baths by 1849 to keep some of the dirt at bay; and in the new Arboretum was there not a nice little pagoda in which to house four Russian cannons captured at the siege of Sebastopol, and a bronze bell filched from a Cantonese temple by the Robin Hood Rifles?

The very fact that such 'extras' existed at all was evidence of Nottingham's growing prosperity now that it was emerging from the doldrums of trade. The hosiery industry had picked up, and even had a few steam-operated factories such as that of Hine & Mundella, opened in 1851 near the Midland Station (and pulled down in 1972). But the stockinger was slow to take to factory life. He prided himself on his independence, however grinding it might be. 'Each man has full liberty to earn what he likes and how he likes and when he likes. We have no factory bell; it is our only blessing,' declared a witness before the Factory Commission in 1833.

By contrast, the lace trade was quick to seize its chance and hitch its wagon to the star of power. It was lace which made Nottingham in the latter half of the nineteenth century; a delicate and frothy product to bloom on the bitter compost of the previous decades. In 1830 Nottingham possessed twenty-two factories and about 1,000 power-driven machines of all kinds. In the seven years starting from 1851 it acquired 110 new factories and forty-six warehouses—most of them for the lace industry.

A multitude of craftsmen had toiled to adapt Lee's knitting frame to drop stitches in a pre-arranged pattern. The result was point-net, an obvious and imperfect imitation of the pillow and cushion laces which had flourished throughout Europe from the Middle Ages. Point-net was swept aside by John Heathcoat, a Derbyshire man who took over a machinery business in Nottingham and, when he was twenty-five, patented the bobbin-net machine which is still the basis of all those in use today. His 'Old Loughborough' model of 1809, which twisted a weft thread completely round a warp thread, produced a plain net that was firm, withstood the rigours of the wash tub and did not run when a thread broke. It is ironic that when it named a street after the inventor of the twist-machine, Nottingham should carelessly twist his name into 'Heathcote'.

A plaque off Derby Road marks where John Leavers, a twenty-seven-year-old Nottingham mechanic, worked in a garret, in 1813, on his famous machine to put intricate patterns into the mesh. Hooton Deverill and others applied their mechanical genius to perfect and control the embroidered motifs, and the stage was set to turn Nottingham into the lace centre of the world. Yarn merchants, finishers, bleachers and dyers, buyers and agents were attracted from the hosiery trade to the new offshoot until the offspring rapidly became independent of the parent. From 1830 onwards a stream of immigrants, mostly German-Jewish, began to arrive in Nottingham, providing it with capital, trade connections and exporting skill. Lewis Heymann came from Mecklenburg-Schwerin with the capital of a Hamburg merchant behind him, and in 1834 founded the mighty lace house of Heymann and Alexander. Bernard Steibel came from

Frankfort. Jacob Weinberg came from Hamburg in 1849 at the behest of his principal Phillip Simon, and founded the great house of Simon May and Co. Moritz Jacoby started another prominent house in 1835. They sent travellers to all parts of the world, opening up and holding the markets of Europe, Latin America and the East in the face of strong French competition. Nottingham lace proved equal to, and even surpassed in quality, the hand-made products—Valenciennes, Torchon, Alençons, Guipure, Malines, Venice—although by the 1880s Nottingham was concentrating on the low-class, cheap, effective article that the mass markets were looking for.

As Nottingham had got noisier and smokier, in the industrial revolution, the nobility had moved out. The mansions and town houses of the gentry around St. Mary's became vacant. Some of them were converted into private schools. The majority became the homes of the merchants, who moved from their smaller and more inconvenient premises in the Norman part of the town around the castle.

As the lace industry swelled, down came the stately homes and up went the factories and the warehouses. The ancient centre of Nottingham became the Lace Market. On the sites of such mansions as Plumptre House, where one leading family had lived for five centuries, grew warehouses—which in some cases were even more elegant. Not content to erect dull, functional buildings, Thomas Chambers Hine—perhaps the most ingenious and imaginative architect who ever stamped his mark on Nottingham—erected warehouses for Richard Birkin and Thomas Adams which were so magnificent that they were criticised as being too good. Hine retorted that they were meant to be edifices worthy of Nottingham, 'noble symbols of the community and its important trade, to encourage every individual member of that community to preserve a corresponding degree of dignity and importance in his own person.'

They can still be seen today, exuding a sooty dignity even through their cannibalisation by various small firms, offices and clubs. The Birkin building, wrapped round both sides of the narrow Broadway, shows a unique, serpentine plasticity and a care for rhythm and proportion in its elongated windows and cantilevered staircases winding round Corinthian columns.

Round the corner in Stoney Street, the five-storey Adams

building could be mistaken for a stately home accidentally transferred from rolling parkland to a city street. Cleverly planned in the form of an 'E', its two wings flank an imposing entrance. Hine provided a carriage court for servicing the building, and an entrance hall with a handsome flight of stairs leading to a thirteen-foot-high salesroom lit by an immense central window.

For the workers of the time, the accommodation was idyllic. They had spacious, well-lighted rooms, warm fresh air, a library, a classroom, a separate tea-room for the men, washing facilities, a workers' dining-room. Most remarkable of all, they had a chapel 'for the spiritual wellbeing of those who have the happiness to be in employment', complete with a chaplain to conduct the services every morning at eight o'clock and 'see after the moral welfare of the workpeople'. Thomas Adams—who used to buy plots of likely land where he thought churches would be required as Nottingham grew—always made a point of being there every morning, praying with his employees.

His warehouse was such a refreshing change from the usual murky conditions that the Factory Commissioners viewed it as one of the most advanced buildings of its kind. One medical visitor from Manchester was so surprised at the happy atmosphere that he commented to an attendant: 'These women look almost as healthy as if they were haymaking.'

From such warehouses went travellers carrying cases of as many as 20,000 pattern samples, bringing the Lace Market to merchants who could not afford to be represented in Nottingham. For sixty years the Lace Market flourished on this site. The departure of the travellers with their cases—most of the houses used to arrange for them to leave for a particular destination on the same day—became a great event. And it was a daily spectacle for the visitor to see the warehouse women and girls stream down into the town every evening. Millions of pounds changed hands—often merely by word of mouth, undocumented. The Market, interlocked with the structure of machinery construction, supply of materials, design and shipment, was so efficient that even in 1860 a piece of lace could be made, bleached, dressed, finished and delivered to London within two days.

Lace brought to Nottingham the money and impetus it needed to catch up with towns which had been able to flex their muscles earlier. The general pattern of the Victorian era obtained, of course. Boom would be followed by slump. But after the Hungry Forties had passed, and the burning zeal of the Chartists had mellowed, Nottingham ceased to be a garrison town and was thought peaceful enough for the troops to abandon their barracks in 1860. Five years later Nottingham acquired—in a single year—the College of Art, the foundation stone of a £1,000 drinking fountain, Nottingham Forest Football Club, a working men's industrial exhibition, and the Theatre Royal. This last—built at the top of the road that at last was being widened from the death-trap of Sheep Lane into Market Street—was provided by two lace dressers, William and John Lambert. Strong churchmen and men of sterling character and compassion, they refused to employ children under thirteen, and introduced staggered hours for their employees in the Talbot Street factory. They were convinced that their fellow citizens could find more civilised uplift in their 2,200 seat Temple of the Muse than in the sodden gin-palaces and boozy music halls. On opening night, the hope was expressed that the theatre could become 'a teacher of the highest morality, nay, even the gentle handmaiden of religion'; a point of view not shared by one clergyman who thundered out a warning that it was bound to deluge the neighbourhood with profanity and vice and urged citizens—particularly 'the poor bird fascinated by the glitter'—not to walk into the expanded jaws of the serpent.

By 1866—notwithstanding the stain of proven bribery in the February elections, which maintained the long corrupt tradition of Nottingham's political life—the town was fit enough to receive the delegates of the British Association. For six days they scuttled with dignity around the local collieries and admired the new theatre, and they held many of their lectures in the Mechanics Institution which, after several false starts, had flourished since 1837.

Nottingham was feeling its confidence flooding back. In the new grounds of the Arboretum (oddly enough, for a town which was eventually to become a tobacco centre, a no-smoking area) the statue erected by admirers of Feargus O'Connor clasped his stone scroll of Chartism. And the stone and iron of Victorian technology rapidly began to shape the future. The town was already quite well lit. From having a single lamp outside the Mayor's house in 1705, and 250 smelly whale-oil lamps half a century later (you can still see the ring of one of the containers outside St. Mary's), gas-lighting had come in as long ago as 1819.

Now it was as if Nottingham were determined that those cast-iron lamp posts should shed their light on a creditable-looking community. The town was accessible enough by rail and water—although it had missed its connections, so to speak, by turning down the idea of a Ship Canal in 1838 and letting Derby pip it to the post as a main line railway centre.

From the 1860s onwards, Nottingham built furiously, both physically and mentally. It was a strange mixture typical of its period, a patchwork of energy and indifference compounded of wishful thinking and growing pride, prodded by compulsion and pressure by men whose industry brought money to the town. Public utilities, for example, were not taken over from private undertakings in one fell swoop but by a series of cat and mouse operations. The Gas Company was bought out in 1874 but the water companies (which in 1873 refused to let the town's medical officer of health take samples from the reservoirs) held out until 1879. The Corporation allowed horse-drawn tramways to be organised by a private concern for twenty years until 1897; it also missed its chance to become the local supplier of telephone services by leaving them—unlike other municipalities—to commercial firms. Yet when it did have the chance to supply electricity in 1882, and blocked all commercial interests, it then procrastinated for at least ten years.

Realising that it must have a decent gateway to the south, Nottingham built a new Trent Bridge in 1871 replacing with a forty-foot wide road (doubled in 1926) the patched-up and obsolete structure which had changed little since the Middle Ages. Its completion gave the town's thrifty soul the pleasure of knowing that it had been done for £1,000 less than the £30,000 estimate.

The need for a bridge was self-evident to men of commerce. Not so obvious were the requirements of the mind. In 1870 it was found that half the children in Nottingham were receiving some sort of elementary education, provided by forty Church of England, sixteen Nonconformist and two Roman Catholic schools. That year's Education Act entrusted compulsory education to School Boards drawing their money partly from the Corporation and partly from the Government. In 1872 Nottingham decided to withhold payment—and only coughed up when threatened with action by the Queen's Bench.

Slow off the mark, too, was help for public libraries. The well-off had their own subscription library, operating since 1820 in Bromley House. So did the Mechanics Institution. Nottingham got its first public library long after the knowledge-hungry rate-payers had petitioned for it. Eighteen years after the Public Libraries Act of 1850 made possible their support from town funds, Nottingham opened its Free Library. But only because it picked up a windfall of 10,000 books when the Artisans' Library, established in 1824, got into financial difficulties.

But though tardy in many ways, the Corporation—inheritor of a tradition of *laissez-faire* and self interest—did show flashes of inspiration. In 1864, the fifth Duke of Newcastle died. The Corporation bounced in with a suggestion to take a 500-year lease on the castle which his unhallowed father had left as a charred reminder of that night in 1831. In July 1878 the Prince of Wales came along and unlocked the doors of the Midland Counties Art Museum, the first of its kind in the country. Not the least of the wonders on view was a huge metal flagstaff, during the construction of which a long search had been made for a riveter small enough to crawl through its inside.

Within three years, Nottingham had another visitor; his Royal Highness Prince Leopold, Duke of Albany, opening the French-Gothic complex in Shakespeare Street which drew together the strands of university college, public library and natural history museum. As in so many instances in Nottingham, it was an achievement pushed through by a blend of far-sighted vision, pressure, howls of protest and a timely offer.

There was an active thirst for knowledge in Nottingham. In the 1850s there were at least half a dozen working men's libraries kept in public houses. Unstamped newspapers and journals had a wide circulation. In 1789 an adult Sunday school 'for Bible reading and the secular arts of writing and arithmetic' was opened in a room belonging to the Methodist New Connection by William Singleton. He had help from a Quaker, Samuel Fox, in whose grocery shop in the High Street all the assistants wore the Quaker garb of lavender gowns, white shawls and bonnets. It was a visit to this school that inspired Joseph Sturge to found his Severn Street Men's School in Birmingham, and inaugurated a nation-wide period of expansion in adult education.

The Mechanics Institution, the friendly societies, and the

People's College set up in 1846 'for the mental and moral improvement of the labouring population', all formed a rich soil for adult education. Educational establishments for children had sprung from private endowment (such as the Boys' High School, founded in 1513 by the widow of a bellfounder), or from religious bodies (High Pavement School was started in 1788 by a splinter group of dissenters who removed their support from the Blue Coat School in Weekday Cross). Some were consciously exclusive (the Girls' High School in 1875 was sixth and second largest of the thirty-eight begun by the Girls' Public Day School Trust). Nottingham was no worse off than most of its contemporaries for education, but by the 1870s and 1880s its governing élite of wealthy businessmen could see the necessity for making it better. If only for technological advancement.

Classes in science and industrial subjects had been pioneered in Nottingham in 1873 with the first University Extension lectures in the country. Hardly were they over than a local solicitor, Richard Enfield, got the idea that an empty factory might be turned into a centre to make such courses permanent. The notion evolved into something much less makeshift. Agog with enthusiasm, Enfield brought the news of an anonymous offer of £10,000 if the Corporation would find the rest. Why not put everything all under one roof—extension courses, the now over-crowded free library, the museum and collections of the Naturalist Society from a couple of rooms in Wheeler Gate, and the evening classes run in the Mechanics Institution? There was, of course, a lot of sharp discussion about the original estimate of £37,000. And derision when the cost ultimately rose to £61,000. But having accepted the challenge, the Corporation weathered the storm. Gladstone, who spoke at the laying of the foundation stone in 1877, envisaged it as a university proper. In fact, that status had to wait until 1948, but Nottingham's University College of 1881 was an astonishing piece of Victorian enterprise—a municipal project paid for almost wholly out of the rates, almost unique in not having been endowed by rich individuals or public appeals.

Calling attention to the provision of the section given to the library, one reporter wrote: 'In this town there are great marshes of stagnant minds; large fields of intellect lying fallow or producing only weeds.' There could be little chance of much else while vast areas of Nottingham were breeding-grounds for stagnant bodies. William Booth, born in Sneinton in 1829, had lived his early life in Nottingham. His first pulpit had been a soap box when he preached as a street-corner Wesleyan. Booth began the Salvation Army in London in 1865, but before he left Nottingham at the age of twenty he had had seared into him the imperative need to save bodies before you can save souls. A spanking new college was all very well, but in the heart of Booth's home town there were still the appalling rookeries where as many as eight people lived in a room eleven feet square.

In The Park, ninety-nine-year leases had been granted for suitably genteel houses fringing the Duke of Newcastle's domain, and since the 1850s these had been laid out in a superior estate of crescents and drives named after the families—Pelham and Clinton and Cavendish. Guarded by gates, staffed by servants who, if they did not 'live in', often went back home to their new slums in the Meadows, these big ornate houses—shut off, discreet and mysterious—were the homes of the lace kings, the hosiery barons, the new aristocracy. But five minutes' walk away, in the Broad Marsh area, nearly 200 out of every 1,000 children born were dying before they were one year old. The fashionable and well-to-do favoured Holy Trinity Church, but a few yards across the road lay festering streets which policemen never entered unless in pairs. Parliament Street—built on the site of the old town wall—was flanked by notorious slums along both sides. It had a music hall at one end, the town gaol at the other, and an assortment of brothels, gin palaces, and squalid tenements along its entire length. For twenty years the piously built Theatre Royal looked over a collection of broken-down pubs, old slaughter houses, and houses that were so rotten that they were condemned as unfit even for the 1880s.

The razing of this warren was Nottingham's first real attempt at slum clearance. The opposition was noisy and bitter, and the owners held out for every penny, but from it emerged the thoroughfares of King Street and Queen Street. Nottingham had the bit between its teeth. Somewhere along the late 'seventies the phrase 'Queen of the Midlands' had crept in. The description was a little premature but it seemed to act as a spur to civic pride.

In 1877, Nottingham suddenly grew bigger.[1] The outlying

[1] See map on p. 123.

parishes of Bulwell, Basford, Lenton, Radford and Sneinton were
taken in within the town boundaries—along with such extra-
parochial appendages as the castle, The Park and Brewhouse
Yard. There were now 11,000 acres instead of 2,000, and 157,000
people to administer instead of 86,000. As befitted its enlarged
status, the Council moved out of the little Guildhall in ancient
Weekday Cross and into the Exchange in the Market Square.
Considering that it was built primarily for civic purposes, it was
strange that the Corporation wanted little to do with the 150-
year-old building. The stuccoed front was very dirty at some
times or very clean at others. The ground floor was taken up
almost entirely by shops; there were five public houses in the
block; and from the dimly-lit corridors below wafted the smells
and noise of sixty-six butchers' stalls in the Shambles. It was
draughty and drab, and the officers of the council complained
that anybody could wander in. Anybody who could raise the
rent was encouraged to stage exhibitions, concerts, dog shows,
waxwork exhibitions, election meetings or lantern lectures in
the Exchange—and the general confusion was augmented by the
latest miracle of science, a time-ball on the roof. This mechanism
wound a big brass globe to the top of a pole. Once a day, at
1 p.m. G.M.T., an electrical impulse from Greenwich tripped a
switch and the ball slid down the pole—an event which always
brought traffic in the Market Place to a standstill until the
Corporation scrapped it in 1887.

The Exchange's Council Chamber possessed poor acoustics,
and the only advantage was that it gave direct access to the
'Feathers' inn directly below. But from it, some attempt was
made—and bravely, too—to shape a reasonable throne for the
new Queen of the Midlands.

The town was fortunate in having particularly notable public
officers to guide the main expansion during the Victorian period.
The Town Clerk for instance, Samuel G. Johnson, set the tone
in enlighted local autonomy. The Medical Officer, Edward
Smeaton, was quick to earmark three of the worst slum areas for
destruction, and got the Corporation to pioneer a block of buildings in Bath Street, of three, two or single rooms, genuinely
intended for the very poor. The Borough Engineer, Marriott
Ogle Tarbotton, and his assistant, Arthur Brown, who became
the Borough Surveyor, campaigned strongly for the wiping out

of the rookeries and saw to it that Nottingham had a fine sewage system at Stoke Bardolph.

In the 1880s, at a time when sixty-foot-wide roads were considered a shocking waste of land, Nottingham built boulevards, giving work to the unemployed and making a tree-lined ring road consisting of Gregory, Radford, Lenton and Castle boulevards; a masterpiece of traffic planning, fifteen years before the first car spluttered into Nottingham.

By the time the new Guildhall (for civic offices and the courts) was built in Burton Street in 1888, the number of new buildings was averaging 2,500 a year. Some of the largest brickworks stood on the high ground of Mapperley—hence the saying that 'Nottingham once stood on Mapperley Plains'. From those brick-yards, exploiting the Keuper marl and the highly porous Bulwell stone, Nottingham largely created itself. Architects like Watson Fothergill fashioned extravagantly fanciful façades which, now that many Victorian buildings are being cleaned of grime, are today revealing refreshingly quaint friezes of creatures and scrollwork.

The Victorian age is a much-maligned period. Certainly Nottingham experienced its full share of its more hideous aspects. Children were worked like brute animals, drawing threads for lace machines from the age of five, sleeping on piles of jackets on the floor. Working up to seventeen hours a day as embroiderers, they suffered from scrofula, defective eyesight and a permanent stoop. They saw the sun through a gap in a filthy and pestilential slum, they grew up in an atmosphere of drunkenness and crime, and they died unwept, uncared for and unknown.

The slum owners of Nottingham have a lot to answer for, and so have all those who exploited the bodies and minds of the people whose labour made them their fortunes. But to condemn them out of hand is to condemn humanity itself. They found themselves grasping a tiger by the tail, lashing about in the darkness. Events in the industrial revolution were too swift and too unpredictable for them to cope with.

And many people did try. They made ghastly mistakes. The gallows, the treadmill, the work-houses—all these were drastic, ill-conceived but genuine attempts to control a situation which seemed to warrant them. Nottingham was not particularly more savage than anywhere else. And indeed it is to its credit that as

Arches of the old Trent Bridge
The new Trent Bridge

THIS
BUILDING
was erected in 1768 and
used for 10 years by
JAMES HARGREAVES
FIRST COTTON MILL
IN THE WORLD

soon as it got its breath back from the rush of affairs in the first thirty or forty years of the nineteenth century, it buckled down and at least groped in the right direction.

With hindsight, it was blundering progress sometimes. The efforts of charity organisations to bring a ray of sunshine into the lives of the poor with such things as outings in the country, woodwork classes, loans of blankets, penny dinners and glee clubs were but a drop in the ocean in a town where ten per cent lived in dire poverty, and twenty per cent in poverty according to fluctuations in trade. The Ragged School of the 1850s, and the Gordon Boys' Home of the 1880s—where in semi-military uniform of forage caps, blue tunics and hobnailed boots, orphan lads were hired out to run errands, push bathchairs, chop wood or pump church organs—may appear pitiful by today's standards. But they were symptomatic of the new attitudes. A social élite grew up in Nottingham concerned with the problems of the late Victorian period. A strong traditional radicalism in religion was strengthened by a stronger radicalism in politics as municipal government became increasingly democratised. New industries were coming along. The 1880s were the early years for Boots, Player's and Raleigh's. The department stores of Jessop, Griffin & Spalding, Farmer, Pearson and Burton were developing. The men behind them swelled the moneyed élite, bringing intelligence, zeal and philanthropy. Not all of those men acquired a national reputation; they preferred to remain large fish in a relatively small pond. But because most of them were self-made men they forced a guilty recognition of poverty and injustice.

Their influence, combined with the technological progress and sheer instinct for trading which had been a characteristic since the time of the Danes, completed the Victorian patchwork. The worst was over. Nottingham could turn the corner into the twentieth century as a fully fledged city. From Anglo-Saxon tribe to electric trams had taken fourteen centuries.

James Hargreaves' cotton mill

SEVEN

CITY LIGHTS

No dark Satanic mills here . . .

—Visitors' Guide

NOTTINGHAM has been a city since Queen Victoria's Jubilee of
1897, and the stags on its delicate coat of arms face outwards, as
if making sure not to be caught napping again.

Few places have managed to put their industrial eggs in so
many baskets. Nottingham makes things. Not only the familiar
'bikes, fags and aspirins', but boilers and beer handles, thermo-
meters and theatre switchboards, cardboard boxes and cricket
bats, pipes and pressure gauges, radiators and railway wagons,
ship's sirens, dishcloths, engine-room fittings, gas meters, cash
registers, hairnets, garden gnomes, knitting patterns, brassières,
ladders, cranes, nougat, sterilisers, typewriters, glue, wallets, neon
signs, pencils, calculators, bricks, relinings for blast furnaces,
refrigerators, electric blankets, ticket rolls and toilet rolls, power
presses, cables, calendars, paper bags, boats, beds, tip-up seats,
piano keyboards, one-armed bandits, baby's bibs, underwear,
slumberwear and cheap tin trays . . .

Before the First World War, fully a third of Nottingham's
prosperity hung by a thread—a strand of lace. At its peak in 1911
the trade employed 22,000; half the national total. Every Thursday afternoon, half-day closing, when traffic was at a minimum,
the packages of lace and fabric would rumble over the cobbles of
the Lace Market for despatch to the railway stations. But then the
revulsion set in. There had been so much lace right through the
Victorian era—curtains, tablecloths, antimacassars, skirts and bed-
spreads. Today the lace trade employs only 5,000, doing a
reasonable £16,000,000 turnover, but mostly shifted ten miles
away to Long Eaton. What is left of the Lace Market is a decaying

warren for dry goods and electrical suppliers, printers and the demolition men. You have to hunt for Nottingham lace in Nottingham. Few shop assistants know the slightest thing about it; far easier to display some of the Raschel lace pouring in from the Continent or the cheap lines from Japan.

Nottingham would probably have become a depressed area if it had relied on lace in the 'twenties. But it became an outstanding example of a city with a well-balanced employment structure. That it happened was basically the doing of a small boy with a widowed mother, a seed and manure merchant who liked to oblige, and a man who was given only a few months to live. One Nottinghamian and two outsiders. The Big Three, the Holy Trinity of Nottingham trade—Boot, Player and Frank Bowden of Raleigh's.

Jesse Boot once summarised his life by saying: 'I fought for a living, and when that was assured I fought for a fortune. When the fortune came I fought against the combined forces of monopoly.' He fought against illness, too. Worn out at thirty-six by a gruelling slog of twenty-three years, he almost let his business go for a song. Then for the last three decades of his life, he was progressively paralysed by rheumatoid arthritis, controlling his empire either from his bed or from an invalid chair inside a specially made car with wide doors. Today his own company could have helped the cripple who became the poor man's doctor; Boots' researchers have come up with Brufen, the first British anti-rheumatic drug.

When Jesse was ten in 1860 his father died, an agricultural labourer who had turned his hobby of herbs into a livelihood in a tiny shop on Goose Gate. Three years later, the boy—barely counter-high—was taken away from school to run the shop for his mother. Jesse, who had picked up a knowledge of the curative properties of the plants he helped his father to gather in the fields, went one better. As soon as the door closed at 9 p.m. on the last customer, he would study books on pharmacy until well into the night. As a bright young druggist of twenty-seven he opened his own shop four doors higher up the street.

His alert brain hit on the truth—contrary to the established commercial outlook of the time—that it was better to sell many articles, each at a small profit, than to sell a few at a big profit.

Cheapness and convenience were his guiding lights. He bought in bulk to save a few pennies—a ton of soft soap, Epsom salts, camphor, bicarbonate of soda—reduced his profits to a minimum, then ploughed them back to buy even larger quantities to sell at even lower prices. He wrapped his goods attractively, and encouraged his customers to buy large boxes instead of twopenny packets, and in pounds rather than in odd ounces. He sold bicarbonate of potash at a penny an ounce, but at 7d. for a pound; and 6d. a pound—less than $\frac{1}{2}$d. an ounce—for larger quantities. A Napoleon of commerce had arrived, with conquest eventually coming to him in every town and city in Britain.

His war on prices caused a storm. His competitors regarded him as an outlaw. They even accused him of selling drugs that were not pure—a taunt which made him insist, when he started to manufacture his own packed medicines in 1888, on adding the word 'Pure' to the company name. It was recently dropped as superfluous.

Pugnacious, brusque and outspoken, Boot kicked hard at opposing forces. When, as Baron Trent in 1929, he had to choose a coat of arms, it was not simply as a pun on his surname that he picked a jackboot for his crest. He battered at the public's prejudice against entrusting doctors' prescriptions to a shop that sold cut-price drugs. He took a qualified chemist into the business; the pair of them lived to see the firm handling five million prescriptions a year. He bashed away at novel methods of selling—filling his window with sponges and sending sixpenny telegrams about it to 200 potential customers. He proclaimed himself as a ready-cash chemist at a time when it was the 'gentlemanly' thing to do to settle bills weeks later. For a whole generation he grappled with the Pharmaceutical Society when it stuffily compelled his chemists to resign from their professional societies.

By the time he was thirty-three, Boot had opened ten shops in Nottingham, Sheffield and Lincoln and could claim to be the founder of the modern chain store. In 1896 there were sixty-one shops in twenty-eight towns—the largest retail chemist's trade in the world and one which involved 'preposterous' sidelines such as stationery, library books, jewellery, silverware and art—but not, for some illogical reason, any toothbrushes to go with the toothpaste. Boot started his own factories and warehouses in Nottingham. Every morning each section opened five minutes after the one before—the time it took the owner's carriage to make the tour of inspection. Despite his benevolence as an employer and a philanthropist, Boot was a stickler; anybody not at work when he arrived was locked out.

For a spell, the firm which had become part of the British town landscape went American. Because of his age and his health, the seventy-year-old Boot sold it in 1920, staying on as chairman for six years until he handed over to his son. (Nowadays there is no member of the family on the board.) The Wall Street crash in the 'thirties compelled the Americans to sell their holdings back. The period of transatlantic ownership proved no disadvantage; it saw the opening of the 1,000th branch, and the building of the pharmaceutical and chemical works at Beeston, the most advanced factories of their time in Europe.

Fifteen thousand visitors a year are shepherded round those factories on their 300-acre site along the flat north bank of the Trent. A day out at Boots is such a popular item on the calendar of women's organisations that there is a three-year waiting list of people eager to marvel at the buildings prosaically-named 'Wets' (for liquids, pastes and creams) and 'Drys' (powders, tablets and lozenges). More than one in eight of the company's 42,000 employees works on this West Nottingham site. Dozens of assembly lines flow to great packing halls beneath a honeycomb of bottle-green glass portholes. In the soap factory, huge pans turn out sixteen tons of toilet soap at each boiling. A £2,000,000 open-plan head office is be-foliaged and be-carpeted every inch of the way. Down in the basements, perfume ingredients are stored in massive earthenware jars, each big enough for half a dozen of the Forty Thieves. Boots, who on D-Day were making one third of the country's total supply of penicillin, spill out anything from insulin and cortisone to hot-water bottles and home-made beer kits. They have discovered drugs to control amoebic dysentery in cattle and sleeping sickness in humans. They are the world's leading manufacturers of potassium permanganate and saccharin. They send 4,000 brand lines to their shops. They have their own pedigree herds and concentrate on hormones and remedies for internal and external parasites. They are adept at producing anything from insecticides and fungicides to a weekly ten tons of that old favourite, Winter Candy.

The man who made possible this cornucopia of commerce

died in 1931. His bust outside the University carries the inscription: 'Before him lies a monument to his industry; behind him an everlasting monument to his benevolence.' To the 'everlasting monument'—the University—he gave not only the site but £150,000 towards the building and the endowment fund; with, naturally, a fine pharmacy department. It is estimated that his benefactions to his city amounted to more than £2,000,000; these included a pleasure park, £50,000 to the general hospital, £200,000 for a new boulevard, the stately war memorial along the Embankment, workmen's houses, and the biggest open-air swimming bath in the country. When King George V took a golden key, in 1928, and opened the University College (it had to wait another twenty years for full status), its crippled provider lay alone in a small private room, unable to attend the ceremony.

The bronze eyes of Jesse Boot stare at the complex of factories under the 'handwritten' neon symbol of his industry, with yearly sales of £220,000,000. Over a million people go into Boots the Chemists every day for anything from a prescription to a potted plant. There is no need to summon them by telegram to buy their sponges. Boots shops go marching on from the Orkneys to Jersey where their originator lies buried. Fourteen hundred of them. In 1968 along came several hundred more from a merger with the Timothy White organisation. The first one to be converted in Nottingham opened—appropriately—on the spot in Goose Gate where Jesse Boot fought his good fight. And won.

The jobs of some 5,000 people in Nottingham today float on a puff of smoke. Tobacco—worshipped by the Aztecs and Red Indians, considered vile and stinking by James I, and deemed a hanging matter in seventeenth-century Russia—has been a mainstay of Nottingham for nearly a hundred years. (Not to mention the free education on cigarette-cards about Notable British Heroes or Butterflies Of The World).

Player's £8,000,000 Horizon factory, built on forty-five acres of an erstwhile Corporation rubbish dump at Lenton, opened in November 1972. It came complete with a specially composed overture, a single doorway for everybody from director to office boy, a democratic one-class restaurant, built-in resistance to the tobacco beetle, and an award from the Royal Institute of British Architects. Two thousand people will work in this air-conditioned palace, the first in Europe to enjoy a system where natural-gas powers turbines to make electricity and uses the hot-waste gases to provide steam for the air-conditioning. The nearest thing to perpetual motion.

Nottingham Castle—which John Player chose as his first trademark in 1877—would fit several times into it. Or into the three other factories at Radford. Or the slit-windowed bonded warehouse on Ilkeston Road, to which lorries stream from the Liverpool docks with their gigantic casks of compressed leaf, and subsequently depart bearing Weights, Gold Leaf, No. 6, Perfectos, Bachelors and the rest designed to please one third of British smokers.

The son of a solicitor in Saffron Walden, the twenty-year-old Player came to Nottingham looking for work in 1859. He tried being a draper, but by 1861 had set up on Beastmarket Hill near the Market Square as an agent for manures and seeds. The shop was next to the cattle market, and Player obliged the dealers by keeping handy a tin or two of tobacco to sell in 'screws' of a few pence each. By 1868—while the teenage Jesse Boot was poring over his pharmacy books up in Goose Gate—he had abandoned agriculture and sown the seeds of his own future. What gave him the edge over the twenty others in the local tobacco trade was the same quick grasp as his chemist contemporary. Cheapness, convenience, and a flair for advertising.

Buying a small factory in Broad Marsh founded fifty years earlier by William Wright, he started packaging his own Flaked Honeydew instead of selling it loose as everybody else did. He provided customers with ready-rolled cigarettes, wrapped in convenient sizes for quick counter sale. And he made the packets rapidly identifiable with his name and a bold sketch of the castle. The famous bearded sailor (not a real person but painted by a Clapham artist from imagination) was registered in 1883. Five years later the lifebuoy was added with the words PLAYER'S NAVY CUT—the phrase taken from the sailors' old custom of squeezing a plug of tobacco in a piece of canvas, binding it tightly with rope, then cutting off a slice as required. The method is still used today.

With three shops prospering, Player took land in the un-developed area of Radford and built three factory blocks—shrewdly leasing two of them to lace manufacturers until the time when he would need them. He died in 1884 of cancer. His two sons, then eighteen and twenty, carried on. By 1900 they had reclaimed the lace factories and their firm was one of the biggest employers of labour in the East Midlands—with their factory girls, known as 'Player's Angels', each turning out up to 2,000 cigarettes a day by hand. The firm was one of the founder members when the Imperial Tobacco Company was formed in 1901 to protect the British trade from attack by American manufacturers.

The third side of Nottingham's mighty triangle was completed by Frank Bowden. In 1887, Bowden—after fifteen profitable years in the Far East, was sent home from Hong Kong with the gloomy report that he could live only a few more months. But Bowden was advised by a doctor to take up the new fad of cycling. Fit in six months, he was so impressed that he gratefully tracked down the maker of the machine which had given him back his health. He found a dozen mechanics laboriously turning out three cycles a week in a shed in Raleigh Street. Bowden not only thanked them. He bought the business and made it the Raleigh Cycle Company. Nine years from the time he should have been in his coffin, he had built at Lenton what was then—and still is—the biggest bicycle factory in the world. Sixty other little firms had tried their hands at making cycles in Nottingham, since William Campion started this as a sideline to his hosiery business in 1860. One of Campion's employees, a blacksmith moulder called Thomas Humber, set up at Beeston, pioneering rubber tyres, roller bearings and wire spokes. Although several others made cars and motor cycles (the motorbike that T. E. Lawrence of Arabia was riding when he was killed was a Nottingham-made Brough) Raleighs concentrated on setting the world pedalling. They produced the first all-steel bicycle, took the hard work out of it with Sturmey-Archer variable gears, and brought out a first-class machine for as little as £4. The two wars gave the company an indirect boost, for after each it was found that the machinery installed for munitions (in World War II the 10,000-strong (now 4,000) Raleigh plant was the Government's biggest individual supplier of small shells, cases and fuses) was eminently suitable for producing cycle components.

Raleigh Industries—as part of the enormous Tube Investments Group—now make eighty-five per cent of all British bicycles, selling under fifty famous names including Hercules, Moulton,

The Lace Market in 1914
(overleaf) Aerial view of central Nottingham

Rudge, Humber, Triumph, Sun and Carlton. A million and a half
machines are wheeled off the production lines every year. Three-
quarters of them go for export in five continents and in 140
markets—from sit-up-and-beg models for General Amin's soldiers
in Uganda to the ungainly and unconventional Choppers
adored by youngsters in the U.S.A. Dynohub lighting sets . . .
items for every car made in Britain . . . prams, pushchairs and
toys . . . they all pour out of Raleighs. Thanks to the unknown
doctor who once told Frank Bowden to throw his leg over a
saddle.

At the turn of the century another new industry was brought
to Nottingham and became a major enterprise. Ericsson Telephones—now part of the Plessey Group—prospered at Beeston, a
semi-industrialised district where land was cheap. Four thousand
employees today keep the lines of the world's communications
open, tackling anything from the reorganisation of Whitehall's
telephone network to an exchange capable of standing up to the
corrosive atmosphere of New Zealand's sulphur springs.

Firms like Ericsson and Raleigh have been the nucleus of
Nottingham's growth as a considerable engineering centre. A
quarter of its industry is engaged in engineering. Nottingham,
of course, has equipped most of the countries where lace manufacture is carried on; but lace machines last a long time, and
native skills were diversified into a vast selection of products from
lifts to laundry equipment, from stainless steel sinks to hydraulic
pit-props. Heavy engineering is represented by a Royal Ordnance
Depot which has outlasted its parent at Woolwich.

In contrast to lace, the hosiery and knitwear trades and the
clothing industry expanded rapidly between the wars. In and
around Nottingham a quarter of the entire British output of
ladies' and children's clothing is produced. A fifth of all girls
leaving school go into the trade. Hosiery and knitwear (which,
with 50,000 operatives in city and county, have more than a third
of the industry's national labour force) clock up over £200,000,000
a year in Nottingham alone. Half the people involved work for
modest concerns with between twenty and a hundred employees;
something of the independent spirit of the eighteenth-century
stockinger, toiling in his long-windowed cottage, still lingers.

Dip at random, and out of Nottingham's bag you can pull any
number of celebrated brand names—Vedonis, Bairnswear,

Hounds Gate and St Peter's Church
Emett water clock at Victoria Centre

Morley, Viyella, Meridian, Marathon, Witchcraft, Stag, Wheat-croft, Gunn & Moore, Bow. . . . But all over the city the streak of enterprise flourishes in less-known ways. The shop at the bottom of Hockley which made scissors 130 years ago for the lace trade, and still has 300 types on sale; the factory at Bulwell making drinking straws, for which the owner got the idea by absentmindedly twirling a bus ticket in his fingers; the fishing-tackle shop on Radford Road which sells live maggots in a converted milk-vending machine. . . .

One way and another, Nottingham has everything going for it. Communications are good, with the M1 on the doorstep, the East Midlands airport ten miles away, at Castle Donington, handling all but Jumbo-jets, British Rail's freightliners doing a heavy traffic, and that old artery the Trent bringing in ships 140 feet long and eighteen-and-a-half feet in beam. Notting-ham's miners travel out into the county to the richest coalfield in Britain, knowing that, with a daily output per man of a con-sistent fifteen hundredweight above the national average, their twenty-five million tons give the Trent valley power stations the country's cheapest electricity. And (still digging) even the sand and gravel pits—one firm alone supplies ten per cent of the national production—are transformed to advantage, like the nature reserve at Attenborough or the 2,000-metre rowing course at Holme Pierrepont.

The thirteenth-largest city in the kingdom, Nottingham is the focus of a more or less continuously built-up conurbation of over half a million people. Thousands flow in daily from the immediately adjacent areas of West Bridgford (population 27,000), Carlton (39,000), Beeston and Stapleford (57,000), and Arnold (27,000), together with Hucknall (24,000) and Long Eaton (30,000) in Derbyshire. These places, developing from large villages into major industrial or residential satellites in the late nineteenth century, have remained independent despite the interchange of workers and social life. Like Nottingham, they are now watching cautiously to see that, in the restructuring of local government, they will not be kneaded into a huge ball of admini-strative dough.

Similar communities with individual personalities—Bulwell, Sneinton, Hyson Green, and the like—must have felt the same when they were welded into the city in 1877. They managed to

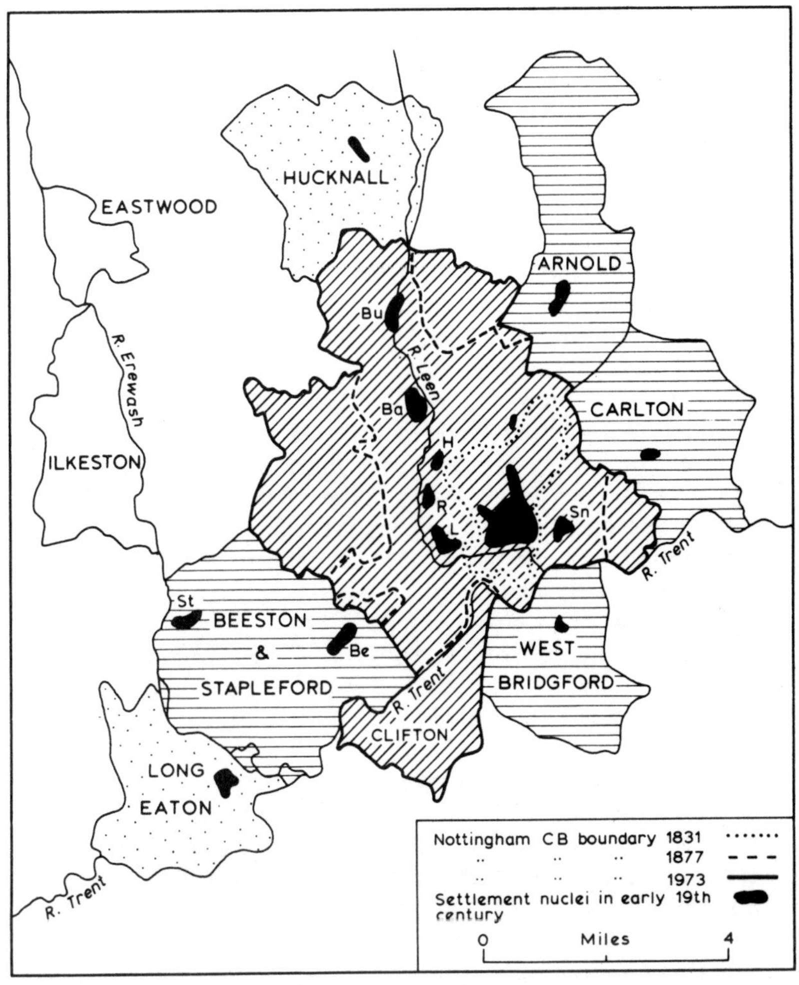

Key: Ba—Basford; Be—Beeston; Bu—Bulwell; H—Hyson Green; L—Lenton; R—Radford; Sn—Sneinton; St.—Stapleford.

In the local government re-organisation of 1974, the urban district councils surrounding the city of Nottingham were grouped to form seven of the eight administrative areas in the county. The eighth, Nottingham itself, now elects twenty-seven of the eighty-nine members of the new Nottinghamshire County Council. Arnold and Carlton went into Gedling district. Beeston & Stapleford U.D. merged with Eastwood into Broxtowe. Hucknall became part of the Ashfield district. West Bridgford (housing the County Council HQ) coupled with Bingham as part of a large area south of the Trent known as Rushcliffe. Ilkeston and Long Eaton are in Derbyshire.

hang on to their own flavours; particularly at Bulwell where the strong sense of individuality is helped by the sheer fact of holding a bustling street-market.

One of the first things Nottingham did when it achieved city status was to let the Great Central build its extension. Nottingham's railway history is unique in that no other large town has had services to London on eight different routes. The £1,000,000 line drove through under the heart of the Lace Market, laying bare the ancient dungeons; and in return for the demolition of its historic Guildhall Nottingham got the Victoria Station (opened on the Queen's birthday in 1900) together with the disappearance of twenty-four pubs, the work-house, and 1,300 of the slum dwellings in its worst rookery. It also did a deal with the railway company for a strip of river bank which, in 1901, it made into one of the finest riverside drives in the country.

Poverty lapped like a dirty tide according to the fortunes of the lace industry. Barefoot boys sold papers in the gutters of Long Row. Many a family breakfasted from the top of a cottage loaf and a farthing's worth of lard.

But with the end of the 1914–18 War, Nottingham really rolled up its sleeves and attacked its slums. It immediately rid itself of its 31,000 antiquated pail closets. It rooted out most of the back-to-backs, jammed in at 500 to the acre, and laid out model estates at twelve to the acre. If Nottingham was the shame of the British Empire in the early nineteenth century, it was its pride a hundred years later. Planners from all over the world came to admire the bold, spacious way in which the city re-housed large sections of its population with a standard of amenity equal to any in the world. Between the wars it built 17,500 houses, and as many since 1945. Thirty thousand people were re-housed in the brand-new estate of Clifton which was taken into the city boundary in 1951. Well over a half of Nottinghamians now live in council-built homes.

St. Ann's—into which 10,000 houses were packed in the 1890s, of which two-thirds had no hot water and three-quarters no bath —has come tumbling down. In the 1970s, this area where King James I used to sample the health-giving waters, had its sleazy walls pounded to rubble at long last. Whether the community spirit which infused the squalor of St. Ann's has likewise been erased is another matter. But at least the population, reduced by a third, have civilised houses without the smoke pall that has always hung over them.

The slums of The Meadows, too, are on their way out. The brick clutter which pulverised the crocus fields after their mid-Victorian enclosure is to be replaced, by the early 1980s, by new buildings complete with a district heating system, and by the transformation of Arkwright Street into a traffic-free pedestrian route between the city centre and the Embankment. Nottingham learned a bitter lesson in 1947 when spring floodwaters of the Trent inundated 2,500 acres, and twenty-eight miles of streets, in the low-lying Meadows. The Trent River Authority's massive flood schemes have since tamed that threat; it is now up to Nottingham to bring back some dignity—if not a little greenery —to The Meadows which were once its most beautiful aspect.

Even at the rate of 2,000 new houses a year, it is unlikely that Nottingham will be in the position of having, as one optimistic alderman declared, 'more than enough by 1980'. It is still near the bottom of the league. One-fifth of its 100,000 homes are still without baths.

But the 'seventies has been a period of almost frenzied activity. Hand in hand with the slum clearance programme has come the realisation that the social services have been shamefully neglected. From less than £1,000,000 in 1966–67—lagging £300,000 behind comparable places like Bradford or Stoke—the city trebled its budget and since 1974 has come under the County wing.

Soon only a handful of outdated primary schools will remain, after the strenuous efforts of an education department determined to rid the city of the ancient premises that existed only a decade ago. Now the acute shortage of nursery places (2,000 instead of the necessary 6,000) is being tackled. Thirty years ago, the city did not have a single new building for further education. Now it has the College of Education at Clifton (one of the largest in the country with 1,300 students) the People's College, Basford Hall, Clarendon College and the 3,300-student Trent Polytechnic. This has grown like a field of mushrooms since 1945, and is now in the midst of a £20,000,000 expansion which will bring to fruition an ambitious civic centre plan drawn up in wartime when few cities were so forward-looking. By 1980 the Poly had over 8,000 students.

With over 5,000 students at the University, and gigantic new hospital complexes, which include a £1,500,000 maternity block at the City Hospital, and Britain's first medical school to be built since 1892, Nottingham is taking its logical place as the centre of what could be the most influential region in Britain.

In 1972 it got the £17,000,000 Victoria shopping centre, and by 1974 its £10,000,000 twin at Broad Marsh. With narrow streets such as Clumber Street, Lister Gate, St James's Street, Low Pavement and Wheeler Gate paved over, park-and-ride traffic schemes, a five-minute bus shuttle (free until 1977) between the Victoria and Broad Marsh Centres, and ambitious efforts to stave off the cars in the middle of the city, Nottingham is striving to make the pedestrian king, and not the machine.

And it caters for its cultural leisure by going ahead in 1982 with a magnificent 2,500-seat concert hall of shimmering glass attached to the 1,100-seat Theatre Royal, a complex envied throughout the country.

The statue of Queen Victoria, removed from the market square when the traffic grew too much for her, reigns silently over the goldfish in the quiet gardens along the river. If she came back to town she would never know the old place.

EIGHT

OBJECTION!

The people of Nottingham have always been spirited and vocal, and have always been in a ferment and disputatious. . . .

—Town Clerk, 1965

NOTTINGHAM has never been a place where they suffer in silence, and the burnt-out castle illustrated the point for over forty years. Its sacking may have been the most spectacular of protests, but it was only an incident in a long history of resistance and dissension; religious, political, industrial and individual.

Maybe the town's parentage has had something to do with it. First the Anglo-Saxons, then the Danes. And no sooner had the Anglo-Danes got a thriving community going than William the Conqueror's Normans arrived and made two distinct towns in one. Clash and argument have been Nottingham's birthright ever since, and at any given time there is usually a row of some sort going on. Why should a little rest-garden be pinched for a car park? What right have 'they' to ban a film? How dare this doctor strike me off his list? Why can't that road be somewhere else?

The precedents of protest are profuse. Early in the thirteenth century, people were so annoyed with the Mayor for giving help to an unpopular Constable of the castle that they killed him and blockaded the fortress for more than a week.

In a traditionally Whig town, the doctrine of the right to resist tyranny was applied literally. Through most of the eighteenth and nineteenth centuries, the characteristic sounds in Nottingham were the noise of jeering crowds, the whine of musket balls and the smashing of glass. In 1766 a riot was sparked off at Goose Fair by farmers asking a high price for cheese. The crowds grabbed the huge cheeses and either carted them off or rolled them like hoops down Wheeler Gate, bowling over the Mayor in the process. In 1788 and 1792 it was the cost of meat which made the butchers flee their shambles, and leave their joints to a mob which not only took advantage of free meals but ripped off the shop shutters and made greasy bonfires of them. The bakers had their turn in 1800 when for three days all bakeries, granaries and breadshops came under attack and mothers scuttled away with filched corn in their aprons.

The misery of the hosiery workers runs like a dirty thread through Nottingham's industrial life. In 1799 an army chaplain commented that in the seventeen years he had been in Nottingham there had been seventeen riots. But it did not always need food or wages to touch off trouble. Religion and politics were always incendiary topics, as the mayor, Alderman Thomas Hawksley discovered in 1715. Flushed with the success of the first Jacobite rebellion, he gave a party at home and 'went down on his bare knees and drank to the House of Stuart'. As if that wasn't bad enough, he damned all their enemies; and soon found himself being hauled off to the House of Correction by a brother magistrate who happened to belong to the opposition. Several people had their noses bashed in and the whole corporate body got to fighting before Alderman Hawksley was voted out of office. Three lawsuits for false imprisonment got him nowhere.

Like the other nonconformists before them (George Fox, founder of the Quakers, had been flung into gaol, but while there managed to convert the Sheriff) Charles and John Wesley had a hard time of it in Nottingham. Ultimately they preached to thousands in the market place, and in a chapel so crammed that a hole had to be knocked in the ceiling so that crowds upstairs could hear. But in the 1740s the early Methodists were pelted with filth and 'the scourings of all things' by 'wild beasts'. Scenes which made Charles comment ruefully in his journal: 'I cannot help observing that we ought to wait upon God for direction when and where to preach much more than we do.'

By 1777, however, his brother John was writing: 'I preached to a serious, loving congregation. There is something in the people of this town which I cannot but much approve of; although most of our Society are of the lower class, chiefly employed in the stocking manufacture, yet there is generally an uncommon gentleness and sweetness in their temper and something of an

Thomas Adams' lace warehouse
Birkin building, in the Lace Market

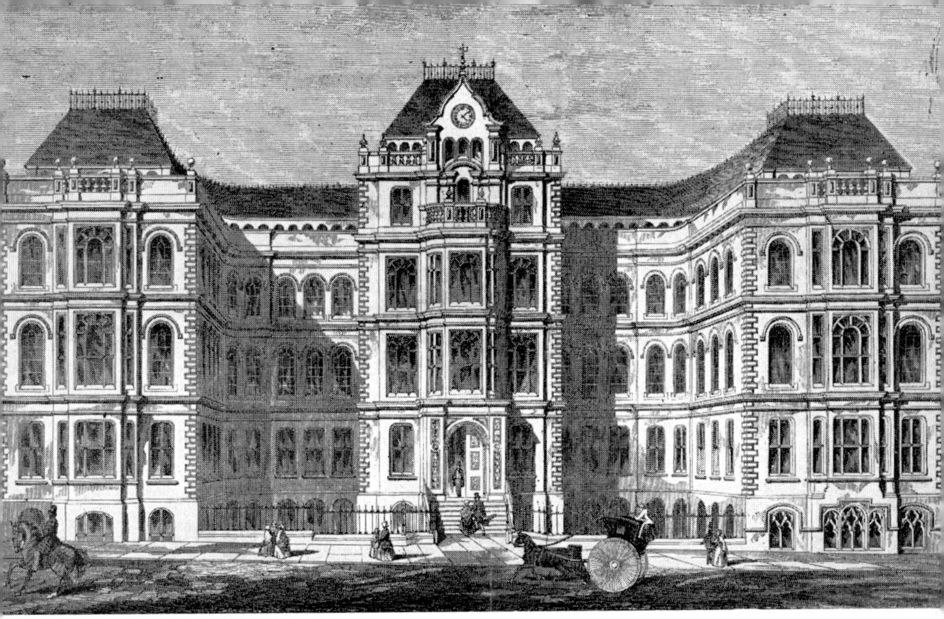

elegance in their behaviour which, added to solid, vital religion, makes them an ornament to their profession.'

But for all the gentleness and sweetness, the people of Nottingham proceeded on their riotous way, usually in desperation. They showed their feelings in ways which all too often brought down the sabre-swishing military and ended in a few corpses being added to the rubble.

They emptied revengeful chamber pots over the soldiers as they filed through narrow streets. They formed 'Loyalist' mobs to hold running battles with the 'Democrats' who sympathised with the French Revolutionaries. With the tacit consent of the magistrates, hooligans were organised into ducking parties to 'baptise' Democrats under the pumps or in the river. At least one victim drowned from such a christening. The Democrats took their revenge when, at the election of 1803, they had both mob and magistrates on their side and towed their opponents round town in carts, pelting them with mud. Elections were high old times in Nottingham, and full scope was offered—and taken—for corruption. Locally, the ruling clique of the Corporation, drawing its members from a handful of families attending the same few chapels, saw to it that it shared the perks of power—the evening parties at public expense, the contracts. Likewise it fixed the parliamentary returns.

The Whigs were so determined in 1802 that they came up with a candidate, Joseph Birch, who was not even aware of his nomination and had to be fetched from Liverpool. Since a few wild spirits had begun to saw through the joists of the Exchange, the poll was held in a wooden booth in the market place. Whereupon Birch's supporters climbed on the roof, called out the names of electors and how they voted, and shouted down whether the crowd should let them through or beat them up. The Tory candidate, Daniel Parker Coke, was abused and threatened so much that he abandoned the fight in eight days. But the Tories petitioned Parliament (with a list that included people abroad on holiday) and the election was declared null and void. Coke and Birch re-submitted themselves for election, entering town with massive entourages of horsemen, and postillions in blue and yellow respectively. This time, the Tories won.

Pitched battles between hired armies—the Blue Innocents and the Yellow Lambs—were part and parcel of the Nottingham

Player's Horizon factory
The Theatre Royal

election scene. Nottingham became a hotbed of agitation by the Chartists. In 1842 an excited throng of 16,000 witnessed the dramatic meeting when O'Connor jumped from his wagon and threshed his way towards his opponent, the once-Chartist fire-brand, now renegade, Reverend J. R. Stephens, and sent him haring for refuge in The Bell Inn. Such violence was typical of the explosive state to which Nottingham had been building up through the Luddite troubles, and the Reform Bill burnings, and the accumulation of poverty and hunger. Only a few weeks later, several hundred men stopped work in an attempt to organise a general strike. Thousands assembled on the heights of Mapperley, ripping the Riot Act from the magistrates' hands and stoning the police. The hussars and the dragoons charged. There was a panicky getaway over hedges and ditches. Four hundred strikers were bundled off. Nottingham could easily have become the flashpoint for another civil war. The will was there but not the means.

The 'Battle of Mapperley Hills' was Nottingham's highwater-mark of insurrection. Fortunately the tide was on the turn. Changes in the political structure had sensibly relaxed the hold of the 'select body' of freemen, and living-space would be given to the strangled town by the enclosure measures of 1845. Actual riots dwindled after that, give or take an election fracas. What Byron in 1806 had termed 'that political pandemonium, Notting-ham' was not to be hushed up overnight.

After all, the town's leaders had always set the tone, doggedly building up their privileges and demonstrating a canny refusal to be beaten, either by royal overlords or by annoyances like electors. In 1813 and again in 1819, for example, the Corporation secured Whig party dominance by simply conferring honorary freedom of the town on 300 squared and safe non-residents. Most of the time it had shown a united front, however stormy the background battles. (A year after Colonel Hutchinson had been confirmed as Governor of the castle, the Corporation petitioned Parliament against 'his impious demands and passionate and violent carriage'.)

Nowadays the united front sometimes cracks. Some sharp words occasionally fly about the council chamber, and the odd literal blow is struck. But for all the political manœuvrings of today, one can only live in fond hope of a flash of the seventeenth-century spirit, as when the whole Council tangled in a free fight in 1682. On that occasion, a Tory mayor had broken open the triple-locked box containing the town seal, in order to surrender the hard-won charters to Charles II. There was an unseemly scramble to carry off the mace, an alderman had his best waistcoat ruined, and the Sheriff's Sergeant 'received a full swop over the face'; and twenty-three protesting Whigs were tried by Judge Jeffreys and fined anything up to £333 for rioting.

The lamp of liberty has always burned bright in Nottingham. The town's first charter, granted by Henry II around 1155, declared that any man who had lived there unchallenged for a year and a day earned the freedom of the borough and could not be dragged back to his master even if he was a runaway serf. Bureaucracy managed to erode that one; in 1612, Nottingham took pains to get rid of anybody who might prove a burden on the 'inhabytantes of the better sorte'. It was forbidden to build 'poore habytacions', and a long list was drawn up of poor 'foreigners', sent back to Kent and Northamptonshire after being settled in Nottingham for two years.

Even though an effigy of Thomas Paine, who had worked as a corset maker in Nottingham, was hanged and burned in 1793 to denigrate the author of *The Rights of Man*—only a few yards, incidentally, from where two-and-a-half centuries previously, two monks of Lenton Priory were really hanged—Nottingham persisted in its right of free expression. At the height of frame-smashing, the *Nottingham Review* was remarkably outspoken in its defence of the Luddites. Its editor, Charles Sutton, was gaoled for a year in 1816 for publishing a letter 'signed' by General Ludd which reported that his son Ned was now whirling his hammer smashing presses, and pillaging in America with Government licence.

Nottinghamians were always steeped in the notion of quick protest, whether complaining, in 1588, against the wife of a drunken wastrel who milked other people's cows in the night, or, like the town waits of 1672, going on strike against attending the mayor on Sundays. A crowd in 1785 became so impatient to see a balloon ascent from the Forest that they tossed out the aeronaut, made a bonfire of his gear, cut the balloon's tether, and let it soar away. It eventually came down in Lincolnshire where farm labourers attacked the flabby monster with pitchforks. In

1852, during the rivalry between railway companies, a Great Northern locomotive steamed into the Midland station, where the superintendent ordered every available engine to engage the enemy. Amid a hissing and whistling the hapless green intruder was pushed into a siding; and the Midland men made sure of their prize by ripping up the rails round it.

Nothing has got by without vociferous comment. One newspaper in 1818 declared that gas lighting was actually wicked: God made the night dark and we ought not to try to upset His order. . . . Another was against it because drunkards, knowing that they could see their way home, would stay in the pubs longer. And when the first lamps were lit, some nervous citizens pointed out the grave risk from the burning gas that must be travelling through the pipes.

The Victorians got het up about attendants missing divine service when the Castle Museum opened on Sunday, about the 'appliances for riotous enjoyment' if bands were allowed on Good Friday, and about the wisdom of building a University College. The Edwardians got het up about noisy trams, motor taxis, and the wisdom of putting newspapers containing betting news in the library reading-rooms. There was a great to-do in the 1920s when the market traders were shifted from the Old Market Square, another when the Council House was built in place of the ancient Exchange, and an even greater one when the Goose Fair was given its marching orders to the Forest.

People have been getting het up and causing a lot of to-do about every mortal thing since. There exists still a stratum of violence that will erupt over Wesley's 'uncommon gentleness and sweetness'. There was an ugly business in 1958 when, in the decaying district called Robin Hood Chase, a stabbing affray between whites and West Indians escalated into a couple of weekends of violence. The Ku-Klux-Klan, reviving in this country, whipped up the flames with pamphlets about 'the black apes', local Teddy Boys fixed a rendezvous with bicycle chains and razors, and about 4,000 sightseers, reporters and TV crews turned out to watch. The resultant clash proved a white-*v*-white affair, with not a coloured man on the streets. There ensued a few 'nigger-baiting' incidents, which were enough to make a bus company in Leicester advertise coach tours of 'Nottingham terror-spots', but the city's anti-colour hysteria fizzled out, no doubt because, for all its argumentative nature, Nottingham is basically a reasonable place. But it insists on shouting the odds. There can be few towns more vocal, few tongues in better working order.

Every town has its little band of letter-writers; Nottingham is well endowed with those whose pens are poised to pounce on rude bus conductors, long-haired yobs, bedroom scenes on television, and dogs fouling pavements. But in addition to such hardy annuals, Nottingham somehow offers a constant variety of circumstances to protest about, something that *Vox Populi* and *Disgusted* can get their teeth into. People positively queue up to air their views in the *Editor's Postbag* of the papers and on the local BBC Radio Nottingham. And the commercial Radio Trent.

Most of it, inevitably, is directed at the City Fathers whose every move is lambasted. And with good reason sometimes. The man in 1738 who was indicted for 'cursing and highly reflecting on the Corporation', and the butcher who, ten years later, wound up at the Quarter Sessions for calling on the Devil to 'blow them up with gunpowder' were but forerunners of today's citizens, bewildered and angry by the seeming high-handedness of their representatives and servants.

Nottingham hears the death knells all over the city as yet another historic or beautiful portion is voted away in committee, and then done to death after a token inquiry which never seems to have the slightest effect. The lovely Collin's Almshouses in Friar Lane were whipped away before anybody knew about it. The Georgian area round the castle was hacked through by Maid Marian Way. The mediaeval Drury Hill and Middle Hill districts were butchered, even though the planners knew how fond Nottingham people were of them. Bitter words are said on piece-meal planning, expediency and the erasing of history in exchange for yet another shopping mall or half-empty office block. They make hardly any difference. A councillor will reply, an official explain. But by and large the protests meet an aloofness astonishing in a city which ought to be setting an example. 'What is it about Nottingham,' asked one despairing campaigner, 'that the planners hate so much?'

Naturally, it is not always a case of Them-versus-The Rest. Nottingham is notoriously split-minded. The Radicals, who sang the *Marseillaise* and tried to plant a Tree of Liberty in the square in 1802, met as many opponents as supporters. For the many who pour scorn on the prim bannings of the Public Protection Committee, there are as many who applaud the safeguarding of morals. Civic societies may be filled with dismay when legacies of the past are carved up, but traders are not. Critics, opposed to letting children appear in an army training film for troops in Northern Ireland, got caught in a backlash from parents who wanted the children to take part.

It will be a rare day, then, when Nottinghamians are unanimous, so one should not be too disgruntled when their council members reflect this disputatious quality. The urge to argue, to challenge, to disagree, to dissent is a lively and attractive and hopeful streak in the Nottingham temperament. It is refreshing to see the spirit of protest still going strong. To know that thousands of theatregoers at the Playhouse signed a colossal petition to keep a favourite director, John Neville. To see 'Welcome to Slum City' posters during a visit by the Duchess of Kent. To learn of tenants in damp, rat-infested houses refusing to pay rent. To watch councillors objecting to wearing evening dress, and turning up for a civic ball in lounge suits. To know that undertakers recoil from time-and-motion methods at Wilford Hill crematorium, and reject 'quickie' funerals, timed by stopwatch. To hear of old-age pensioners planning a bread-and-cheese lunch, in protest against £5-a-head lunches for councillors to celebrate the opening of an incineration plant. And to know that Nottingham's tradition has been passed down to children staging a 'sit-in' to save a street bonfire on Guy Fawkes night.

As long as Nottingham can raise a squawk, or even two fingers, there is hope for it.

NINE

SECRET OF SUCCESS

Hail, Fair Nottingham, albeit thy name
Is not poetical, yet from thee rise
Names mounting up to virtue and to fame.
　　　　　—Robert Millhouse, 'The Burns of
　　　　　　Sherwood Forest', 1783–1839

IF NOTTINGHAM happened to be in Texas, there would be no holding it. Over there, they would appreciate having the world's biggest cycle factory or the world's most advanced cigarette factory. Texas can come up with the world's biggest steaks; Nottingham can come up with an incredible stake in inventions, innovations and ideas. If I had my way I would press on every traveller to Nottingham a leaflet listing the things that have originated in this astonishingly ingenious city.

Scattered through the pages of this book are already a few of them, from the world's first spinning mill to the latest and biggest branch of Boots, from the start of knitting- and lace-machines to Europe's biggest discotheque, from the beginnings of banking in England to the arrival of automated cinemas.

There are quite a few more. Nottingham produced the first fully-fashioned stocking; and, in 1789, the first school for adults in the country. Children's libraries followed the one founded in 1882 by Samuel Morley—hosiery man, Member of Parliament and philanthropist, who saw that 'the working classes are deluged and poisoned with cheap, noxious fiction'. Nottingham was the first place in England to record an earthquake—in 1180. It had the first national police forensic science laboratory in 1934. Two years earlier, the first message of its kind in the country was sent over a police car radio. The city now has the biggest and most modern parcels sorting-office in Britain (even if the crematorium is merely the second biggest).

Nottingham had the first street subway outside of London in

1862. The first regional branch of the National Film Theatre was opened there in 1966, and the BBC's Radio Nottingham was among the first batch of local radio stations on the air, in 1968. A Nottingham man, Charles Shaw, went up in a Farman biplane with a bulky plate camera, and took Britain's first aerial photograph on September 30, 1910. After laying the first proper rails—two miles of wooden ones as a permanent wagonway through Wollaton from the coalpits at Strelley, in 1604—Nottingham put on the first railway excursion in the world. In July 1840, members of the Mechanics Institution visited the Leicester Institution. They paid a single fare for the double journey. Thomas Cook picked up the idea a year later.

Nottingham was the first town in England to have a half-day closing association, when a baker, shoe-dealer and grocer at Basford got together and shut up shop on Thursday afternoons. As well as starting the first non-sectarian grammar school, the city acquired the first Department of Adult Education in 1920; this in 1964 laid the foundations of the Open University, the first full-scale experiment in teaching by a combination of television programmes, correspondence course, and face-to-face meetings with tutors. Nottingham University appointed, in 1966, the country's first lecturer in insurance and established the first Chair of Health Education in Europe seven years later.

An Urdu Library, the only one in Britain, opened in a small shop in 1967. And the following year a Pakistani named Mohammed Ajeeb—former bus conductor and driver—became the first full-time salaried housing officer for coloured immigrants. A West Indian, Eric Irons, appointed the first race relations officer in 1958, took his seat on the Guildhall bench as Britain's first coloured magistrate in 1962 and even had a calypso written about him. One of the Ukrainian community, Volodymyr Choma, made history in 1973 by becoming the first Ukrainian Catholic priest to be ordained in England. Another Ukrainian, Victor Krokosz, who retired in 1972 after fifteen years with the City Engineer's department, was recognised as Britain's best-dressed roadsweeper. Anthony John Mundella—the son of a poor Italian immigrant—came to Nottingham as a young man and, as a Liberal M.P. and a member of Gladstone's government, introduced the revolutionary Factories Act for children, and made school attendance compulsory.

The first greenhouse in the country was built at Wollaton, and it has never been disproved that the first rose show was held—in a pub named after the Crimean War general, Cathcart—on Easter Monday, 1859. Dean Hole himself, who became the first president of the Royal National Rose Society, battled through hail, rain, wind and snow from Caunton, near Newark, to see for himself the fragrant products of the tiny allotments tended by stockingers on the terraces of the Hungerhills. And still in the horticultural line, the finest rockery stone in the kingdom is Bulwell stone, which hardens under water, and germinates moss a year or two before any other kind. For several generations, it has always been used in the royal gardens. The country's most prolific producer of garden pottery is at Bulwell.

Thanks to the water-engineer Thomas Hawkesley, Victorian Nottingham was the first town to have a constant supply of water by mains and always under pressure. With a staff of one man and a boy, Hawkesley, who achieved a world-wide reputation as a civil engineer, provided a piped supply to 8,000 houses for a penny a week each. Without his genius the horror of the slums would have been incalculably worse.

St. Pancras station was built of Nottingham bricks. The sailors who fought at Trafalgar wore shrink-proof jackets, made from double-lap worsted on Nottingham warp-frames. The first major building to be designed in Britain in the metric system in readiness for the Common Market came from the Nottingham firm of Simms, Sons and Cooke, whose pre-fabricated buildings can be found at the South Pole.

Mental hospitals all over the world took a lead from Mapperley where the 'open doors' principle was evolved. And, definitely on a locked-doors principle, Nottingham's prison was the first prison workshop to install injection moulding machinery so that the inmates could make plimsolls and slippers.

Working away at the soft gypsum of the Trent Valley, with an affection felt by their Italian contemporaries for the marble of Carrara, Nottingham craftsmen in alabaster were pre-eminent until the mid-sixteenth century. Their lovingly carved Madonnas and altarpieces had a vast export trade—to France, Spain, Italy, Denmark and even to Iceland. On a more mundane and hardly so beautiful level, nowadays there is a vast export trade for the Bell Fruit Company, the country's biggest manufacturer of gaming machines, which hit the jackpot anywhere from Nottingham to Nevada.

Pick practically any subject and the chances are that Nottingham will crop up in it somehow. Banking? Thomas Smith's bank was the first private bank in the country to issue paper money. Telephones? The Plessey Group at Beeston is turning out the world's first mobile exchanges. Supermarkets? The two-acre GEM (now ASDA) supercentre at West Bridgford pioneered the American trend towards one-stop suburban shopping as long ago as 1965. Football? Shin-guards were invented in 1880 by Samuel Widdowson, a Nottingham Forest forward. And goal-nets (dreamed up by a Liverpudlian) were first used in a North-*v*-South match at Nottingham in 1891, before the Cup Final that year. Town planning? In the eighteenth century, one of the earliest examples of planning was when a triangular market place-cum-children's play area was laid out, at Carrington as a sort of shopping precinct; in the days when it was dangerous to cross the forest on the edge of Nottingham.

Fishing? Any angler appreciates the ease of the Nottingham cast. Contract Bridge? Who's for a rubber of the Nottingham System? Toys? The University's Child Development Research Unit has encouraged manufacturers to produce a whole range of special toys for youngsters suffering from blindness, spina bifida and other handicaps. Autographs? Probably the biggest collection in the world belongs to N.C.B. worker Wilson Barratt of Bulwell, who in thirty years has stalked—by post and in person—20,000 famous folk from Ghandi to Getty. Maps? A Blind Mobility Unit, again from the University, has fitted over one hundred braille plates to pillars in the Victoria Centre to tell blind people where everything is. Kayaks? Daring Nottinghamians first paddled them round Cape Horn in 1977.

Any city, of course, is basically the product of the men (and in this chapter I mean men literally) who shape it and are shaped by it. Who can measure the extent of Nottingham's influence on them and what Nottingham in turn has received from them? In a long, turbulent and inventive history, Nottingham has been like a huge battery, charging its cells from its own and outside current alike, supplying power not only to itself but to the national and international grid.

That most eminent of literary figures associated with Nottingham—George Gordon, Lord Byron—could hardly be classed as a Nottingham man, being born in London, living in Scotland, being educated at Harrow, and roaming the world until his restless heart found peace as the thunder rolled from mountain to mountain in Greece. But although he loved the crumbling magnificence of Newstead, nine miles away, Nottingham must have played a considerable part in his impressionable youth. We have seen already how the poverty and squalor he saw fired him to plead for the desperation of the Luddites. Byron, clubfooted from birth, was sent—at the age of ten, in 1798—to lodge in Nottingham, at 76 St. James's Street. He went frequently to the theatre in St. Mary's Gate. On one occasion his nurse Mary Gray took him to see *The Taming of the Shrew*. In the scene where Catherine is contradicted by Petruchio and says 'Nay you lie, it is the blessed sun', young Geordie, as they called him, jumped excitedly to his feet and cried: 'But I say it is the moon, sir!'

A clash with an elderly eccentric produced what is held to be his earliest effort in poetry. Irritated by her talk about the soul, and how it took flight to the moon after death, the young Byron wrote:

> In Nottingham town, very near to Swine Green
> Lives as curst an old lady as ever was seen,
> And when she does die, which I hope will be soon,
> She firmly believes she will go to the moon.

Looked after by Mrs. Gray, who often beat him or left him unsupervised while she went boozing, Byron had treatment for his foot from a Mr. Lavender, who styled himself a surgeon but who was merely a maker of surgical appliances for the new general hospital across the road. His idea of straightening the twisted foot was to rub it with oil and clamp it agonisingly into a wooden frame. It did irreparable harm.

When the thirty-six-year-old poet died in 1824, killed by incompetent doctors who bled him to death three months after his arrival to lead the Greeks in their insurrection, his body was brought back to England immersed in 180 gallons of spirits. Denied burial by the Dean of Westminster, this 'notorious libertine' set off on the long, last ride to Nottinghamshire. For the first mile or two, the cortège—headed by the hearse, and a coach carrying an urn containing the poet's heart and brain under a velvet pall—was escorted out of London by a procession of fifty carriages. Most of them were empty. The 'best people', who years before had lionised him, stayed away. But Nottingham remembered. As the body lay in state in 'The Blackamoor's Head', the parish church bells tolled, masses of stockingers filed through the room in respectful groups of twenty to pay their last respects to the aristocrat who had fought for them, and next day the mourners stretched for a quarter of a mile.

The Byron vault at Hucknall Torkard was reopened in 1938, and a dozen people gazed down at the taut, yellowing skin of the man who had been the handsome genius of his age. The coffin was stacked on top of that of his grand-uncle, the 'wicked' fifth Baron who, heated with claret after dinner, got into an argument about the best way of preserving game and ran his sword through his kinsman and neighbour William Chaworth.

Today, along a drive heavy with the scent of pines and rhodo-dendrons, the spirit and memories of Byron are preserved by the city of Nottingham. In 1931 Sir Julien Cahn and a previous owner of Newstead, Charles Ian Fraser, gave the historic ruin and its house to the Corporation. The Prime Minister of Greece came to pay homage at the presentation ceremony. The poet's sitting-room and bedroom are as he left them. There are his boxing gloves and fencing sword, the sword and plumed helmet he took to Greece, the collar of his dog Boatswain for whom he erected the elaborate tomb outside, some letters including the one break-ing the news of his death to his half-sister Augusta, some portraits —and a pair of wooden shoe lasts, made for a lame boy.

The chance to enshrine a writer in a stately home is rare. More humble homes are lucky to be left standing at all before fame is assured, and in Nottingham you would have to be very lucky indeed before anybody got round to putting up such a thing as a commemorative plaque. On the old offices of the *Journal* in Pelham Street it is mentioned that Sir James Barrie worked there as a leader-writer in 1883, and there are one or two wishful theories that he got his inspiration for *Peter Pan* while walking in the riverside beauty spot of Clifton Grove. But the native-born writers are given little or no tangible honour. The Victorians did their bit by placing busts in the castle colonnade of Philip James Bailey (1816–1902) who, spasmodically over half a century, eventually doubled his epic poem *Festus* to 40,000 lines; of

William and Mary Howitt; and of Henry Kirke White, ex-butcher's-boy in whom the poet laureate Southey discovered strong marks of genius, but who burned himself out with study at Cambridge at the age of twenty-two, in 1806.

Nottingham has a creditable quota of literary men, although so far only one has been given the Freedom of the City—Cecil Roberts, who received it in 1965, and sometime later found that a mouse, attracted by the waxy parchment, had nibbled the ceremonial scroll. Roberts, who began as a corporation clerk for eight shillings a week when he was fifteen, vowed that he would make £10,000 before he was thirty-five. Turning out novels and plays, lecturing, and becoming the country's youngest daily paper editor (of the Nottingham *Journal*) at twenty-seven, he achieved his aim to be financially independent so that he could live and write anywhere in the world. This spry octogenarian best-seller lived and worked in his beloved Alassio until his death in 1977. His forty books sold twenty-one million copies.

Like him, although born just outside the city in Stapleford, Arthur Mee was another Nottingham newspaperman with a prodigious turn of mind. The son of a militant nonconformist, Mee had a job as a proof-reader's copy-holder on the *Evening Post*, but he sent his first news story—a chapel sermon—to the opposition, the *Express*, where the political outlook was more in sympathy with the opinions of both the preacher and the note-taker. He moved over, as a reporter, to the *Express* when he was sixteen, and five years later was promoted editor of its evening paper the *News* for £2 a week, augmenting his salary with articles for *Titbits*. Mee became journalist-in-chief to British youth with his *Children's Newspaper*, *Children's Encyclopaedia* (fifty fortnightly parts at sevenpence each), *Children's Shakespeare*, and *Children's Bible*. He got through at least a million words a year, giving ten years of his life to his *King's England* survey of 10,000 towns and villages. Throughout eighty volumes, this Peter Pan figure kept his wide-eyed sense of wonder, and although he tended to lay it on thickly about England (his 'little Treasure Island'), he sparked youngsters throughout the world with a thirst for knowledge. He died, aged sixty-eight, in 1943, having refused a title several times.

Nottingham journalism has fostered many celebrated literary birds of passage—Graham Greene, Sir John Hammerton, Sir

Linton Andrews *et al*—following in the exuberant footsteps of Herbert Ingram, a Chapel Bar stationer who founded the *Illustrated London News*, and of George Burbage who for thirty years was owner and printer of the *Journal*. In the Napoleonic wars he would simply add an 'o' or two to the enemy casualty figures, and in this way killed twice as many Frenchmen as there were in France.

But one of the country's best young writers of today—Alan Sillitoe—slogged away making a full-frontal attack on the world of books. Born in 1928 on a council estate in Lenton Abbey, but brought up mainly in the huddled terraces of Radford, Sillitoe failed his eleven-plus twice, took a job drilling holes in plywood, became a capstan lathe operator down the road at Raleighs, and got most of his education reading books while recovering from T.B. with the R.A.F. in Malaya. He served his literary apprenticeship at near-starvation level in a tumbledown cottage on Majorca. His manuscripts rejected countless times, he was on the point of admitting defeat when he tried one last despairing throw. He wrote about what he knew best, his home town. *Saturday Night and Sunday Morning*, published in 1958, filmed two years later, and selling over a million copies in paperback in 1964, was rough and real. Sillitoe wrote his story of a young, hard-drinking, womanising, cycle-worker 'as if with a carpenter's pencil on wallpaper'. With later pieces like the rebellious *Loneliness of the Long Distance Runner* and the strangely tender *The Ragman's Daughter*—for both of which he also wrote the screenplays—Sillitoe, whose seventeenth book came out in 1973, bears indelible marks of his Nottingham background.

Sillitoe's honest, uncompromising defiance has strong bonds with that of D. H. Lawrence, whose genius is appreciated more in Nottingham—'that dismal town where I went to school and college'—than in his home town of Eastwood, nine miles away. They aren't very keen on him in Eastwood. Too many families recognise themselves in the descriptions by 'this mucky man'. Even with Lawrence's tombstone mounted on the wall of the council chamber, the Eastwood Urban District Council refused in 1972 to recommend that his childhood home in Garden Road (The Breach that served as his model for the miners' houses in *Sons and Lovers*) be put on the Historical Buildings preservation list. Left derelict, a target for vandals and an eyesore for tourists,

the house was snapped up for £1,100 when the Association for
Young Writers spotted an unobtrusive advertisement in a Nottingham paper, and only a fierce campaign has since persuaded
the council to turn it and his birthplace into museums.

It would have tickled Lawrence to think of Eastwood still
smarting from its Philistinic image, while Nottingham goes to
town with its massive displays about 'Young Bert' and per-
formances at the Playhouse of *The Daughter-in-law* and *A
Collier's Friday Night*. A new office block has just been christened
'D. H. Lawrence House', a few minutes' walk from the writer's
early haunts in the city.

Actually, Nottingham brought about the creation of Lawrence
himself. His collier father Arthur was a keen dancer who first
met his future wife Lydia Beardsall, freshly jilted by a schoolmaster, in a Nottingham dance hall. In a tape-recorded recollec-
tion, the late Professor David Chambers, whose sister Jessie was
the Miriam of *Sons and Lovers*, remembered: 'When Lydia asked
him what he did for a living, he said he was a contractor. Now
that was strictly true. As a "butty" he contracted to get coal,
employed his own workmen and sold it . . . But of course he
worked down the pit and came home black.'

Young Bert—'a delicate brat with a snuffy nose'—was the first
Eastwood boy to win a scholarship to Nottingham High School.
In the column of the school register describing 'Father's Occupation' the word 'miner' stuck out like a grimy fingerprint
among so many doctors and lawyers and lace manufacturers.
Lawrence spent three years there, until he was fifteen in 1901,
missing daily prayers because of the train timetables from Eastwood, carving his name on a stone windowsill, and having a
quiet and undistinguished career. In his final year he came
fifteenth in his class of nineteen.

For some months he worked as a clerk, translating business
letters for the surgical appliance warehouse of Haywood's in
Castle Gate, Nottingham—the 'insanitary and ancient place' of
Thos. Jordan and Sons in *Sons and Lovers*. He found the high-
spirited, teasing factory girls 'coarse', and it seemed to him
monstrous that a business could be run on wooden legs. But
Haywood's—pulled down in 1960—had an oddly artistic air. For
no other reason than decorative exuberance, the firm's catalogue
interspersed its trusses and elastic stockings with pictures of polar

bears, Zulus, and what Lawrence was to take as his trademark—a phoenix.

Ill with pneumonia, he went back to Eastwood with its 'wilful black dreariness', became an uncertificated teacher at his local chapel, and in 1906 returned for a two-year training course at Nottingham University College. 'To be sure,' he wrote in *The Rainbow*, 'the arches were ugly, the chimney-piece of cardboard-like carved stone with its armorial decoration looked silly just opposite the bicycle stand and the radiator, whilst the great notice board with the fluttering papers seemed to slam away all sense of retreat and mystery from the far wall. Nevertheless, amorphous as it might be, there was in it a reminiscence of the wondrous, cloistral origin of education.'

He had little respect for any of his formal education. 'The profs. in coll.,' he wrote in 1908, 'went on in such a miserable jogtrot, earn-your-money manner that I was startled; then I came to feel that I might as well be taught by gramophones. . . . I doubted them. I began to despise or distrust things. I lost my rather deep religious faith. I lost my idealism and my wistfulness.'

Nottingham University College's final assessment of Lawrence was more charitable. He was 'well read, scholarly and refined', would make an excellent teacher of upper classes, but 'for a large class of boys in a rough district he would not have sufficient persistence and enthusiasm but would become disgusted'.

Nottingham, for all the alleged non-impact of its educational institutions, had as much influence on the budding author as did the area round Eastwood, 'the country of my heart'. His first story was published in the *Weekly Guardian* in 1907—a Christmas tale *A Prelude*—sent under the name of Jessie Chambers. His early books, particularly *The White Peacock* and *Sons and Lovers* are full of references to the city. With his band of Pagans—young teachers and trainees with whom he discussed and dissected life and art—he went frequently to exhibitions of painting at the Castle Museum, or to the Theatre Royal where he saw Sarah Bernhardt in *La Dame aux Camelias* in 1908, and declared that he could love such a woman to madness.

And in 1912, in Nottingham, he found the woman he did love, vividly, stormily, until his death in Vence in 1930. She was thirty-three-year-old Frieda Weekley—wife of his former French professor at the University College; mother of three, a cousin of the

The University; with a bust of Jesse Boot

J. BOOT
FOUNTAIN PLA
DRUGS AND
PROPRIETARY ARTICLES
AT REDUCED PRICES.

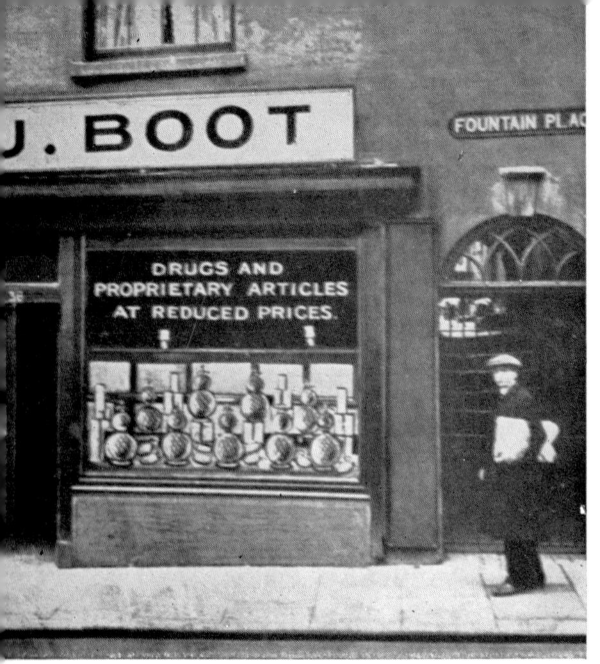

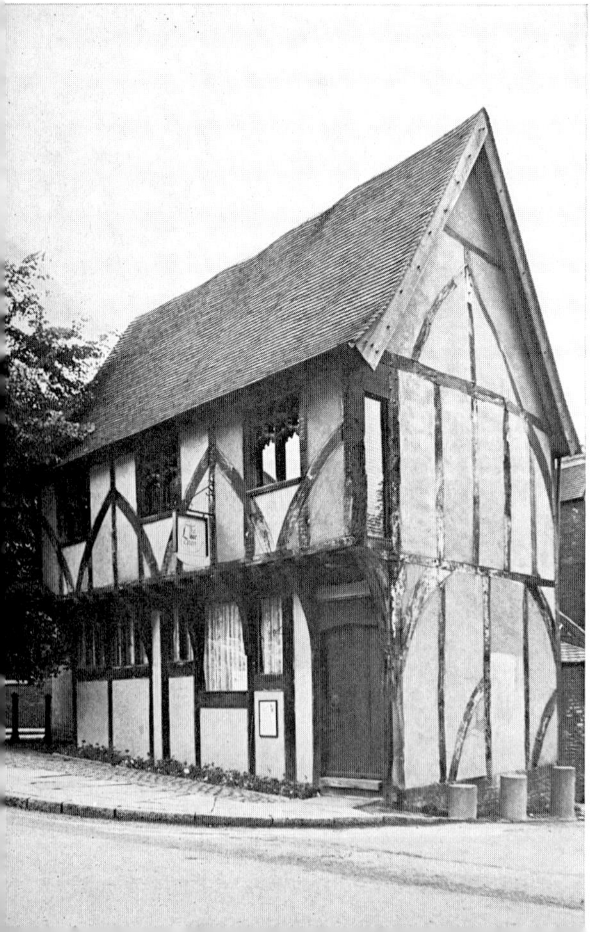

German flying ace Baron von Richthofen, and 'a magnificent, blonde, tall animal'. The ex-student came to lunch at the Weekley's home in Victoria Crescent, Mapperley. Within a month, the collier's son and the aristocrat had run away from Nottingham for ever. He was twenty-seven.

With spectacular figures like Byron and Lawrence on the door-step, one might overlook the less flamboyant. Nottingham, however, has other writers, quietly but vigorously adding to the city's literary laurels.

People such as Stanley Middleton, turning out his novels and scripts in the evenings while by day he teaches English at High Pavement School; Eric Malpass of Long Eaton, who gave up the security of banking to become a professional writer; Malcolm Elwin,[1] with his elegant biographies of Thackeray, De Quincey, and Robert Louis Stevenson.

Like Elwin, Geoffrey Trease is a Nottingham exile—living in a village in the Malvern Hills, but a firm believer in returning to his grass roots at least once a year. His sojourn at Nottingham High School was somewhat happier than that of D. H. Lawrence—he was head boy—and he won a coveted scholarship in classics to Oxford. Gently determined, he carefully cancelled the academic life after a year and plumped for making his living as an author. He struggled along until Robin Hood—in characteristic style—came to his rescue. *Bows Against the Barons*, published in 1934 when he was twenty-five, was a breakthrough in books for children, giving the Sherwood Forest stories a realistically intelligent flavour far removed from the patriotic *Boys' Own Paper* pap usually served up. Since then, Trease has earned his just reputation as one of the country's most respected and prolific writers. Of his ninety-two books, over forty are still in print, a record unsurpassed by any living British author. They range from adventure yarns for children to lucid studies of Byron and Lawrence for teenagers. And his loving sketches of Nottingham make him an eminently fit companion for such historians as Thoroton, Deering, Blackner, Wood and Gray and for all the others who have laboured to chronicle this town with scholarship.

These historians could fill volumes about the 'migrants' who, arriving from other parts of the country, have tapped the energy

[1] Died October, 1973.

Jesse Boot's first shop, in Goose Gate
"Severn's" medieval building near the castle

of Nottingham and in return have given it a boost. The poet John Drinkwater who at sixteen worked as an insurance company's office boy; so poor that he bought rotten fruit to eke out his threepenny lunch. The hopeful Donald Wolfit, playing truant from Newark to cycle over for matinées at the Theatre Royal. Hugh Gaitskell, teaching out-of-work miners at the Workers' Educational Association in the 'twenties. John Neville, ex-darling of the Old Vic, turning his back on the West End to prove that Nottingham Playhouse was better. William Wallett, the circus clown who recited chunks of Shakespeare, who amused Queen Victoria so much that he called himself 'The Queen's Jester', and who once stepped into a Nottingham pawnbroker's shop and pledged himself for £10 as a publicity stunt. Composer Eric Coates from nearby Hucknall.

But even without the obvious choices—an angry William Booth, marching verminous outcasts into the respectable pews of his Wesleyan chapel . . . the crippled millionaire Jesse Boot, able to summon his secretary only by inserting an arthritic finger in a loop in his coat lapel—what of the real Nottinghamians?

The net is cast wide. The Archbishop of York, Richard Sterne, who died in 1684, was from Nottingham. And so is the present Dean of Westminster, the Very Reverend Eric Abbott. Queen Elizabeth's royal beasts were specially carved for her Coronation by James Woodford—whose work includes his city's Robin Hood statue and decorations for S.S. *Queen Mary*. Sculptor to the Prince Regent and to King William IV, John Charles Felix Rossi (son of a Sienna-born doctor in Nottingham) provided many of the finest pieces in Buckingham Palace and St. Paul's Cathedral. William Clayton is the world's leading exponent of the *trompe l'œil* style of painting.

Harry Rowe, one of the most famous puppet showmen of the eighteenth century, was originally intended for the Church by his schoolmaster father. But he ran away to join the army, fought at Culloden, and knocked about the country as a 'groaner', or fake patient to quack doctors, before marrying a widow who owned a touring puppet company.

There was nothing of the fake about Dr. John Higginbottom, Fellow of the Royal Society and a pioneer in the use of nitrate of silver in nineteenth-century medicine. As long ago as 1844 he published warnings about the dangers of smoking.

For twenty-five years, until 1798, another F.R.S., the Reverend George Walker, the silver-tongued minister of High Pavement Chapel, led the intellectual life in Nottingham. One of his petitions for Parliamentary reform in 1793 was so free in its language that the Prime Minister, William Pitt, condemned it as disrespectful to the House.

Like Byron, the Arnold-born artist Richard Parkes Bonington (1802–28) spent most of his life abroad, but before he died at twenty-six he ranked with the landscape painters Turner and Constable. The eighteenth-century brothers Paul and Thomas Sandby had an immense influence on English water-colour painting. Nottingham artists also gave to the world some of the most famous cartoon characters of the twentieth century. Tom Fisher was responsible for the cap-askew, socks-down William of the Richmal Crompton books. Tom Browne, who as a teenage lithographic apprentice often sketched the Cervantes characters of Don Quixote and Sancho Panza, used them to create those lovable tramps Weary Willie and Tired Tim. Born in 1896 as Weary Waddles and Tired Timmy, they took over the front page of the comic *Chips* for fifty years. And Dudley Watkins, who died in 1969, came up with a host of people, from Lord Snooty to Desperate Dan, for the *Beano* and *Dandy* comics.

George Green, a miller's son from Sneinton, was hardly recognised in his lifetime (1793–1841), but his mathematical researches in electricity and magnetism have won him acclaim as an innovator in scientific progress. The Willoughbys of Wollaton produced their crop of explorers and naturalists; the Lowes, with their mansion at Highfields hung with Rembrandts and Gainsboroughs, fostered a crop of botanists and meteorologists. It was a Nottingham man, Sir Charles Fellows, who brought the Xanthian Marbles to the British Museum. And another, George Vason—who went out to Tonga as a missionary in 1796—was the first white man ever to be made a South Sea Island's chief. By that time he had packed up his missionary aims and turned native—tattoos, several wives and all. Homesick for Nottingham, he worked his passage back via China and finished up as keeper of the work-house and governor of Nottingham gaol.

The number of 'local boys' now making good in national life is considerable. The new chairman of the Bank of England, Gordon William Richardson; the Official Solicitor Norman

Turner; the trades union organiser Frank Cousins; Douglas Houghton from Long Eaton, who became chairman of the Parliamentary Labour Party in 1967 and a life peer in 1974.

The world of show business is full of them—dancer Douglas Squires (another Long Eaton product) of television's *Young Generation* fame; comedian Leslie Crowther; opera singer John Brecknock (long Eaton); actors Richard Beckinsale*, Michael Jayston, John Turner, Brian Smith, Barry Foster, John Bird; dramatist Roy Minton; octogenarian 'drag' comedian Douglas Byng, who in the heyday of the Cochrane and Charlot revues starred in cabaret at the Cafe de Paris longer than anybody.

Nottingham has always loved a colourful character—whether Ned Dawson, the true-blue Tory of 1828 who kept that blue coffin as a cupboard; or rose grower Harry Wheatcroft with his eye-opening check suits, overblown side-whiskers and rose-pink Rolls.

But perhaps best of all, it admires a fighter. Albert Ball, the boy wonder of the Royal Flying Corps, who dodged about the skies of France—sometimes in his pyjamas—shooting down forty-two enemy planes, collecting the V.C., the M.C., two D.S.O.s and death in the process. Tom Blower, who in 1947, defied the waves to become the first man to swim the Irish Channel. Doug Scott, in 1975 the first to conquer Everest by the fearsome south west face. Or Bendigo. . . .

Bendigo was a boxer, the bare-knuckle champion of England in the days when pugilists hammered at each other with their fists. One of triplets, from a slum brood of twenty-one, he got his nickname when a friend called the trio Shadrach, Meshach and Abednego. His real name was William Thompson; a tough lad, knocking about with the Lambs in their tussles with the police. He could throw a cricket ball 115 yards and a stone 200 yards. He tossed a half-brick, left-handed, 75 yards across the Trent, won second, third, fourth and fifth prizes in an All-England fishing match, and saved three people from drowning. A racehorse, a town in Australia, and bottled beer have been named after him.

The first recorded southpaw in the annals of the ring, he would mill it with his opponents for a hundred rounds or more. To win the championship belt took over three hours. When his fighting

Died March 1979.

days were over, Bendigo, somewhat punch-drunk, turned to the
bottle. Sometimes he would strip a butcher's shop and toss out
all the joints into the street. Or seek out a policeman who happened to bear the same name as an old rival and beat him up. He
was gaoled twenty-eight times.

But as he grew older he grew gentler, fishing quietly with his
pet monkey on his shoulder. Then at the age of sixty he saw the
light. Converted at a revivalist meeting, he became a star per-
former on gospel platforms, delivering racy testimony that King
Jesus had licked him in the first round. The well-known hymn
was amended:

> Praise God from whom all blessings flow,
> Praise Him for Brother Bendigo . . .

He had his own way of dealing with troublemakers, laying his
Bible on one side and wading in 'until the Ebenezer Chapel
looked more like a knacker's yard' while he ensured that:

> Five repentant fighting men were sitting in a row,
> Listenin' to words of grace from Mister Bendigo.
> Listenin' to his reverence, all as good as gold—
> Pretty little baa-lambs gathered to the fold.

In his seventieth year, Bendigo fought his last round. He died
in 1880, his huge gnarled fist clasping that of an old fellow
pugilist. His funeral cortège was followed by thousands, in a
procession a mile long, who stopped to sing hymns such as
Welcome Home and *The Sweet Bye and Bye*. And on his grave in
Bath Street cemetery they placed a gleaming, white, recumbent
stone lion.

Tough, brave, hard drinking, reformed, religious Bendigo. In
many ways he was the typical Nottinghamian.

TEN

IN PRAISE OF WOMEN

The train of coaches filled with the beauties of the north . . .
—Daniel Defoe at Nottingham races

NOTTINGHAM is famous for its pretty girls, plenty of them. Two for every man, I was assured with a nudge and a wink when I said I was going to live there. I doubt if the proportion was ever that high, even though the 1901 census showed a preponderance of 16,000 women in a city of 240,000 people. Today the sexes seem roughly equal, but the women have the slight edge—104 to every 100 males.

The prettiness of the girls, of course, is open to challenge, depending on the boasts of your own town. It is one of those claims which have sunk into the folklore of Nottingham and are perpetuated with pride. Requests for pen-pals (with pin-up pictures) continue to arrive steadily from men—mostly sailors—who quote the legend and demand to be put in touch.

There is no denying that Nottingham girls are handsome. They are also well built and jolly. The intermingling of Anglo-Saxon, Danish and Norman blood has somehow produced a soft, peach-like complexion, with hair that varies from striking blonde to an intriguing, blue-black sheen. And the settling of over 20,000 immigrants, from anywhere from Jamaica to the Ukraine, is contributing to the variety. For 'pretty', perhaps read 'happy'. Nottingham's women live in a women's town. Conscious of their reputation, they demand—and get—good clothes, good shops, good design and, on the whole, good wages. And why not? They make them all possible.

The city's manufacturers depend hugely on women and always have done. There were over 12,000 factory girls way back in the 1880s. Of today's Big Three, Boots' 8,000 employees are mostly women. So are over half of Player's 8,000. Out of a work force of 7,000, Raleigh's have 1,500 women. They would all be in dire trouble if the married ones alone decided to down tools. So would the hosiery trade—three-quarters female—or the lace and net industry in which women account for sixty per cent of the employees. Because of its light industries, Nottingham employs twice the percentage of women in manufacturing as does its close neighbour Derby.

In the Nottingham area, some forty-one per cent of the occupied population is engaged in transport and public utilities, the distributive trades, banking, insurance, educational and professional services and public administration. Nearly half of these are women and girls. Throughout the country, the proportion of women in jobs is about thirty-five per cent. Nottingham goes four per cent higher.

So the city woos its women, anxious to supply convenient hours such as the early evening 'twilight shift', the lure of hairdressing facilities, swimming pools and visits from pop stars, and the occasional provision of nurseries like the twenty-four-hour crêche at the City Hospital to tempt married nurses back into the wards.

The men of Nottingham could hardly have been so 'spirited and disputatious' without the backing of their womenfolk. Eighteenth- and nineteenth-century Nottingham women gained a national reputation for their reactions against their depressing living conditions. When the government refused to do anything about the failing hosiery industry, they led the rush to break every pane of glass in the hosiers' houses. In 1812 it was women who started a riot over the price of bread, brandishing a ha'penny loaf which had been streaked with red ochre, draped with black and stuck on a fishing rod, emblematic of 'Bleeding Famine Decked In Sackcloth'. At a time when women were of little account except as mere toilers and breeders, Nottingham women formed a political union in support of Chartism. Their militancy is made clear in a letter they wrote in 1838 to the Chartist newspaper *The Northern Star* in which they told of 'millions sickened and wearied of an existence embittered to the last moment by cruelty, misrule and oppression'. Rather than die by famine they 'would glory in seeing every working man in England selling his coat to buy a sword or a rifle'. Only thirty years previously, a wife and her two children had been meekly sold in Nottingham Market Place for 27/6d.

The present generation of women comes from ancestors who believed in doing things and having their say—if only like Tom Booth's wife in the 1750s. Booth was a poacher, and so proud of it that he had a tombstone carved before his death, eulogising his exploits. He left spaces for the dates of his demise and that of his wife. His was duly filled in in 1752 but the widow, annoyed at having her name on a tombstone while she was still living, gave instructions that she be buried elsewhere. The inscription in St. Nicholas's churchyard is incomplete to this day.

The town's history is peppered with memories of strong-minded women. In 1513 Dame Agnes Mellers used some of her late husband's fortune from bellfounding to endow the most important school in Nottingham, the Boys' High School, whose castellated walls now overlook the Arboretum. She was pre-pared to endow the whole school herself but, as businesslike as her husband had been, persuaded practically every other notable to help—accepting anything from a mayoral gift to the odd six-pence. She drew up elaborate documents for a Corporation Trust to manage the school, and arranged for Masses for herself and spouse at commemoration services, including such items as four shillings and sixpence for cheese and ale on Founder's Day. It is a custom still kept up on June 16 in the Lord Mayor's parlour, when groats are handed over to councillors who can prove that they sat through all of the service at St. Mary's that morning.

A more humble bequest literally comes ringing across the ages, at St. Peter's church, through a bell presented in 1543 by an ex-washerwoman called Margaret Doubleday. She added a legacy of 20/– a year for the sexton to ring the bell at 4 a.m. so that the washerwomen would not be late for work. Fortunately he doesn't, nowadays.

A couple of dozen widows and unmarried people over sixty have a home on London Road—once the only entrance from the south—thanks to the almshouses built in 1859 by a quiet spinster. Ann Burton inherited her fortune from her father, a prosperous saddler. She had plans for more almshouses—but she died sud-denly before signing the will, and her cousin (whom she disliked intensely, and who was far less charity-minded) inherited the lot.

The health of Nottingham children owes much to Lady Mary

Wortley Montague, daughter of the Earl of Kingston, whose mansion was in Stoney Street before it was taken over by lace men. Living in Turkey with her ambassador husband she learned about inoculation against smallpox and faced a clamour of protest when in 1718 she introduced it to this country by testing it on her own child. The clergy rose in wrath in their pulpits against this tampering with providence, but her example emboldened a Nottingham surgeon to practise inoculation in the town in 1766, a year after her death.

Not all the Kingston family were as sweetly disposed as Lady Mary. The second Earl married a woman who—apart from being a bigamist—spent most of her time tormenting him. Her final wish was that her coffin be chained to his in the vault of Holme Pierrepont church, just outside Nottingham. The wish was never granted.

More edifying is the story of the romance between a Royalist and a Roundhead. During the Civil War, which spluttered intensely around Nottingham, innumerable country houses were held for one side or the other by small bodies of troops. In the highest romantic tradition, Agnes Willoughby—from the Royalist Aspley Hall, near the family seat at Wollaton—was saved from three rapists by a gallant young Captain Thornhagh who commanded the Parliamentary garrison at Broxtowe Hall, a mile or so away. He was sauntering in quiet meditation, Bible in hand, when he heard her cries. Pocketing his Bible and exchanging it for a pistol, he leapt to the rescue. Despite the peril to himself, he escorted her back home and kept calling on her, and they fell in love. He was a rebel and a heretic; she a royalist and a papist. Each was convinced that the other's beliefs could lead only to damnation.

The affair finished abruptly when Thornhagh was ordered to join Colonel Hutchinson at Nottingham Castle, and was killed in the assault on Shelford Hall. The heartbroken Agnes put on her shabbiest dress, resolved never to marry, and for the next sixty years devoted her life to piety and charity.

It was a woman who started the Children's Hospital in 1869. And the extensive Royal Midland Institution for the Blind at the top of Chaucer Street came about through the small house for the blind which Mary Chambers set up in Park Street. She died in 1848, totally blind, an expert in ancient and modern languages.

Her raised globe and arithmetic working board are kept on view in the Institution.

In her way, Kitty Hudson, too, contributed to Nottingham's medical knowledge. In 1783 Kitty was admitted to the new general hospital where she was its ninth and oddest patient. From the age of six she had swept the pews and aisles of churches. Any pins she found she would store in her mouth. After accidentally swallowing a few she eventually got to like the taste—and reached the point when she could not sleep or eat without gulping a few. The surgeons removed hundreds of pins and needles from her, and dozens more kept surfacing through the flesh over a period of two years. This human pincushion was twenty when finally declared pin-free and discharged. She lived to bear nineteen children, not one of them resembling a hedgehog.

She was not the only tough woman in Nottingham. Mary Ryley, who died in the work-house in 1739 aged at least a hundred, was more than ninety when she last left it and walked to London to visit relatives. Having tired of them, she walked back. In the same institution there died in 1797 another woman pauper who was always thought to have been a man. She had been a jockey and the 'father' of several illegitimate children.

The women of Nottingham have a long tradition of asserting their equality, even if sometimes they took it to extremes. Such as Joan Phillips who was hanged as a highwaywoman at the end of Wilford Lane in 1685; or Phoebe Harris, a century later, who provided a crowd of 20,000 outside London's Newgate Gaol with a memorable spectacle when she was half strangled then burnt alive as a forger of coins.

Women's Lib, as such, may not then have existed in the form of an organised movement, but Nottingham women have never been found lacking in spirit. When, during the Civil War, there arose the danger of royalist saboteurs setting fire to the town, posses of fifty sharp-eyed women patrolled the streets with the vigilance of today's lady traffic wardens. In the early eighteenth century, Anne Ayscough carried on not only her late husband's newspaper but his fiery, radical spirit as well. Like him, she was summonsed for 'printing and publishing several scandalous and indecent expressions tending to bring the King's ministers of state into contempt'.

Many others have suffered for their beliefs. In 1785 the foetid cells beneath the Shire Hall held two sisters, Protestant dissenters from the village of Calverton—of knitting machine fame—who refused to accept the validity of the Church of England's wedding ceremony. They were actually incarcerated for ten years until, embarrassed by John Howard's exposure of the case, the authorities 'accidentally' left the gaol gates open long enough for them to escape.

It was women who were most active in the field of early education. In 1885, they ran sixty-nine of the eighty private schools in Nottingham. Five years later they campaigned to bring about the General School for Women, a type of domestic science college formed by the amalgamation of the School of Cookery and the medical-sounding 'Ladies Sanitary Association'. And when the call came from the Suffragette movement, Nottingham women girded up their voluminous skirts, burned down the Boat Club, tried to blow up the G.P.O., dropped tubes of phosphorus into pillar boxes, and braved heckling and stink-bombs. Mrs. Edith Annie Lees, a founder member of the city's branch of the National Council of Women, left her husband and two small children so that she might break windows in London and be carted off to Bow Street.

The same kind of energy manifests itself in many other ways . . . the setting up of a Women's Centre where women can find out about anything from abortion to family allowances . . . a keenness to start football teams . . . a vast interest in health and keep-fit classes . . . an avid joining of evening classes, to study ancient architecture or modern management methods. The women of the city will have a go at most things—learning Russian, writing short stories, running Brownie packs, staging plays, going fishing, joining music clubs or smashing about in Bomber Cars. The place is alive with their interests.

It would be hard to find a city more liberally stocked with women's clubs and societies and committees—The Towns-women's Guild, The Abstinence Union, political groups, The Soroptimists, The Zionist Women's Association, The Gas Federation, Miners' Welfare, ladies' circles, business and professional clubs, widows' clubs, Young Homemakers, The Mothers' Union, Women's Institutes—everything from the Railway Women's Guild to the Electrical Association for Women. And they do not meet merely to eye each other's hats, either.

They get down to studying the eroding effects of loneliness; the neuroses of living in high-rise flats; the problem of losing friends in slum clearance schemes. They are concerned with the plight of the old, the sixteen per cent rise in the V.D. rate, the increase in 'battered baby' cases. They make their feelings known about underpaid woman hosiery workers who take home £9 for a forty-hour week; criticise Nottingham for having only five family-planning clinics for 40,000 women—and get the number doubled. Collectively their influence can be considerable. The Nottingham Standing Conference of Women's Organisations, for example, sends delegates from forty-nine organisations in the area, representing 30,000 women, framing resolutions on topics from drug addiction to dog licences.

Women's groups keep a wary eye on the planners. They help sonsumer councils in surveys, and designers in details. It is one thing to make an aloof judgement and phrase a vague resolution; and another to block a road with prams to point the need for a school-crossing warden. Nottingham women are quick to adopt both methods of approach. And they keep up a constant and prodigious flow of help for the handicapped, the needy and the deprived. The mainsprings behind the voluntary movements are women.

They have an honourable tradition going back to the last quarter of the last century, when it became clear that social injustice would not be remedied overnight but that the sufferings of the poor demanded immediate action. Women—who at an earlier date could not have ventured alone in some parts of the town without risk of theft or harm—began to take over much of the day-to-day work of relief and charity. Typical of their day were the Nottingham Town and County Social Guild (modelled in 1875 on the lines of Octavia Hill's Charity Organisation Society in London six years earlier), and the Nottingham Society for Organising Charity. Both were designed to locate the 'deserving poor' and co-ordinate the efforts of philanthropists and the Poor Law authorities. One of their methods of finding the deserving poor, incidentally, was to offer any applicant for relief as much bread as he could eat, on the principle that if he could make a meal of bread and water it was pretty good evidence that he was deserving.

In the face of a tidal wave of poverty, it was like sweeping back the sea. But the well-meaning middle-class ladies of Nottingham battled on, organising soup kitchens, convalescent homes and recreation rooms, loan clubs and cheap meals. At least they threw out a life-line.

The volunteer helpers of today are by no means confined to middle-class do-gooders with time on their hands and their sights on an O.B.E. Women of all classes and all ages know that, despite the Welfare State and the general affluence of Nottingham, poverty, squalor and loneliness are plentiful—if writ smaller. Accordingly, the city's women—most of them busy enough in their own homes anyway—put in countless hours behind the scenes to help others. For every one of the social set, whose photos recur in the glossy magazines—raising spectacular funds for charities to the accompaniment of champagne suppers—there are a hundred anonymous helpers flogging tickets for coffee-mornings, collecting cast-off clothes for a jumble sale, scrubbing out bedpans in hospitals, cleaning up smelly old houses, patching a crumbling marriage, listening to the rambling of a lonely pensioner, talking a would-be suicide out of it, mending broken toys to fetch a few pence in a charity shop, winkling gifts from firms for the tombola stall, borrowing treasured lists of those who will rally round, or dreaming up fresh ideas so that fatherless children can go to the seaside or spastics will get their mini-bus.

Nottingham took a step in advance of many towns by encouraging women to enrol at its University College right from the start. The Nottingham School of Art had already flourished since 1865, although with characteristic Victorian modesty it refused to let its female students paint from nude models. The most illustrious woman trained there—Laura Knight, the only painter ever to be created a Dame—had to wait until she and her husband Harold had gone to live on the Yorkshire coast before they could paint the female nude. They took their models swimming, in the sunlight among remote rocks.

Dame Laura, who died in 1970 a month before her ninety-third birthday, lived in Nottingham from the time when she was a small child and her family moved from neighbouring Long Eaton. Until she left the town at the age of twenty, she often shouldered her way through the raucous splendour of the Goose Fair, as the steam organs blared in the Market Square. But she never painted it. Instead the gaudy excitement seeped into her heart and eyes, storing up for the pictures that made her famous—the paintings of acrobats and scenes backstage in theatres, the warm, vigorous studies of circus people and gipsies. But her first pictures in Nottingham were of children, youngsters willing to model for her for a penny a morning and a cup of coffee with a biscuit, all the young artist could afford.

Dame Laura Knight, Royal Academician since 1903, and commissioned to paint the Nuremburg war criminals' trials, was an exceptional woman for any country or any city. Nottingham has fostered a smattering of women of reasonable success in the fields of art and writing—for example Mary Gillick who sculpted the Queen Elizabeth II head on our coinage; the Victorian children's artist Kate Greenaway, who was educated at the University College; Hilda Lewis, whose book about a deaf child called Mandy made a compassionate film; Helen Cresswell, with her stories for children. . . . But Nottingham has failed to supply many notable actresses, singers (with the glowing exception of Constance Shacklock, Covent Garden's principal mezzo-soprano for ten years until 1956), dancers, or even—surprising in view of that reputation for pulchritude—beauty queens, until Miss Great Britain in 1972.

But within the confines of the city, the influence of Nottingham's women is still sweetly formidable, just as it was in the eighteenth century when the soirées of the gentry at the Assembly Rooms on Low Pavement were run by a ladies committee with such rules as 'No attorney's clerk shall be admitted' or 'No lady is allowed to dance in a long white apron'. Nottingham has more than its share of female doctors, lawyers, management executives, taxi drivers, and even company chairmen. 'The media'—newspapers, magazines, radio, advertising and public relations—are full of them. The central library owes its vast local history section, of 30,000 volumes, to the labour and perky zeal of Lucy Edwards who, often sitting at D. H. Lawrence's old desk, has built up and catalogued a unique collection of material consulted by scholars throughout the world. Thanks to her fourteen-year stint with the section, Nottingham has the finest collection of Lawrentiana in the world outside of America. After forty-four years with the library, Miss Edwards retired at the beginning of 1973, and, as an expert on Byron (she is an officer of the Byron Society) immediately fell to organising a multi-nation trip to

Missolonghi in the following year, the 150th anniversary of the poet's death.

Over at the University, Dr. Elizabeth Newson, with her doctor husband, has been conducting important surveys in child training and development, including long-term research with 700 Nottingham mothers and their offspring. Another doctor, Jocelyn Rose, proved her point as an authority on natural child-birth by panting a running commentary into radio microphones as her fifth baby was born.

Technically, Ailsa Stanley is a Yorkshire woman, but she has been in Nottingham long enough to claim citizenship. The weekly column which she has conducted for years in the local press gathers much material from organisations which she not only reports but in which she plays a leading part. As well as being a leading light in practically every local activity involving women, and a J.P., she has made her mark nationally by serving with the British Standards Institute and being for the first three years the only woman on the Metrication Board.

Alderman Joan Case brought new lustre and warmth to Nottingham's politics by being the first woman to don the Lord Mayor's chain of office in 1968–9. (Gallantly the Corporation bought her a feminine tricorne.) She commanded the respect and admiration of fellow councillors and officials steeped in generations of masculine domination—and enchanted hundreds of children by encouraging them to have a look round the hallowed fastness of the Council House. Across the river at County Hall her counterpart Alderman Anne Yates joined her in showing that politics were all the better for a woman's touch, or rather grasp. As first woman chairman of the Nottinghamshire County Council, Mrs Yates cheerily took on a 'housekeeping' budget of £32,000,000. With a flair for publicity, and the number plate ANN 1 on her official limousine, she gamely flew in aeroplanes and climbed firemen's ladders—and was elected for a second three-year term of office. (The number plate, incidentally, was given to Princess Anne as a wedding present.)

The Nottingham woman has survived history with patience and resilience. She has been flogged in the market place, ducked as a scold, burned as a witch, auctioned for as little as a shilling; she has suffered the treadmill and the work-house, and hauled coal-tubs with chains biting into her pregnant belly. Ravaged by 'phossy jaw', she has earned 5/– a week in the phosphorus-match factories of the 1850s and seen her children haunt-eyed and swollen with starvation.

She has come through it all remarkably unbitter. After a generation or two of comparative prosperity she is confident, relaxed, well informed and well cared for.

A Nottingham woman shows warmth and ready neighbourliness without crashing into other people's privacy. Without being Amazonian, she is still tough. As any cinema manager can testify, she weeps at sentimental films; but when the gory scenes come on it is the men who do the passing out.

She is resourceful—and one factory worker has reason to be grateful for it. Accidentally sprayed by acid, he rushed into a room staffed by girls who stripped every stitch from him, hosed him down, and saved his skin if not his blushes.

She is kind—like the nurse who spent her entire leave making 3,000 jars of marmalade to pay off the debt on a church hall. She is active—like the girl who nips off to Wales most weekends to clean locomotives and shovel coal on the Festiniog Railway.

She can be jealous. The city's public analyst can vouch for that from those wives who bring in their husbands' hankies to check lipstick marks. She has a sense of humour—like the woman who left the note for her milkman: Please close the gate after you, as the birds get in and peck the tops off the bottles.

As in the case of Jesse Boot's wife, who gave him the idea of selling cosmetics and lending books in his chemist's shops, she is ambitious for her man but not to the point of henpeckery. Independent, she is not fanatical about it. The buses rarely bristle with hostile females glaring down at seated men. Yet when she encounters male stupidity—such as installing a television camera 'for security reasons' in the ladies' lavatory of a new factory—she sounds off with acid derision.

No one has ever done a Kinsey-type study of the Nottingham woman's sex life. But her attitude is liberally forthright without being crude. She can take a blue joke, but knows when to get gently starchy with exuberant *raconteurs*. There is no evidence that she is any more 'easy' than anybody else. The high illegitimacy figures—which as recently as 1968 were twice the national average—seem to indicate lack of knowledge rather than lack of morals.

Lord Byron's house in St. James's Street

ST JAMES'S STREET

Considering their famed good looks, Nottingham's girls are not very keen on parading themselves. It is a constant source of amazement that the majority of entrants in the Nottingham heats of beauty contests are from elsewhere. Women were less bashful in 1717, if this advertisement in the *Nottingham Weekly Courant* is anything to go by:

Any able Young Man, strong in the Back and endow'd with a good Carnal Weapon with all the appurtenances thereto belonging in good repair, may have half-a-Crown per Night, a pair of clean sheets and other necessaries, to perform Nocturnal Services on one Sarah Yates, whose husband having for these nine Months past lost the use of his Peacemaker, the unhappy woman is thereby driven to the last Extremity.

Gone like the kiss of first love is that day in the 1750s when the entire town turned out to see Mayor Trigge's daughter married to her dashing Lord Lyttelton. The Hen Cross in the square, where the women sold their poultry and garden produce, was garlanded with flowers and loveknots. The bride had a dowry of £30,000, and the wedding procession included the empty carriage —drawn by horses in black harness and a coachman in deep mourning—of an erstwhile suitor who had caught a chill and died on their proposed wedding day. But Nottingham women are still as romantic. They prefer to marry in church, although 1,400 a year pass through the old registry office in Shakespeare Street, now tarted up with soft lights and sweet music. There is still a fondness for bridal archways—even though they range from uplifted T.V. tubes to the crossed jibs of a brace of building cranes.

Organisers of a national contest once discovered that Nottingham men write the best love letters; no doubt because the women of Nottingham know how to inspire them.

Interior of the Nottingham Playhouse

ELEVEN

AS SHE IS SPOKE

'Ay up, mester!'
—Nottinghamese for 'Good morning, Sir'

ONE of the first plays staged by the Nottingham Playhouse when it moved into its new theatre was, almost inevitably, an adaptation of *Saturday Night and Sunday Morning*. Already the film version had given a view of the city rather different from its usual role as mediaeval backdrop to a spring-heeled Robin Hood. Not without a certain resulting coolness, either. During the location shooting of Karel Reisz's film, one local brewery declined to have its products in a pub scene because *Saturday Night and Sunday Morning*, with its beer-swilling 'hero' and its backstreet abortions, was obviously going to give Nottingham a bad name.

The film men pressed on, typical of the post-war wave of potent new writers, directors and actors, who had set about the posh accents of the arts, their talents as sharp as flick-knives. The Queen of the Midlands emerged with a face that was homely, tough and raddled—but real. And with a real voice, too; or as real as you could get without a cast of genuine Nottinghamians.

There is something about the way Nottingham people speak which eludes actors. Albert Finney (who comes from Salford) played the cycle worker Arthur Seaton with cantankerous virility, knocking off bike spindles and mate's wife with equal aplomb. But even with the advantage of having the authentic article by his side—author Alan Sillitoe who wrote his own screenplay—Mr. Finney couldn't quite get the accent. Neither could Londoner Ian McKellen, when Frank Dunlop directed the live play in 1964. The film and stage people studied hours of conversations tape-recorded by a Nottingham family, including a Mrs. Gubbins type Grandma. But the result was still that hybrid blend of Yorkshire/Lancashire which satisfies most of the country.

Not that your native Nottinghamian could really tell you what his accent sounds like. It has not the outlandish quality of the Geordie's, the distinction of the Irishman's, the clarity of the Scot's. A man in Devon or Norfolk can be so unintelligible that the stranger staggers away and writes off the conversation. But even at its worst, broad Nottingham is still comprehensible. With certain key words you can get by without much strain. If, that is, you are prepared to accept that Nottinghamese has something of the harsh clatter of the Brummie, gleanings of t'Northerner, spatterings of the Derbyshire yokel—and imports from outlying districts which, even ten miles from the Old Market Square, have a flavour of their own.

No one could blame the actors in *Saturday Night and Sunday Morning*. Even the true *homo Nottinghamensis*, once he has slipped out of his mother speech, finds it hard to slip back in.

The people of Nottingham have never been ones to ape the tones of the home counties, and are too independent to let their speech slide into what could be called 'Northern'. The end product, like so many things in Nottingham, is neither one thing nor the other—not fiercely individual, nor yet weak enough to be nondescript.

But a Nottingham accent is stubbornly there, and the visitor cannot go far wrong if he has a grasp of two basic essentials.

The first is that any person in Nottingham—man, woman or child—can be referred to as 'Me duck'; a nice, cosy, inoffensive description if ever there was one. The second thing to remember is the key greeting 'Ay up!', meaning, subject to shades of subtlety, 'Hello'. If it came to a push, a man could live most of his life in Nottingham with a vocabulary restricted to 'Ay up' and 'Me duck!' And by adding a single 'then' to 'Ay up!', he need never utter another word.

For 'Ay up, then!' is capable of infinite variation. According to inflection, it can convey, with ease and beautiful economy, the whole range of emotion. A couple of early morning workers, passing each other in the dawn, can put a wealth of meaning into this laconic exchange.

'Ay up, then!' says one of them, levelly and unemotionally. He is saying 'Good morning! Nice to see you. Hope you're all right.'

'Ay up, then!' replies the other. But depending on tone, raised eyebrow or jerk of the lip, he is conveying information ranging from 'Hurry up, you're late!' to 'It's been a hell of a shift and No. 3 turbine has been playing up again, to say nothing of the foreman's ulcer.'

Said cheerily, 'Ay up, then!' is recognised as a torrent of verbiage. ('I trust the world is going well with you and yours' . . . 'Kindly give my regards to your wife and family' . . . 'Yes, I'm feeling on top of the world' . . . Every expression of goodwill you care to mention.)

By the most delicate elevation or depression of timbre this eloquent phrase can be used to cover the gamut of feeling, from tenderness to raging anger, from incredulity to resignation. It serves equally well a policeman pushing his way through a crowd to a fight on Saturday night, and a youth on a Sunday morning stroll watching the girls and weighing up his chances of 'gerrin' off' with one of them.

For the more advanced student, the following is a glossary of useful words and syntax that will stand him in good stead in Nottingham. (Pronounced, by the way, '*Nott*-ingum', never in the American style 'Notting-*ham*'):

MEMBERS OF THE FAMILY

Our Mam . . . My dear mother
Our Dad . . . My beloved father
Our Sis . . . My charming sister
Our Fred, Ron, Bert, etc. . . . . My stupid brother

COMMON WORDS

Bobbo . . . horse
Corsă . . . pavement
Frit . . . afraid
Mardy . . . surly, complaining, malcontent, disgruntled, etc.
Mester . . . Sir, Mr., head of the house, gentleman, teacher, policeman, visitor, rent collector, etc.
Nesh . . . squeamish, afraid of cold, faint-hearted, half mardy and half frit
Pumpture . . . puncture
Snap . . . food

Sustificut . . . certificate (usually medical)
Twitchell . . . lane, cut-through
Welloes . . . rubber boots
Wok . . . work
Yo . . . you

TERMS OF ABUSE (*equally ENDEARMENT*)

Nig-nog . . . usually 'Yo right nig-nog!' (non-racial)
Nit . . . usually 'Yo great steamin' nit!'
Bogger . . . usually 'Yo'm gettin' a nesh, mardy bogger!'

USEFUL PHRASES

What's gooin' off? . . . What's going on?
Wairza boozer? . . . Could you direct me to the local?
Innit cowd . . . Rather chilly today
Intitot . . . Rather warm today
Arkattit . . . Listen to the rain
Ah, shut your whittlin'! . . . Would you mind not complaining
  so much!
Itz black over Bill's Muthaz . . . It looks like rain
D'yah g'dahn, then? . . . Have you been to the football match
  involving Nottingham Forest F.C.?
Wotsupp? . . . Is something amiss?
Our Dad hadda goo dartin' wi' our Fred in 'is pit muck an'
  Welloes . . . Father was obliged to go straight from work in
  his working clothes to fulfil a sporting engagement—to wit,
  a game of darts—in the company of my brother Frederick
Gerroff . . . Please go away
Aya masht, meduck? . . . Have you made the tea, dear?
Mek it g'backudds . . . Put it into reverse
Our Dad went an' gor' issen chucked outa the Trip for thumpin'
  the Mester . . . Father was ejected from a local hostelry follow-
  ing an altercation in which he was so moved by the sentiments
  expressed by the landlord that he struck him a resounding
  blow
Gizarfonnitt . . . Share and share alike
Oo worree wee? . . . Who was he with?
Worree wee issen? . . . Was he alone?

Wigorn av uz dinnaz . . . We are about to take lunch
Arn't ya gornta eetitt? . . . Are you not hungry?
Y'alluz wanna gerra sustificut . . . You should get a doctor's note
It wur gin me . . . I had it given to me
Aya gorra wee ya? . . . Is your wife with you?
Am gooin' wee missen . . . I am going alone
Atode im eekudd pleez issen . . . I told him the choice was his
Yowl koppit . . . You'll be in trouble
Kenni cum anorl? . . . May I come too?
Thiz summat up wee 'im . . . I think he may be ill
Ez ee sed owt? . . . Did he say anything?
Shurrup an' gerrin . . . Don't talk so much and climb inside the car
Aya gorrote? . . . Have you got anything?
Owzeeno? . . . What makes him think he is qualified to speak on
   the subject?
Ta-rar, then! . . . Goodbye for now!

EXERCISES FOR FURTHER STUDY

Gerrup, yo, elsal bat yatabb
Smarrerwee im?
Azeeginniter?
Purrimineer
Thallafter gerra newun
Eesezitintiz burraberritiziz
Summonemz gorragerroff
Lerrus gerrus andswesht
Tantad nowt dunnatitt as I nose
Eedursnt purrized underworter
Atoldim burreewunt lissen
Gerrarri tergeeyandweeitt
Eez nowt burrababbi
Comforuz atarpastate

TWELVE

FUN AND GAMES

Nottingham ale, boys, Nottingham ale!
No liquor on earth is like Nottingham ale.
>   —Traditional song

NOTTINGHAM is a light-hearted town with plenty of time on its hands. Its citizens work comfortably rather than desperately. And there is a Mediterranean streak in their character which keeps the brake on too furious labour. Even in the dark days of the eighteenth century, some hosiery masters remarked that the stockingers worked such long hours because of their fondness for taking time off. In 1710 *The Tatler* reported on Nottingham's liking for high jinks, citing young ladies deprived of sleep by 'riotous lovers who have infested the streets with violins and bass viols between the hours of twelve and four in the morning'.

The holiday feeling about the city is constant and unmistakable. Always plenty of people to wander the well-stocked shops, or to stroll the castle green, or study the dahlias in the Arboretum, or walk the dog on the Forest, or take a boat out on the University lake, or simply to supervise the spurting of the fountains in the Old Market Square.

There is not much you can't do in Nottingham. Where two or three dozen are gathered together, a club gets formed, furthering the interests of anything from alpine plants to flying-saucers. Cacti and Cub Scouts, train-spotting and toy-soldiering, winemaking and weight-watching, doll-dressing and dinghy-sailing ... name it and Nottingham will have it, find it, or start it.

A town which for generations had grown accustomed to gawping at the passing show of kings and queens making their entrances and exits, is not going to remain dull between-times. Accordingly, Nottingham has built up a vast variety from which to choose. Depending on your pocket, you may fly your private aircraft at Tollerton and Castle Donington; or your pigeon from an air-conditioned transporter, holding 5,999 others. The biggest ten-pin bowling centre in Europe awaits you, and, if your ears can take it, the biggest discotheque. The Corporation runs ten indoor swimming baths all the year round, and three open-air lidos (the one at the University is the largest in the country). There are two theatres—one lately refurbished by the city, the other the acknowledged National Theatre of the provinces —and lately a rash of nightclubs, including one for homosexuals. Four cinemas offer a total of fourteen screens. You may lose your feet at the ice-stadium or find your sea-legs at the £1,500,000 water leisure centre at Holme Pierrepont, the first to have an Olympic rowing course. Nottingham has Ukrainian dancers, a nest of the Handlebar Club where members compare the bushy luxuriance of their moustaches, people who go jousting, people who dress up as cavaliers, a Russian Church in Exile, half a dozen karate clubs, men keen on trams, women keen on bell-ringing, and a Ukelele Society. For three months, in the autumn, the plug is pulled out at the Victoria Baths and the exhibitors of cats, dogs and model engineering take over. It is clearly understood that a hobby, whether racing a kayak or building a miniature cathedral in matchsticks, can be indulged to the full; although there was one man who had to be gently restrained from premature use of his grave in the general cemetery. Having had it dug, he would sit in it, reading; but he attracted too many crowds. On a less spectacular scale, I remember an official gathering in the Council House when all the men came in shirtsleeves to show off their fancy waistcoats. No one thought it strange. The Lord Mayor of the time was interested in fancy waistcoats.

Nottingham abounds in amateur dramatics. Since 1893 the Operatic Society has sung its way through Gilbert and Sullivan, Ivor Novello, and Rodgers and Hammerstein; its annual productions pack out the Theatre Royal. The Arts Theatre in George Street, opened in 1948 and the only theatre run by the Co-op, has been a nursery for dozens who have made good on the professional stage. The drama director for its first five years was Sir Hugh Willatt, a former Secretary-General of the Arts Council of Great Britain. Practically every works and every church has its own drama group; but one of the foremost examples of self-help has been the Theatre Club, which since 1927 has had its members literally taking off their coats and converting exciting little theatres, successively, from the most unlikely premises. First a garage, then a brewer's malt store, and now a Lace Market warehouse.

The city isn't as fanatical about music as, say, Manchester or Huddersfield. But the English Sinfonia has made its home here, wearing green cummerbunds and lace jabots as tokens of belonging. The *Messiah* of the Harmonic Society—formed in 1856— would stand comparison with most; and the miners of the Nottinghamshire coalfield have upheld the best traditions of sounding brass. Bands like the Black Diamonds flourish, even though some of the collieries have fizzled out. And although the Corporation's economies have stopped the concerts in the parks, the bandsmen still converge on the Albert Hall (with its adjudicator locked up all day in his judging box) for a yearly blow-out.

Considering that Nottingham was enlightened enough in the fourteenth century to pay for its own musical 'waits', and in 1697 appointed a 'Town's Husband' to organise festivities, the city shows canny caution over its cultural and artistic life.

The prime example has been the Playhouse, which has become an important theatre in spite of—not because of—the city whose life it enriches. With no civic backing, except for a small gift from the education authority, the Playhouse got going in 1948 in a tiny theatre (now a furniture shop) which had opened in 1910 as Pringle's Picture Palace and had been through the gamut of clog dancers, performing poodles and Tod Slaughter melodrama. Steered by directors of the calibre of André Van Gyseghem, John Harrison, Val May and Frank Dunlop, that draughty little theatre in Goldsmith Street achieved fortnightly miracles. It became one of the country's leading repertory theatres, battling with a vest-pocket stage, dressing-rooms foetid with boiler fumes, wings so puny that scenery had to be put out in the street, and the sort of acoustics which meant that whenever a fire engine left the station nearby it drowned the actors' lines.

After deliberating for four years, the controlling Labour group on the City Council proposed again the age-old idea of a civic theatre. The cost would be met from a municipal nest-egg, the money paid on nationalisation for the city's gas undertaking. Instant Conservative cries of 'feckless and reckless!' were later modified to 'splendid idea but we can't afford it!' National personalities, theatrical knights, dames, and playwrights waded in with letters and rallying calls. A petition to cease the political warfare and get on with the job collected 3,500 signatures in a fortnight. Opposition letter-writers were equally vociferous, quoting the needs of the homeless and the aged. Most unliterary councillors delivered the occasional passage from Shakespeare.

It was not until 1961—by the single casting vote of the Labour Lord Mayor, just before the Tories got back into power—that the nest-egg was finally broken into the frying pan and the city committed to its £380,000 theatre. Even then, the Corporation, which paid £310,000 and kept the building, was not charging a mere peppercorn rent. The spearhead of theatre outside London, the best post-war theatre in Britain—architecturally and artistically—was saddled with £31,000 a year in rent and rates. It has taken years of battling by such directors as John Neville, Stuart Burge, Richard Eyre and Richard Digby Day to make Nottingham slowly cancel that out by increased subsidies. But such parsimony may already have clipped the Playhouse's wings.

The case is not unique. Nottingham has been notoriously mean in anything to do with the arts, and is only just beginning to wake up slightly, with such ideas as the plan to turn Brewhouse Yard into a new type of people's museum. As recently as 1972 the castle museum was described as having the air of a depressed area, with treasures shoved into store for lack of sufficient space or showcases. Until county funds provided the Angel Row Library, valuable documents piled up as if in a junk shop, and were even stored in a coke-hole at Basford dustbin depot. A shudder seems to go through Corporation and public alike when expense is considered on matters that show no tangible return. They've been arguing for years about a concert hall; the complex planned by Labour near the Theatre Royal was scuppered by the Tories in 1976. So the city has to make do with the Albert Hall, a Methodist Mission of 1906 which, naturally, can veto any booking it may consider unsuitable. On slender budgets, such superb exhibitions as those on D. H. Lawrence, bicycles and clowns at the castle are few and far between.

Goodness knows if Nottingham will brace itself to pay for a decent Festival again. After letting the Playhouse—with the patronage of business firms—provide an arts festival for a year or two, the city took the plunge: in 1970, again in 1971 and 1972 staged a fortnight of gaiety, ranging from leading orchestras to hot-air balloons. Like all festivals these lost money. In characteristic style, the affair turned into a political war, and the Corporation came under heavy fire when it jibbed at paying the debts of the Festival Association which ran the festivals for it. Many creditors were caught in the crossfire when the Association was wound up, including artists of international repute. The city's festivals since then have lacked a certain flair.

But though unimaginative in many ways, Nottingham is reasonably generous with its parks, its bowling greens, its tennis courts. The Harvey Hadden Stadium at Bilborough (boosted by the gift of an ex-Nottinghamian in Canada) is used for major cycling and athletic events, despite its draughtiness which gives it the nickname of the Siberia of the Midlands. There are plans for a new sports complex at Bulwell, and unanimous support for a mighty project at Colwick which may involve a major football stadium for 50,000 spectators, dog racing, show jumping, and water sports linked to the county's Holme Pierrepont marina. If followed through, it could lead to Nottingham becoming one of England's biggest sports centres.

Which is as it should be, for the city has always been keen on such activity. Not all of the sport has been reputable. Every bull was once baited before being slaughtered (the mayoress used to get 1/- for providing the rope to tether it). Two packs of hounds were quartered in the town in 1750, yelping after stags for as far as thirty miles. Dog-fights drew ready crowds, as did the bare-knuckle marathons of 100 rounds in which the legendary Bendigo figured. One passing diversion was to hurl sticks at a tethered hen. And cock-fighting was so common that in 1763 an association was set up in 'The Red Lion' in Pelham Street to protect breeders from people 'stealing or detrimenting' their fowls. Somebody had nobbled a visiting team of cocks from London by slipping arsenic into their water.

The more legitimate sports have flourished for centuries. The suburb of Hyson Green grew up around the large race-course dating from 1690, extending westwards from the present Forest into the adjoining parts of Radford and Lenton and attracting saddlers, wheelwrights and straw dealers, and developing Vauxhallian pleasure gardens with tea-rooms and an artificial lake fenced by a coloured panorama of the Bay of Naples. The race-course was removed in 1895 to Colwick, where its one-and-a-half-mile track is leased by the Corporation for a nominal £1 a year; a rent ruefully noted by the Playhouse.

Cricket had been played regularly between Nottingham and Sheffield since 1771—sixteen years before the foundation of the M.C.C., when a wicket was used that looked like a croquet hoop. Twenty years later, a thousand guinea match between eleven local noblemen and gentlemen from the Marylebone club drew a crowd of 10,000, fully half the population, to the Meadows. In his *Rural Life of England*, of 1837, William Howitt draws an evocative picture of cricket on the Forest, with its windmills crowning a scene of tents and ginger beer stalls, nut-sellers, and pots boiling on fires, and finally—among a deafening roar—a carrier pigeon soaring away to the visiting team's town with a red ribbon, the signal of loss, tied to its tail.

Just over Trent Bridge lies the revered ground of the Notting-hamshire Cricket Club, venue of nearly thirty Test Matches since William Clarke—who had married the landlady of the adjacent inn—laid it out in 1838. True, it has not the grandeur of Lord's, but it has been called the best in England and retains its charm even though a block of offices and flats has been built to raise badly needed cash. The Trent Bridge arena aches with memories; of the big Gunns, William, George and John . . . the ex pit-pony boy Harold Larwood doing his long, menacing run-up for the bodyline bowling which caused such a furore . . . the whirlwind left-armed Bill Voce . . . stylists Reg Simpson and Joe Hardstaff . . . captain Gary Sobers. It was on these hallowed six-and-a-half acres that W. G. Grace scored the first century of a first-class match.

The Nottinghamshire side, which could once apply a birth qualification almost as rigid as that of Yorkshire, and whose place in county cricket's Big Six was never threatened, had in its Victorian heyday a glamour that Manchester United footballers enjoyed a century later. More people watched Nottinghamshire take on Gloucestershire at Trent Bridge in 1872 than saw England play Scotland in the soccer international of the same year.

A vandal could nearly chuck a half-brick from the turf of Trent Bridge to the goalposts of Nottingham Forest and Notts. County football grounds. Both of them originally used the cricket pitch.

Notts. County—black and white stripes providing the nickname 'The Magpies'—is the oldest league club in the world, having started in 1862. Forest—'The Reds'—is the third oldest, following three years later but beating County by getting its own ground in 1898. Its Bedfordshire turf makes it the greenest ground in the country. Paradoxically, Forest's city ground is over the boundary in the county, while Notts. County's ground is in Meadow Lane —in the city. If ever the two clubs—'potential bankrupts' as one sports columnist has put it—share the same stadium at Colwick Park, then the traditional Nottingham inquiry 'D'yah g'dahn, then?' will have to be amended to 'D'yah g'oop, then?'

Nottingham is a sight to behold when both teams are at home and their crowds are disgorged, for record gates amount to 50,000 each. Of the two, the County lot are better behaved. Forest's 'Trent Enders'—tossing bottles among the toilet rolls, raising a wall of two-finger salutes and shouting obscenities at the referee— present a greater problem than was met in 1755 when a Grand Jury ordered 'some active, nimble constables to be sent to the churchyards every Sabbath to prevent boys playing'. They tend to be hauled into court for their sins more often than their softer-centred neighbours across the river.

But apart from the odd foray into hooliganism, such as shower-ing the visiting team's coach with mud and stones, and shoulder-ing old ladies off the pavements on the way home, Nottingham takes its football seriously. Some pubs keep a set of reference books to settle arguments on the finer points. And the Bishop of Sherwood was once asked to delay the consecration of a cemetery for three hours because the ceremony coincided with a Cup Final.

The leisure energy of Nottinghamians is burned up in a bewildering array of pursuits, mostly active. They learn to ski on a ninety-six-foot rubber slope at the Carlton Forum sports centre. Activities range from the orthodox to the oddball, like pushing peas with the nose, playing table-tennis for a week, and estab-lishing records for hand-shaking or running barefoot to London. Tender care is lavished on budgerigars, chinchillas and chrysan-themums. The surfaces of the Trent and other waterways bustle with yachtsmen and water-skiers; the banks blossom with the big green flowers of anglers' umbrellas.

Most events—whether cultural or physical—entail some degree of financial outlay, and in recent years local industry has come to the rescue. In particular, Player's organise a sub-industry, channelling help to theatres, art galleries, festivals, film clubs, schools, charities and sport. Some of it goes modestly unpublicised, but Player's are the first to admit that it is not altruistic to lend their name and insignia to Sunday league cricket, racing cars, aeronautic displays, steam-engine rallies, golf tournaments, regattas, cycle marathons and tennis matches. (It is quite a thought that much of our open-air enjoyment and fitness is made possible by products which carry a Government warning about damage to health.)

Indoor enjoyment, too, has carried its health risks in Nottingham. When James Whiteley built an elegant, thousand-seat Theatre Royal near St. Mary's church, the theatre was regarded as a hotbed of vice and dissipation. The opening night, in 1760, was unfortunate to say the least. An alderman violently opposed to the whole idea sent round four constables to drag away the leading actor. Proprietor Whiteley attempted a rescue but ended in the House of Correction with a bleeding nose. Indignantly he composed a poetic blast which began:

> Dear Town of Commerce, once the Muses' seat
> Where Players tasted happiness complete
> Till dark stupidity usurped the Throne . . .

No doubt with his blackened eye on future more successful productions, he finished it:

> Yet however wounded and oppressed,
> Be thou, O Nottingham, forever blest!

After that, Whiteley played it cool for a while, giving 'concerts of vocal and instrumental musick' for the benefit of the poor, and thereby gaining the support of the public and the church. Into one of these admirable interludes, four years later, he slipped a 'highly moral play'; and took it from there.

It was remarkable how swiftly Nottingham got the London productions and their stars. Mrs. Siddons came up in 1807 to play Lady Macbeth; at double the usual prices. A month later the attraction was Master Betty, the Young Roscius. Edmund Kean played Richard III, his greatest role. Byron was in the audience that night, riding out from his estate at Newstead and later penning pages of praise.

But by 1835—after such varied attractions as MacReady in *Hamlet*, Paganini's farewell concert, and an on-stage race between five real ponies—the rot was setting in. One writer complained about 'this gloomy barnlike building near a graveyard, more like a prison'. The theatre-going middle classes had become theatre-averse dissenters. Besides, manners were falling off. 'The process of imbibing and mastication,' sniffed a writer in 1860, 'would do credit to the occupants of a beleaguered city.' He had further caustic comments about the volleys of orange peel, the uncorking of bottles, the catcalls and piping of penny whistles, the shouts of recognition, and the jostling by the 'glaring vulgarity of a class too obtrusively prominent in all public places'.

The old theatre limped along, but the focus had shifted. Caught up in the boisterous boom of industry, the working classes evolved a culture of their own. From the scores of pubs, the 'free and easies' where anybody could jump up and regale the company with song and story until 5 a.m., came the music halls, complete with chairman in white tie and tails, banging his gavel, wiping the beer froth from his moustache, fruitily announcing the turns, and inviting himself to another drink by announcing a polite but firm intention to 'take wine with his friend in the cloth cap and choker'.

Chairman at St. George's Hall (the Co-op now stands there) was a former Worcester china-worker named Harry Ball. In 1868 his little daughter made her début on that stage. 'Don't be frightened,' he told her. 'Sing as if you meant it. Don't cough, and sing clearly.' She was four. And she became Vesta Tilley.

The old Theatre Royal, renamed the Alhambra, became a music hall. So did the Talbot Palace, which for a time went over to the forces of temperance. To those three halls came most of the great artists of the day. Fred Karno, once a lace worker, started his career as an acrobat. Charles Coburn, the man who broke the bank at Monte Carlo, hardly broke the bank with a salary of £3–£10 a week. Another notable hall, the Royal Coliseum, was not so impressive as its name. Its audience consisted of 'boys and girls from twelve to twenty, thoughtless and dissipated young men and rakish-looking middle-aged individuals, the women wearing clouds of crinoline and Brummagem jewellery'. And when the show began it was not uncommon for a brace of policemen to go round, yanking out a pickpocket or two.

But the music halls did not have it all their own way. The

Lambert brothers built their new Theatre Royal as 'a place of innocent recreation and moral and intellectual culture', despite warnings that to 'expend £15,000 upon a playhouse in a town where efforts are daily put forth to improve the morals and religion of the young is the height of folly and sin'. Six months from the time of clearing of the site, it rang up its first curtain in a blaze of gaslit glory, on September 25, 1865. And although M.P. Sir Robert Clifton was hissed as he entered, it was a good night—unlike the occasion in St. Mary's Gate 105 years previously. A special prologue was uttered by seventeen-year-old Madge Robertson (she became Dame Madge Kendall), and when the curtain fell on *The School for Scandal* it was promised that after the solids of the banquet would come the trifle—'the gay burlesque, the witty farce, and in due season King Pantomime'.

And so it has proved. The Theatre Royal can hardly be called 'a gentle handmaiden of religion'—even after a visit by Cliff Richard wearing his crucifix. But it stands four-square among the litter of less durable theatres, welcoming everybody from Agatha Christie to Glyndebourne Opera, Margot Fonteyn to the Black and White Minstrels. When the Moss Empires lease ran out in 1977, its owners, Nottingham Corporation, took the bull by the horns and splashed out £5,000,000 to restore it to its Victorian splendour, demolishing the County Hotel for dressing rooms and in 1982 adding the superb £12-million concert hall next door, directed with flair by Barrie Stead.

Its contemporaries have become ghosts. The next-door Empire was once the Royal's car park. Built by Sir Oswald Stoll, of London Coliseum fame, this 'stately pleasure dome' lasted sixty years. Little Tich flipped his big boots, Harry Tate wiggled his moustache, George Robey drew a postcard cartoon of himself for every member of the audience on his eightieth birthday. Everybody came to the Empire, Marie Lloyd and Harry Houdini, Will Hay and Tony Hancock, Chico Marx and Max Miller, Fields (W. C.) and Fields (Gracie), Champion and Chaplin, Nottingham's own Billy Merson. Bludgeoned by T.V. pop shows, and seedy strippers, it finally curled up, ashamed, and died in June 1958. Its carcass rotted for eleven years.

The Grand at Hyson Green, to which horse trams jogged in 1886, had a dozen palmy years with Henry Irving, and the original

University Medical School
The new concert hall (right)

D'Oyly Carte operas, became a cinema, essayed a brave experiment in repertory with the Compton family in the 1920s, turned
back into a cinema and faded out in 1956. The Bulwell Olympia
tried variety for seven years from 1915, lurched on as a cinema
until 1952, and is now a Woolworth's. The Hippodrome variety
theatre had a heady nineteen years from 1908, became the
Gaumont cinema until 1971 and was knocked down in 1973 to
make yet another office block.

Spawned in controversy, the glass-and-concrete Playhouse,
designed by Peter Moro (of the Royal Festival Hall), was opened
by Lord Snowdon in December 1963, who hoped that it would
spark off a lot of argument. It certainly has. For its first five years
the 750-seat Playhouse was hardly ever out of the headlines,
culminating in a head-on clash between the actor John Neville,
its passionately dedicated director, and members of the Playhouse
Board. Neville—whose dynamic drive had helped maintain con-
sistent attendances of eighty-five per cent—'screamed blue
murder' when the Arts Council pegged the theatre's grants, and
resigned. Board, Arts Minister Jennie Lee, and Lord Goodman,
chairman of the Arts Council, urged him to reconsider. He offered
to withdraw his resignation—but his régime came to a shatter-
ing end when the Board, feeling by then that they, and not a
director, should decide overall policy, dug in their heels and let
him go. It was an acrimonious struggle for power and principle,
with massive petitions from Neville supporters and lobbying of
Parliament, which shook the entire British theatre.

With the novelty of the new theatre worn off, the personality-
plus figures gone, and the sharpness of politics softened, the Playhouse settled into a gentler era. Ready to meet the challenge of
other new theatres, it now follows its steadfast policy of providing
the best of the classic and modern. High-calibre actors and pro-
ducers are prepared to bring their talents for a fraction of the
money they could get in television or in the West End. Apart
from Stratford-upon-Avon, Nottingham was the first major
theatre outside London to operate the repertoire system which
gives audiences a choice of plays, instead of a short single run.
Under Stuart Burge and later Richard Eyre, the Playhouse's
record of transfers to places like the National Theatre has shown
that 'provincial' is no longer a dirty word. Plans are quietly
moving on for expansion, particularly with young audiences in

Goose Fair, on the Forest

mind. The Playhouse, right from its beginnings in 1948, has pioneered work among youngsters, putting on special matinees from the ordinary repertoire, and taking specially written shows —about anything from canals to the lace industry—round schools in the county, and letting the pupils themselves take part. The result is that audiences at Nottingham Playhouse are among the most youthful in the country. Alive, alert, critical, perceptive and excited. Shakespeare himself may have come to Nottingham when the King's Players made a visit in 1615. It would do his heart good to see hundred-per-cent audiences at the Playhouse for his plays.

Not everybody, of course, is interested in the theatre, as the Prince's Players discovered in the seventeenth century when they collected 13/- for actually staying out of town. But Nottinghamians are always interested in food and drink. They have always been good trenchermen, putting on spreads of fifty dishes at banquets in the Assembly Rooms. Council business was at one time mostly done over dinner at the town's expense. The most celebrated freeloader was a miserly clockmaker who, in 1770, stuck with an oversize clock from a cancelled order, presented it to the old Exchange and was made an honorary burgess. He turned up at one civic banquet, found all the seats taken, and plunged under the table, trying to force his way up into a place but being tapped smartly on the head by spoon-wielding councillors.

There are sixty different sorts of sausage on sale in Nottingham. One firm, Pork Farms, turns out seventeen tons a week, along with a quarter of a million rolls, steak and kidney pies and Cornish pasties, as well as 128,000 pork pies. For as the saying goes: 'The true, the perfect pork pie is made from a recipe stored in Heaven and known only to the people of Nottingham.' It may have some bearing on a recent Schools' Medical Officer's report that the city has 900 Billy and Bessie Bunters, children— as heavy as twenty stone—overweight through over-eating.

Much of the success of Burtons, which occupies most of the Council House arcade with banks of eatables, was built cn their practice, since 1864, of letting the customer taste before he bought.

Nottingham can offer a cosmopolitan menu these days, from pizza bars to Chinese fish and chips. In the space of a hundred yards up the narrowness of St. James's Street you may enjoy a smart grill, olde Englishe quiet, a beefburger, a French bistro or a perfect Italian cuisine. Further up the hill you may, in the same place, carve yourself as much meat as you can eat for a modest price or indulge in a feast which almost seems to warrant taking out a mortgage. Hotel food has vastly improved in recent years. 'The Black Boy', whose rococo charm on Long Row is now flattened into a store, has had its name (and famous Negro statue) enshrined at the top of Market Street in an ingenious selection of dining rooms. The 'Victoria', once threatened by the overpowering presence of the new centre, is happily intact. Not so the 'County' taken for the Theatre Royal. New hotels such as the 'Albany', 'Bridgford', 'Strathdon' and 'Savoy' give ultra modern service, and the ancient calm of the 'Flying Horse' has turned into a noisier atmosphere—with better food. The Berni brothers have studded the city with neat, quick and comfortable restaurants.

Fond as Nottingham is of its stomach, its drink comes first. Nottingham ale is the stuff of which real men are made. Bacchus himself, according to the song which Oliver Goldsmith and his cronies used to bellow out in their London taverns, sprang from a barrel of Nottingham ale. When inspired with a bumper of it, bishops and curates can open their throats and preach without notes. Doctors who:

> More executions have done
> With powder and bolus, with potion and pill,
> Than hangman with halter or soldier with gun,
> Than miser with famine or lawyer with quill.

are ordered the panacea of a comforting dose.

Indeed, local doctors took the advice. Nottingham's General Hospital had its own brewery, and had extended its cellars by 1833. Irate ratepayers in 1860 were complaining that the expenditure of £430 on beer was 'a sinful waste, the means of perpetuating intemperance and producing poverty, crime, disease and death'.

Time was, when the test for the strength of ale was for a Customs and Excise man to sit in a puddle of it wearing a pair of leather trousers. If they stuck, it was strong enough. In 1701 the Excise men were grumbling that Nottingham ale was so powerful that less was drunk, with a consequent fall in tax revenue. But brewing has always been a source of profit and pleasure to Nottingham. A Saxon chronicle of A.D. 728 speaks of ale houses in the town—and the even temperature of the sand-stone caves still makes them ideal brewing and storage spaces. It was technique learned in Nottingham that made the fame of at least one brewery in Burton, where the water is slightly better.

A Trent-sized torrent of ale has flowed down Nottingham gullets throughout the years, but the pubs have been used for other things than sheer drinking. They were recruiting centres; 'The Eight Bells' near St. Peter's Church promised volunteers, in 1778, a bountiful meal of roast beef and plum pudding and a ticket to the theatre. Stocking frames were auctioned at 'The Flying Horse' in 1785. A society was set up in one to make flannel waistcoats for soldiers. At one time there were sixty Friendly Societies, all based on pubs. They were also the H.Q. of political life. The landlady of 'The Sun' in Pelham Street received a letter in 1792 saying that her premises would be burned down if she continued to harbour sympathisers with the French Revolution. One pamphleteer suggested in 1803 that Nottingham pubs were 'seminaries of disloyalty and Jacobinism where the maxims of revolution have been inculcated into the young and unwary, roaring through the streets the republican songs of their abominable orgies'. Signs 'No Jacobin admitted here' were plentiful, and a suspected Democrat would be ferreted out by someone sniffing raucously and muttering, 'I smell a Jacobin!' in his direction. If he failed to respond to an anti-Jacobin toast, it was a matter of either shooting out of the door or risking a dousing under the pump. High society patronised 'The Blackamoor's Head' (where Byron's coffin rested in 1824), and so did Oliver the spy, who also mingled with customers in 'The Golden Fleece' and 'The Three Salmons' to glean the plotted details of the Pentrich Rising in 1817.

Today, Nottingham has some 750 licensed premises to pick from—ranging from the quaint legacies near the castle such as the gabled 'Salutation' where King Charles's recruiters tried to whip up support, to the plastic roadhouses where plugged-in guitars now try to whip up enthusiasm. It is still possible to drink behind cut-glass windows and have your beer pulled by a porcelain lever rather than squirted from a hose.

At 'The George' they keep the cheque with which Dickens paid his bill. And outside 'The Old General' on Radford Road they keep in a glass case the statue of Ben Mayo, an eccentric who died in 1864. He used to round up a battalion of schoolchildren and get them to pelt the school with mud until their teachers gave them a holiday or bribed him with twopence to call off the attack.

A determined soul could enjoy himself for years working his way through Nottingham's history via its pubs. He could see the mounting-blocks on the pavement outside 'The White Hart' at Lenton, from whose walls starving debtors used to plead for bread. Still in Lenton he could find the brand-new, fortress-like '17/21st Lancer' with its mural of the Charge of the Light Brigade, and its perpetuation of the regiment which recruits in Nottinghamshire. He would learn that 'The Gondola' has nothing to do with Venice; it is simply in Balloon Woods—and a gondola is a balloonist's basket. He would find out that 'The Earl Howe' remembers the admiral who crushed the French fleet in 1794 on 'the glorious first of June', and that 'The Sir John Borlace Warren' is named after another local naval man (also an M.P.) whose frigates destroyed or captured 220 ships in 1796. Up Ilkeston Road 'The Jolly Higglers' refers to eighteenth-century water-carriers. 'The Cross Keys' in the Lace Market area of Byard Lane found its stock dwindling when navvies building the Great Central railway tunnel burrowed into its cellars.

But perhaps our researcher of hostelries would best appreciate the story of the instant cure. The Victorian owner of what is now Yates' Wine Lodge used to be very fond of marble statuary, which he scattered around the premises. At closing time one night, an extremely tanked-up patron was accidentally locked in, slumped beneath a table. He regained consciousness in the deserted bar to the sight of the moon glimmering eerily on the white figures.

From that moment, Nottingham ale lost one of its best customers.

THIRTEEN

SWINGS AND ROUNDABOUTS

The Public are respectfully informed that each Flea is
securely chained.
> —Professor England's Royal Exhibition
> of Educated Performing Fleas. 1892.

EVERY October, Nottingham keeps a date with madness. On the
first Thursday of the month, the Lord Mayor, flanked by the
Sheriff and his macebearers, steps on to a wooden scaffold and
tries to look as solemn as any man can when standing near The
House of Dracula and the Two-Headed Man From Paraguay in
the middle of the Forest recreation ground. At noon, the Town
Clerk, gowned and bewigged, reads a proclamation to several
hundred people who are concentrating more on the posters for
the Golden Goddess of the Nile; the Mayor rings heartily on a
pair of silver bells, and the civic party take a dignified bump on
the Dodgems.

It is Goose Fair again, Nottingham's own Saturnalia, the
Mardi gras of the Midlands, a three-day Walpurgisnacht when
the banshee shriek of The Ghost Train fights the screams of girls
on the Hurricane Jets. Between now and Saturday midnight, over
a quarter of a million people will shove, struggle or slosh their
way round this eighteen-acre canvas city, happy to be stunned
by the lights and the din. Their stomachs lined with chips and
hot peas, soft nougat, candy-floss, brandysnap, winkles, beer,
marzipan, onions, lemonade and hot dogs, they will pay to be
pinned to the centrifugal cage of the Rotor, twisted upside down,
shaken, rattled, rolled and tilted until their eyes turn like pin-table
balls and their livers threaten to snap their moorings.

Some 300 of them will get tossed out, bruised, cut, or stung
by the wasps attracted by the toffee-apples. A small regiment of
tiny lost children will push through the swirl of legs in ever-

rising panic until scooped into the Lost and Found tent and rejoined to their parents. Bold youths, with fringed Stetsons and experienced eyes, will mount the roller-coasters and ride the rifle ranges, impressing the giggly girls they hope to seduce later among the dark trees on the edge of the golden garish clamour. The scrubby front gardens of the houses round the rim of the ground will bloom with hope, light and rental money from the palmists and phrenologists. And for three days the environs of Nottingham will carry the annual trademarks of plastic police-helmets, furry monkeys bobbing on elastic, Robin Hood caps, Japanese dolls wearing gowns of Nottingham lace, and balloons straining so eagerly with gas that they stand as stiff as Belisha Beacons.

Goose Fair probably goes back a thousand years. Certainly the Feast of St. Matthew, an eight-day affair around September 21, was flourishing in 1284 when King Edward I's charter granted official permission for a fifteen-day fair in November. The introduction of the Gregorian calendar in 1752 moved the starting day to October 2 until 1875.

Whatever incidental amusement it brought, the mediaeval Goose Fair was not a mammoth funfair like it is today, but rather a vast supermarket in nice time to stock up for the winter. Its name seems to derive from its acting as a clearing house for stubble-fattened geese brought waddling into Nottingham market place. Twenty thousand of these mobile Michaelmas dinners would be herded in from Lincolnshire or Norfolk—their feet shod with tar and sand.

By the nineteenth century the pioneer showmen had begun to impinge. Wombwell's Wild Beast Show trundled in its wonders in 1805, and by 1821 there were so many sideshows that people were complaining about shortage of space for the sale of food and animals. Madame Tussaud herself arrived with her collection of ninety waxy characters in 1819, and again ten years later. Not for her the rowdy struggle of a fitted-up booth. She took the comfort of a large room in the old Exchange, and charged an unprecedented 1/- for admission.

As yet the magistrates were holding out against 'those disgraceful and dangerous machines called merry-go-rounds' and refusing a place on the site for these 'instruments of folly, immodesty and danger'. It would have been difficult to squeeze them in anyway,

for Goose Fair was still a trade fair in the 1830s, important enough
for army recruits to insist on Goose Fair leave when they enlisted
in the militia.

Two-thirds of the market place was given over to trade; 'the
Sheffielder brought his cutlery, the Barnsley man his linen, the
Halifax and Leeds people their cloth, the Staffordshire man his
china, the Grantham lady her gingerbread.' The stalls fronting
the Exchange were for Nottingham's special products—lace and
hosiery, baskets from the osier beds of the Trent, whipcord, hemp
and heaps of liquorice.

The other third had the showmen. Wombwell's with its
lions and lapdogs, tigers and titmice, serpents and singing birds,
polar bears and polecats; Holloway's Travelling Company of
Comedians with a panorama of prodigies; Hylton's collection of
ugly dwarfs, fat bullocks, learned pigs and assorted magicians.

'The bawlings,' wrote William Howitt, 'the invitings, and
oratorical declamation of a dozen different showmen, with
bellowings of gongs and clashing of symbols, made up sound
enough to drive to distraction more swine than ran into the sea of
Gennesaret, but which seemed, notwithstanding, wonderfully
delightful to ears grown weary of country quiet.'

On Saturday morning the cattle market turned the town into
a huge Smithfield, and the women folk either kept indoors or
'were vastly frightened if they ventured out'. Dancing bears
padded through the mob; hurdy-gurdy girls were as plentiful as
blackberries. A 'triumvirate of barbarous bagpipers' came all the
way from Scotland. A bearded lady was ungallantly refused a
site, on the grounds that she was an unnatural exhibition.

After each fair, the letters of complaint. Outraged moralists
spoke bitterly of 'low theatrical exhibitions', and 'noise and dis-
order destructive to all peace and comfort'. It didn't do them
much good. The Superintendent of Markets was able to report in
1857 that Goose Fair—'which, while losing to a great extent its
trading qualities has been acquiring more and more those of a
pleasure fair'—had netted £107 in revenue from shows alone, a
'sum acquired without any sacrifice beyond that of a slight public
inconvenience which was at that time expected and cheerfully
made'.

Local market traders voiced their objections so forcibly that
they got the eight days of the fair cut to five in 1876. The pressure

continued, mostly from societies and committees alarmed not
merely by the bedlam caused by the growing proliferation of
mechanical roundabouts and rides, but by the influx of shysters,
cardsharps, confidence men and prostitutes. In 1878 a special
inquiry was set up to collect and tabulate evidence as to the moral,
social, sanitary and commercial effects of Goose Fair. 'A perfect
nuisance', was a typical reply from a manufacturer. 'Girls will
not work unless they please, and my man finds it a good opportunity to drink.' A more enlightened employer recognised it as
'a necessary relief from the cares and toils of business and the foul
atmosphere of factory life'. With a lucrative income, the Corporation ignored the opposition who wanted the fair trimmed to one
day or abolished entirely, and in 1880 fixed the duration at
three days.

But it organised things better. Sharp at six o'clock on Monday
of Goose Fair week, the staff of the markets department was
assembled, given a breakfast of ham sandwiches and strong tea
and despatched into the empty market place with buckets of
whitewash, brushes, tape measures, balls of cord and lumps of
chalk. In a few hours the place was covered with neat rectangles
and circles, allocated to Captain Payne's Electric Bioscope, Terry's
Performing Croc., Pat Collins's Venetian Gondolas, Wallace the
Celebrated Lion, Norman's Human Bear, and the rest of the
bizarre migrants who would arrive in the next two days.

And in they poured. Jumbo the English bullock, challenging
the world and offering £1,000 to beat his 1 ton 7¾ cwts. weight
. . . the tattooed sailor, who had endured twenty-four weeks
under the needle to be covered with designs ranging from the
Immaculate Conception to an Irishman Smoking A Pipe . . . the
only boxing kangaroo in Europe . . . Princess Paulina, a living
doll of nineteen inches . . . 'Commandant Synam' the ape who rang
the alarm bell at Mafeking when the Boers shelled the town . . .
Count Orloff, the only living transparent man ('place a candle
against his limbs and you can read a newspaper behind them').

Nottingham wandered entranced, riding sedately on the latest
Pneumatic Steam Bicycles, marvelling at the new cinematograph
which gave them Queen Victoria's Jubilee 'as well as those who
went to London and paid £5 a seat', picking a way through the
smoke and steam of the traction engines whose electric bulbs
outshone the hissing naphtha flares.

But even though the repertoire of the £1,000 Gaviolophone organ included the 'Hallelujah Chorus', the Bishop of Nottingham was not happy about Goose Fair. In 1897 he was particularly worried about 'the organised rushes of the crowd which are said to take place towards midnight'. It did not appear to him to be modest or decent that young women should voluntarily allow themselves to be crushed up and carried along in a dense crowd of all sorts of people. 'I fear,' he wrote gloomily, 'that many a girl owes her first fall into sin, and subsequent ruin, to the crowded rushes in Goose Fair.'

It was evidently a vintage year for similar complaints. The publicans and the gingerbread men might benefit, said one correspondent in the letter columns, and so would the railways. But Nottingham hardly benefited since a considerable proportion of the 80,000 excursionists were 'pickpockets, prostitutes and people of that class'. Pausing only to deliver a side swipe at the stench on the Saturday night, this writer confessed to seeing 'thousands of young people in various stages of intoxication from the frisky stage up to that of beastly drunk'. It was 'likely to be the ruin of thousands, and particularly of young girls'.

Yet Nottingham's young somehow survived, and so, for a time, did the old style Goose Fair. It was sheer mechanical progress which took over the traditional venue. With the new century came the trams, focusing on the Market Square, and although the fair threw up its striped canvas and continued its glittering brass confusion into the 'twenties, its heyday was over. In 1928, the bellowing of its animals long gone, and the slap of tarred goose-feet an ancient memory, it was ousted from the square over which the new white Council House was rearing its girders.

Whether Britain's biggest three-day fair will survive for long depends on the tenacity of the dwindling company of men and women who jolt across the country with their grotesque machines and magical-tawdry booths. Nottingham Goose Fair, 1982 edition, was the 687th in a direct succession broken only by the plague and a couple of world wars. Already the regulations are pretty stringent. No fortune-telling on the ground. No animals, birds or goldfish as prizes. No selling of confetti (an echo of the days when boys used to sweep it up and resell it). Not even a 'tickling stick' that shoots out a feather on a 'scissors' handle.

Police television cameras stare quietly down at pickpockets and car thieves. And since a rumpus in 1971 when a thirteen-year-old schoolgirl shook her hips outside a strip show, all the sideshows are vetted. Markets and Fairs committees do not believe in magic. Eventually, Arlena the Alligator Lady cannot be expected to give of her best in the face of an official label stating that she is really Elsie Nicholls from Barnsley. And the Amazing Abominable Snowman from Tibet will feel foolish when he has to carry a certificate establishing him as Albert Spooner (35), casual showman's labourer of East Acton.

But when the last bearded lady is clean-shaven and the last Indiarubber Man done his final stretch, they can rest secure in the memory of a thousand years. The tumblers who pranced for scraps in the Danish market, the men who led their Mighty Mastodon through the Victorian crowds in the Old Market Square, the plastic-suited barkers who offer a blast-off from Nottingham Forest in an electronic Apollo capsule—they have this in common. They have given Nottingham a lot more fun than geese ever did.

FOURTEEN

QUEEN OF THE MIDLANDS

> I love this people. There is something wonderfully pleasing
> both in their spirit and their behaviour.
>
> —John Wesley, 1786

I HOPE that Nottingham doesn't get too big. One of its attractions for me is that it is the right size—a nice handy area, large enough to give the feel of a considerable city but at the same time as compact as a fair-sized village. It has always surprised me to find how much the people of Nottingham know what is going on. Not for them the feeling of being in an amorphous wen. Nottingham belongs to Nottingham, and the sense of belonging is great.

It is an asset which it ought to hang on to. Not with the insularity that expelled mediaeval 'foreigners' from another parish, or the mulishness of the industrial revolution when it was bursting its heart. In any case, that sort of closed shop is impossible these days.

But a town which gets too big ceases to be a town with an identity. And people with no identity become apathetic, lawless and despairing, increasingly regarded as broiler chickens. It is essential for Nottingham to keep its critical powers sharp, its personality honed, its pride whetted and its identity keen.

The East Midlands is developing at a faster rate than anywhere else except East Anglia. By the year 2,000 there could be three million more people than there are today. Nottingham is the industrial and cultural pivot of that region. It should set both the tone and the example.

In 1974 it was worried, poised on the brink of the biggest shake-up of local government in a century. With a long tradition of independence, it gloomily wondered whether it was being 'taken over' by the new county administration of Nottinghamshire, sunk as a mere unit in 'Area No. 20', robbed of its control of education, libraries and social services.

Yet I somehow cannot see Nottingham throwing in the towel, any more than it surrendered its pride and its spirit to the upheavals and hardships of its history. It is, after all, the biggest district council in the area; any bigger and it would have qualified as a metropolitan zone. Out of the eighty-nine councillors deliberating across the river in County Hall, no fewer than twenty-seven are from Nottingham. And nobody is going to tell me that twenty-seven Nottingham councillors are not a force to be reckoned with.

In 1957 a consortium of local authorities throughout Nottinghamshire came up with something called CLASP, an industrial building system designed for places subject to mining subsidence. It has since proved a world-beater, providing 2,000 quick, efficient and low-priced buildings in Britain and Europe—health centres, churches, railway stations, a hospital in Scotland, a library in Bath, a polytechnic in Wales, a tax office in France.

There seems no reason why the new County Council should not be like CLASP—flexible, speedy, adaptable and cheap. The city of Nottingham brought to it 1,400 years of experience, a vast amount of know-how, a wealth of character, and the sort of inventive vigour which has buoyed it up through the ages. And in return, the sheer fact of having to work in concert with others rather than in glorious isolation is bound to rub off some of Nottingham's own sharp edges.

Goodness knows they need rounding off. Nottingham has been calling itself the Queen of the Midlands for so long that it has often dazzled itself with the title. Under the regal robe has been swept a great deal of poverty. The patterned rows of openplan houses which have replaced the worst of the long, black, slum terraces are an improvement—but many of the occupants can't afford to switch on the central heating. Many garages lie empty and vandalised. Ken Coates and Bill Silburn, whose book *Poverty—The Forgotten Englishmen* was based on their 1967 study of conditions in St. Ann's, now find that the number of families in poverty in that district has jumped from a third to half.

It is to be hoped, too, that Nottingham will turn into a less argumentative personality, cutting down on some of the political chatter and getting on with the job. Most of the rows which have bespattered Nottingham's image have sprung from the clash of personality and party within the council chamber, and have fogged the real issue.

When it becomes more conscious of its position as leader of a region wider than its own boundaries, Nottingham might take some heed about the way it is destroying its individuality. Month by month it grows more faceless. Pleasant and interesting city skylines have been bludgeoned; civilised and worthwhile architecture erased with appalling regularity as yet another piecemeal project rears its ugly head. There is still time to stop short. Nottingham could just—only just—pull up at the actual abyss. Far too much has been grabbed and can never return; there is little incentive or opportunity to sit and stare in Nottingham now that the upturned-soapbox-and-half-empty-filing-cabinet brigade have moved in. No living city can turn itself into a museum, of course. But if Nottingham does not have the guts to halt the developers and keep their greedy paws off conservation areas, then it will be hacked irretrievably within ten years.

As you drive into Nottingham from the south, you encounter clusters of concrete cooling-towers. Waisted, ethereal, they change with the weather. On a leaden winter day they are like black funnels looming into the sky, and in spring sunshine they are so luminous that you can hardly tell which is sky and which is concrete.

To me, those cooling-towers are like Nottingham itself—sometimes dark and powerful and perverse, but mostly light and gay and elusive.

But who can analyse a city? Can it be interpreted from a handful of facts and statistics? Depending on what figures you choose, you can draw a black portrait of Nottingham . . . with more crime per head of population than other cities outside London, frequently heading the suicide list, its V.D. rate touching epidemic proportions, drug addiction rising, illegitimacy well above average. You can quote figures . . . 11,000 people over the age of seventy-five, half of them living alone . . . 500 single homeless persons sleeping rough or in Salvation Army hostels or police cells . . . 7,000 houses so defective that they have a life of only ten years . . . 20,000 houses without baths. . . .

Nottingham is in the most poverty-stricken region in the country in terms of medical provision—3.82 doctors per ten

thousand population, compared with 4.25 elsewhere; one dentist
to 6,854 compared with one to 2,482 in the London area; £6 less
spent, per person, than in London. It is trying desperately to help
its handicapped; its meals-on-wheels service is far below par;
there are not enough geriatric beds; social workers find the aged
existing in pitiful conditions of neglect. Small wonder that with
such things happening within its shadow, it has been said of the
Victoria Centre: 'It is as if the welfare state had visibly materi-
alised itself in an assortment of great plastic musak towers, sym-
bolically embodying the principle of all-transcending mediocrity.
Never before has it been possible for human beings to be boring
on so huge a scale, to elevate philistinism and greed into monuments which can subdue a whole townscape.'

Whether mammoth developments like the Victoria and Broad
Marsh centres can be equated with poverty in other quarters is a
moot point. Stark with concrete in the style of watered-down
elephant-house, they are like twin vacuum-cleaners of commerce,
sucking in shoppers to be entranced by the air-conditioned trendy
wonders and be gently but firmly parted from their money. Isn't
that what all shops want to do? I doubt if their presence has any
bearing on the living conditions of the city's needy. They may,
in the long run, improve them.

It is too early to see what these two great magnets will do to
Nottingham. Their pull may drain some of the life and influence
of the traditional city centre; but, paradoxically, that might lead
to a revitalising surge in the quality of life. The focus of Nottingham's shopping has been shifted bodily, and attention trained
intensely on two widely separated spots; this far more sudden and
dramatic than the slow, evolving change from Saxon gathering
place in Weekday Cross to the big market square. Instead of all
roads leading to a central core, the middle of Nottingham could
actually acquire a quiet grace. Nine streets adjoining the city
centre have been paved over for pedestrians, acknowledging the
fact that people matter even these days.

Instead of slicing up the city as some sort of sacrifice to the god
of the internal combustion engine, Nottingham has abandoned its
ideas on new urban motorways. There will be no new major
highways and no radical improvements to existing roads within
a two-mile radius of the centre. A 'collar' was tried in 1976
to control traffic; main roads to the centre were restricted to

a dozen, and other through-roads sealed off; and an elaborate, computerised system of lights and traffic lanes gave priority to public transport. While other cities throughout the world got hopelessly bogged down with traffic thrombosis, Nottingham—for a time—led the way in saying 'No' to the private car.

Although shelved as premature, it was a heartening straw in the wind in modern Nottingham, a vivid acknowledgement that the city was saying 'Enough!' With it came a taking stock —the realisation that life in a city need not be entirely a mad scramble. The tempo and size of everything is constantly increasing—just as a modern stocking machine can whip along at two million stitches a minute when the best that the Reverend Mr. Lee could do was less than a thousand. Bigness is all—a £5,000,000 incinerator to burn the city's 175,000 tons of rubbish; gigantic shopping malls; vast sports arenas; even the whole educational system gone comprehensive.

Some of it is commendable and desirable. But there is a great yearning for a bit of peace and quiet, a revulsion against huge projects, a resentment at being shouldered and pushed and organised and herded. Human dignity is being dwarfed. People crave an oasis from the rat race. They are starved of whimsy. I find it very significant that along the 100-shop corridors of the Victoria Centre, the thing that gets the most attention is the Rowland Emett water-clock. Every half hour, vast crowds congregate to see the burnished copper petals of its metal sunflower reveal a host of bejewelled creatures. Fountains play from reeds held by frogs, and drive a flower-strewn wheel on which tumble glittering butterflies. A stainless steel squirrel pushes a wheelbarrow, another rides a filigree-winged flying fish, and, as the hour strikes, silver and gem-studded birds cavort and spin to harpsichord music. It is an enchanting, mind-refreshing dream.

Throughout Nottingham one can detect evidence that people— even the much-maligned planners—are moving towards an improvement in the quality of life. The traffic scheme is a first-class beginning. Concentrating on low buildings, instead of stacking families into high-rise towers, is another. Buildings restrictions are becoming tauter. More plans are being rejected as 'disfiguring nonentities'. The social services have improved with a rush, just as health centres and family-planning clinics have done. Parents—

and pupils—are on the governing bodies of secondary schools, in a move believed to be the first of its kind in the country. Campaigns are going on to give buildings a facelift, the streets a smartening-up and the Trent less pollution. The unique Lace Market, listed as an area of outstanding national importance, is luring firms, and even houses, with grants.

It is dawning on the planners, albeit very late, that something is lacking when warm—if drab—communities are hauled out by the roots and installed in strange new houses. Designers are now thinking towards fostering the traditional neighbourliness—to the extent of trying out pre-fabricated 'little corner shops'. There seems, at last, to be a growing awareness of Nottingham's historical assets—the people's museum approved for Brewhouse Yard near the castle contains period furnishings, a museum of childhood, and a long overdue niche for Robin Hood. And the industrial museum at Wollaton Hall stables is at least beginning to trot if not to gallop; £55,000 has been spent there on a special building to house the 120-year-old beam engine from Basford pumping station.

In many ways, then, Nottingham seems to be thinking more imaginatively. In the past it has often been left behind or has made a false start. There is no reason at all why it should now follow anybody else's lead. Time without number it has proved its ingenuity, its adaptability, its ability to rise above swamping odds. Why not show the rest of the country the way?

All the material assets are there, waiting to be used properly. Nottingham is immensely rich industrially, historically, naturally, geographically and socially. Let it conserve its uniqueness and stress it. Let it preserve its past and spread it out for all to see. What good is a history which has no evidence to show?

Let it take a tip from young Jesse Boot and put its wares fully on view. Why not a lace and hosiery hall where visitors could see the stuff, and watch how it is made? Or a cycle centre? Or showrooms for the tobacco industry and Nottingham's other famous products? These are things that Nottingham can be proud of—make them obvious. Let it make use of the Trent to the full; let it be seen to be a playground as well as a power house. Let it encourage its street markets, the individual flavour of its immigrant citizens, its robust character. Let the world know that Nottingham is different, that it does not intend to become sterile and faceless and rubber-stamped. Let Nottingham's qualities or gaiety, commonsense and independence have their head. For then it will become a city in which life is worth the living, a real Queen of the Midlands with a robe that others will finger in envy.

It is over thirty years since I first sat on one of the benches in the Old Market Square, hearing the rush of pigeon wings and noting how confident were the people of this city in which I was about to live. The holiday atmosphere I felt then has persisted surprisingly. But things have speeded up. The crowds have got thicker. They stream rather than stroll, and they have an edgier, more harassed look in their eyes. They certainly appear even more prosperous and well-fed, and their arms hold more parcels. But they seem to be not so much wandering as anxious to reach somewhere else, planning the next move across a crowded crossing through a parade of cars and buses.

Perhaps, when I sit on the same spot soon, the tension will have gone; the crowds will be just as thick, but able to relax without having to skip through the choking traffic. Either way, I know that Nottingham will regard it as a bit of a lark. For this is a good-humoured town.

A fascinating town, too. It does strange things so often that they take on the sort of bizarrerie which makes you label them 'Typical Nottingham'. It is 'Typical Nottingham' to prohibit film-stills outside a cinema if they show a man holding a gun or a knife. Children may walk inside and watch the whole shooting match or brawl, but the pictures outside must carry a piece of paper stuck over the weapon. It is 'Typical Nottingham' for the Public Protection Committee—on getting a complaint from a clergyman who hadn't even seen it—to ban the film *The Devils* after it had already been showing for eight days. It is 'Typical Nottingham' to run the city's official Festival and then to leave creditors stranded through a political squabble.

Some odd, useless scraps of information can be picked up in Nottingham. The police are allowed to wear contact-lenses but not glasses. In 1577 the mayor was dismissed 'for besporting himself with a naughty hussy'. The oldest travel-agency, a century ago used to issue its third-class passengers to America with pistols and cutlasses to help beat off pirates. Whenever Royalty visits by train, the 'Gents' signs at the Midland Station are unscrewed or covered up. More sailors are recruited in Nottingham—over sixty miles from the sea—than anywhere else. Fifteen spectators were once squashed to death at Garner's Hill near the Shire Hall after watching a public execution. There are supposed to be ghosts in the Theatre Royal, the Odeon cinema, and the turbine room of Wilford Power Station. In 1972 a family refused to sleep in their house until the ghost of a cat was exorcised.

Like Autolycus, I am a great snapper-up of unconsidered trifles, and Nottingham has filled a bulky bag for me. I have come across records of children christened Livewell, Penitence, Vinefruite and Friendlesse. Beeston Council has taken a superstitious load off their tenants' minds by having no houses numbered 13. A schoolboy's essay declared that 'The Lord Mayor has many affairs and wears his gilt around his neck . . .' The stone lions outside the Council House are supposed to roar when a virgin walks past. I have not heard them yet.

For years I puzzled over something like an upside-down thermometer affixed to an alley wall off Pelham Street, until I learned that it was a marker for calibrating theodolites—which have an inverted image. I remember the Spaniard who was talked out of stripping to his underpants in the Old Market Square to display 'Gibraltar is Spanish' on his back. In the nineteenth century there were names like the lawyer Caractacus D'Aubigney Shilton, and the surveyor Marriott Ogle Tarbotton. When I arrived in Nottingham I discovered that the Chief Constable was called Captain Athelstan Popkess. It was ecstatic experience to sit in court one morning and hear a flustered prisoner say: 'I would like to thank you from the heart of my bottom, Poptin Catpiss.'

Nottinghamians have a great sense of curiosity but they are also polite and try not to show it. Two students who boarded a bus with a coffin during a university rag found that the patient people in the queue hardly gave it a glance. I myself had occasion to walk into a crowded bar on a Saturday night with a Roman centurion, and nobody turned a hair. We had been involved in a film-advertising-stunt at a cinema, and, after doing a bit of patrolling in the foyer, my colleague—magnificently decked out in leather skirt, sandals, scarlet toga, shield, sword and plumed helmet—suggested we break off for a drink across the road at the County Hotel. So we did, and, except for a few sidelong glances, everybody in the bar behaved as though a member of Julius Caesar's Ninth Legion came in for a pint every night.

Nottingham also has a gleeful sense of humour, particularly where sex is concerned; which may account for so many pronouncements being made about Nottingham's inherent instincts towards moral debauchery, and the attempts to 'protect' it from sin.

But Nottingham still relishes its most classic example of illicit sex. It happened some ninety years ago when a judge—noted for his resolute way of dealing with immorality and vice—was on circuit here. One night, after a hard day at the Assizes, he died in the arms of a prostitute. His body was discreetly taken back to his lodgings and put into bed for his valet to find. At the inquest, he was said to have expired from 'over-excitement'. *The Times* published a glowing obituary notice stressing his sterling qualities and his worth to the legal profession. And as far as the world was concerned, that was the whole story.

But all Nottingham knew. A memorial card for the late judge was brought out. Bordered tastefully in black, it had a vast circulation:

In memory of Mr. Justice ——— ———, who departed this life suddenly at Mrs. Salmond's, Nottingham, Thursday night July 17, 1884. Aged 56 years.

> In eight feet deep of solid earth
> Sir ——— ——— lies.
> He lost his breath, which caused his death
> 'Twixt Nellie Blankey's thighs . . .

Rabelaisian, robust Nottingham. It has come a long way and will go a long way yet. It has shown what it can do, and must inevitably show more. Its people—friendly, spirited, argumentative, warm—have gone through too much to be wasted in some unwieldy, uncohesive urban sprawl with no sense of direction or pride of place.

In my time, the changes have been marked. They've even scrapped the revered old title of Griffin & Spalding's store in the square and 'brought it into line' as Debenham's—but I bet it will be a long time before Nottingham stops calling it Griffin & Spalding's.

These things don't matter all that much. What counts is that

Nottingham should still keep a shape and an identity, and the character which is uniquely its own; refusing to be messed about, by insisting on having its say, by its determination not to drift into a shapeless and dreary duplication of so many other places. One might take timely note of the crime rate in Nottingham—nearly every radio shop keeps a length of chain linking radios and TV sets together, and wanton vandalism is so prevalent as to be commonplace. Could it be that the famous spirit of protest and dissension is emerging through these ugly, distorted channels in revolt against the accelerating sterility of life?

Like any other city, Nottingham has its faults. But its grip on the quality of life is sound. The sense of community is springing up in the rebuilt Meadows and St Ann's, although it has been decided that the hideous and damp Balloon Wood flats should be pulled down. It honours its past more—as in checking the obliteration of the Lace Market and restoring the windmill of the Sneinton miller and mathematical genius George Smith. It has been bold in such things as its theatres and the dazzling concert hall. And it has woken up to promoting tourism with holiday package deals round the countryside of Byron, Lawrence and Robin Hood.

With a sense of proportion, a sense of community and a sense of humour, Nottingham will find its direction. I'm prepared to go along with it. For, with great affection, I have two of its own words to say to the city which I adopted and which adopted me: 'Ta, duck . . . !'

J. D. Chambers: *Modern Nottingham in the Making* (Nottingham Journal Ltd., 1945)

Ken Coates and Richard Silburn: *Poverty: The Forgotten Englishmen* (Penguin Books, 1970)

Guy Denison: *This Is Your Nottingham* (Nottingham Publishing Co. Ltd., 3rd edn. 1969)

Henry Field: *The Datebook of Nottingham 1750–1879* (Henry Field, Nottingham, 1880)

Duncan Gray: *Nottingham Through 500 Years* (City of Nottingham, 1949)

——: *Nottingham: Settlement to City* (Nottingham Co-operative Soc. Ltd., 1953)

Henry C. Hall: *Artists and Sculptors of Nottingham and Notts.* (Herbert Jones & Son Ltd., Nottingham, 1953)

T. C. Hine: *Nottingham: Its Castle* (Hamilton, Adams and Co., London, 1876)

Richard Iliffe and Wilfred Baguley: *Victorian Nottingham*, eleven vols. (Nottingham Historical Film Unit, 1972, 1973)

Peter Lord: *Portrait of the River Trent* (Robert Hale & Co., London, 1968)

Dennis McCarthy: *Local Boy Makes Good* (D. McCarthy & BBC Radio Nottingham, 1971)

Robert Mellors: *In and About Nottinghamshire* (J. H. Bell Ltd., Nottingham, 1908)

John Sheffield: *Nottingham, A Guide* (John Sheffield and Fred Broad, Nottingham, 1977)

Malcolm I. Thomis: *Old Nottingham* (David & Charles Ltd., Newton Abbott, 1968)

Geoffrey Trease: *Byron* (Macmillan & Co. Ltd., London, 1969)

——: *Nottingham: A Biography* (Macmillan, 1970)

——: *A Whiff of Burnt Boats* (Macmillan, 1971)

——: *D. H. Lawrence: The Phoenix and the Flame* (Macmillan, 1973)

University of Nottingham: *Nottingham in the 1880s: a Study in Social Change* (Nottingham University, Department of Adult Education, 1971)

D. E. Varley: *History of the Midland Counties Lace Manufacturers Association* (Lace Productions Ltd. on behalf of the British Leavers Lace Manufacturers Asscn., 1959)

F. A. Wells: *The British Hosiery and Knitwear Industry* (George Allen & Unwin Ltd., London, 1935; revised edition David & Charles Ltd., Newton Abbott, 1972)

A. C. Wood: *A History of Nottinghamshire* (Thoroton Society of Nottinghamshire, 1947; republished by S.R. Publishers Ltd., Wakefield, 1971)

INDEX